THE LEISURE CLASS
IN AMERICA

This is a volume in the Arno Press collection

THE LEISURE CLASS IN AMERICA

Advisory Editor
Leon Stein

A Note About This Volume

For the wealthy, the American hotel has been the scene of events demonstrating their wealth. But for the mass of Americans, starting in the early days of their history, the hotel was the status arena utilized for important ceremonials, a separate world experienced by those who could afford to travel and play, the meeting place of important people, a place of bars, ballroom and marble staircases. No subject "could better reflect the progress of our national customs and tastes," R.L. Duffus observed in reviewing this book in the *New York Times*. About, it, Allan Nevins wrote in the *Saturday Review of Literature*, "a great deal of social history is bound up with the record of these hotels. The list of their rules alone, from the early days, throw a significant light on American mores. Mr. Williamson has a keen eye for items which bear upon this subject. He has provided a trustworthy and sufficiently comprehensive treatment of a not unimportant subject."

See last pages of this volume for a complete list of titles.

THE AMERICAN HOTEL

Jefferson Williamson

ARNO PRESS

A New York Times Company

New York / 1975

E
161
-L4W5J
cop 2

Fordham University
LIBRARY
AT
LINCOLN CENTER
New York, N. Y.

Reprint Edition 1975 by Arno Press Inc.

Reprinted from a copy in
 The Newark Public Library

THE LEISURE CLASS OF AMERICA
ISBN for complete set: 0-405-06900-6
See last pages of this volume for titles.

Manufactured in the United States of America

Library of Congress Cataloging in Publication Data

Williamson, Jefferson, 1885-1930.
  The American hotel.

  (The Leisure class of America)
  Reprint of the 1930 ed. published by Knopf, New York.
  Includes bibliographical references.
  1. Hotels, taverns, etc.--United States--History.
I. Title. II. Series.
TX909.W5 1975   647'.9473   75-1873
ISBN 0-405-06939-1

THE
AMERICAN
HOTEL

THE AMERICAN HOTEL

AN ANECDOTAL HISTORY

Jefferson Williamson

Nineteen hundred and thirty
NEW YORK · ALFRED · A · KNOPF · LONDON

Copyright 1930 by ALFRED A. KNOPF, INC.
All rights reserved — no part of this book may be reprinted in any form without permission in writing from the publisher

NEW YORK

ALFRED A. KNOPF INC.

730 FIFTH AVENUE

&

LONDON

ALFRED A. KNOPF LTD.

37 BEDFORD SQUARE W.C.2

&

TORONTO

LONGMANS, GREEN & COMPANY

128 UNIVERSITY AVENUE

MANUFACTURED IN THE UNITED STATES OF AMERICA

To
MATILDA

CONTENTS

THE INN CROSSES THE RUBICON · 3
An introductory review

I

YE BOWL AND PITCHER PERIOD · 13
The début of the first modern hotels

II

NEWFANGLED NOTIONS · 38
What made the modern hotels modern

III

WESTWARD HO · 73
Hotels of the cities that grew up overnight

IV

WELCOME, STRANGER! · 105
The nineteenth-century hotel guest

V

RAGS TO RICHES · 137
Mine Host of the past and present

VI

DIAMONDS TRUMPS · 169
Some variations of hotel service

VII

THE GROANING BOARD · 192
The rise and fall of the great American-plan meal

VIII

WATER, WATER EVERYWHERE · 224
The resorts, where the belles and beaux made love

IX

LAVENDER AND OLD LACE · 260
Famous old hotels of yester-year

NOTES · 299

INDEX · *Follows page 324*

THE AMERICAN HOTEL

OLD PALMER HOUSE, *Chicago*

THE INN CROSSES THE RUBICON

THE NINETEENTH CENTURY, which saw the most remarkable changes that had ever come over human life, was also the century of the beginning of the modern hotel, an institution that is perhaps the most representative and expressive example of those changes that we have. Prior to the nineteenth century there were only inns — romantic places, no doubt, but as different from a modern first-class hotel as a trip through a wilderness in a stage-coach, in days of old, was from a trip today in a *de luxe* train or a Rolls-Royce. For the modern first-class hotel was an invention, with the old-style inn merely furnishing the root idea — just as the pianoforte was an invention, based on the older clavichord, spinet, and harpsichord; or Stephenson's locomotive, based on Watt's condensing steam-engine and other fundamentals.

Roughly speaking, it took inns twelve thousand years to grow from one to thirty rooms in size, and then, in the next hundred and thirty years — or since about the year 1800 — they have shown a great burst of speed in development and have attained a present maximum of three thousand rooms.[1] Which may, or may not, be the ultimate limit. The probability is that it will not.

But it is not merely its hugeness that makes the modern hotel such a striking contrast to the old inns. The real difference lies in the grandeur, the comfort, and the service that one gets in a modern hotel. And all this comfort, grandeur, and service date little further back than the beginning of the nineteenth century. It was then, all of a sudden, after so many centuries of static existence, that the old-style inn began to change — almost overnight — into the new-style hotel and brought into the dictionary a new word, defined: " Hotel — A superior kind of inn."

Nor did the coming of the modern hotel entail any loss of those romantic connotations which surrounded the old inns, for the modern hotel has always been a center of all sorts of colorful life. Its annals are filled with romantic memorabilia. This is particularly true of America, where the modern first-class hotel made its first appearance. Our hotels have been, as one writer said, " the thermometers and barometers of our national civilization," and have wielded a great influence on the manners and tastes of the country. It will be long before the memory of the fine old hostelries of the past century fades away. Legend and tradition and many a song and story will save them from oblivion, and they will have, too, their modest morsel of space in the pages of history — especially the social and political history for which they have provided so much stage setting.

The great and the near-great have lived in all of them and haunted their corridors, banquet-rooms, lobbies, and bars. Presidents and statesmen have lived and died in them, and emperors, kings and queens, princes and grand dukes, rajahs and maharajas, and crowned heads of all sorts have received democracy's adulation at their banquet boards. Most of the great stage stars have spent their entire adult lives in hotels, and politicians have always made them their rallying and plotting grounds. There have been other events, too — tragic and comic, important and unimportant — that will serve to perpetuate the memory of these old hotels.

Tinsel and all, our ornate hotels symbolize and typify

THE INN CROSSES THE RUBICON

the spirit of America. They have been, perhaps, the most distinctively American of all our institutions, for they were nourished and brought to flower solely in American soil and borrowed practically nothing from abroad. The spotlight does not beat on them now as it once did, and they are not so wondrous as they were fifty or a hundred years ago — when they were almost alone in their grandeur — for this is a sophisticated age of too many marvels for a mere hotel, no matter how huge and magnificent, to make anyone stand in awe.

There are, of course, several perfectly good reasons why inns and innkeeping remained at nearly a standstill for so many thousands of years and why they have developed so fast in the last hundred years or so. In order to exemplify those reasons let us project our minds for a few moments back into the dim prehistoric past — back to the days of the one-room caravansary that was the beginning of innkeeping.

Undoubtedly Mine Host was one of the world's first Tired Business Men, on the job as early as the time of the old stone age. Back in the year 10000 B.C., let us say — or just about twelve thousand years ago — a caravan of pre-Adamic men trudged down from the forest uplands to the seashore, carrying pelts, polished flints, horn and bone knickknacks, and other fruits of their prowess and handiwork. As they came within sight of a cluster of huts and dug-outs along the shore, they discreetly sounded the halloo of friendship and were answered in kind by their hairy kinsmen of the cliffs and salt marshes. For this was a periodical visit to the beach, to exchange hinterland merchandise for the general provisions of the sea. The forest-dwellers also wanted some of the strange, pretty shells and colored pebbles, to take back to the women and children they had left behind to keep the home fires burning.

They were weary, these prehistoric travelers, for the

trekking had been slow and strenuous. Their primitive cousins extended the crude hospitality of the day, giving the visitors the use of a guest-hut, where they could sleep together, huddled on some reeds strewn on the floor. The visitors paid for this rude lodging, but not, of course, in money, for Crœsus, or whoever deserves the credit, had not yet invented the root of all evil. In those far-away days, most likely, the guests paid their reckoning in voluntary gifts, for they wanted to make sure of a welcome the next time they put in an appearance. Thus Mine Host's first guests probably fixed their own hotel rates — which in itself shows what a neat lapse of time there has been between that day and this.[2]

Such, in a general way, is probably how innkeeping began, twelve thousand years ago, more or less. But as a regular business, innkeeping was not possible until some standardized and compact medium of exchange had come into existence. This was about the sixth century, B.C.[3] The invention of money brought about a sudden expansion of the trading radius of the ancient world and occasioned the real birth of travel. Not, however, the easy, nonchalant flitting about that prevails today. The perils of going a few miles away from home were still too great, and, as in the days of the cave-man, all travel was strictly for business purposes, undertaken only by men of heroic mold. Sailors plied between ports in small, frail ships. Groups of traders, " sword in hand and prayers on their lips," led their pack-horses (the wheel had not yet been invented) from one little city to another, over trails that would mire a snipe, and that were infested with robbers. They were looked upon with fear and suspicion wherever they went. Besides these, high officials went on tax-collecting tours, accompanied by well-armed retinues. Eventually beggars and pilgrims took to the road.

Centuries rolled by and highways became a little better,

cities larger, and travel greater in volume. There was a surprising amount of it during the Middle Ages, all things considered. Finally the stage-coach came thundering down the road, for its few crowded hours of glory, until it fell a rather easy prey to the iron horse. It was during this brief sway of the stage-coach that the hotel, then always called an inn or tavern in Anglo-Saxon countries, began its remarkable growth.[4] The stage-coach came on the scene long after the dawn of the modern era, five hundred years ago, and meanwhile down through all the ages from beyond Biblical times inns had changed very little. They were as they had been from time immemorial — self-service establishments, for the most part, run on a one-horse basis by generally disreputable and unprogressive landlords. Cleanliness was rare and a low standard of conditions prevailed throughout. It was not such a very far cry, so far as comforts and service were concerned, back to the bare, comfortless shelter provided by Mine Host of the old stone age. About the best one can say of the old inns, in the light of contemporary records, is that although all were bad, some were a little better than others.

Then England began to be industrialized, and in and around London and a few other places a general improvement began, about 1750. Mine Host began to provide more general lackeying and paid more attention to the cleanliness and comfort of his house. Parlors and bedrooms, exclusively for the post-chaise trade, were better furnished. A *vase de nuit* (as De Quincey called it) was sometimes provided, and, in course of time, even a bowl and pitcher. A gentleman, if he was clamorous enough, could occasionally get a single room.[5] During this era the English inns began to gain the reputation of being the best in the world, and seem to have deserved it. It was not, however, until about 1815, when the main highways began to be macadamized, that the spirit of improvement reached the countryside houses of call.[6] These were the inns of the Pickwickian period, about which so much moonshine, irreconcilable with the evidence of records, has been written.

But the English inns never went beyond a certain point, and the English innkeeper remained a traditionalist, unwilling or unable to get out of his ages-old rut, and content to let well enough alone. Meanwhile the American landlord showed not the slightest fear of turning all sorts of new corners. He had become an expansionist and an innovator, first surpassing his English contemporary in the size of his estabishments and eventually eclipsing him in other respects. In the principal American cities — Boston, New York, Philadelphia, Baltimore, and Charleston — the inns of the later Colonial period had merely kept pace with those of the mother country, but did not differ from them in any special way, except for such differences as were due to the general conditions in the two countries. They were inns of the approved London style. All were residences, some with additions built on. The best of them were like an average well-kept home and were not much larger. But soon after the Revolution Mine Host began to expand, in the cities of the north Atlantic seaboard, the only section that had consolidated its civilization sufficiently to be no longer part of the frontier. The first result of this was a crop of large-scale inns, or taverns, out of which the modern hotel quickly evolved, with Boston its birthplace and 1829 the year of its birth.

Thus the golden era of American hotels and hotel-keeping came on. During the thirty years preceding the Civil War caravansaries larger and finer than any the world had ever seen were built in all the older cities and in boom towns that had been non-existent a score of years before. They were kept in the best of style and were full of luxurious innovations of all sorts to pamper the long-neglected guest.

THE INN CROSSES THE RUBICON

There were several conditions wholly peculiar to America that tended to give this country leadership in the development of the modern first-class hotel. E. L. Godkin, the editor of the *Nation,* touched upon two of them — the American habit of permanent living in hotels, and the fact that hotels in Europe were conducted on the assumption that only great folks were entitled to comfort and luxury. America's hotels, on the other hand, were built for equalitarian enjoyment. The view in this new democracy was that Brown, Jones, and Robinson had as much right to comfort and luxury as anyone — provided they could pay for it. And the rates were within the means of almost everybody. Indeed, the public could enjoy much in America's hotels without its costing them a cent — the lobby, for example, and even the bar-room.

Then, too, there was the fact that America's hotels were the great social centers of the general public, the favorite places for balls, banquets, and other affairs. This was a heritage of the old inn days, when there was a lack of private mansions in which social affairs could be held on any sizable scale. Democracy's leaven, admitting all classes to these events, made it necessary to use the Long Rooms of the inns. In addition to being the accepted centers of social activity, the hotels also were the centers of political, business, and other forms of activity.

Moreover, there was the fact that the average American did much more traveling than did the people of other countries. Americans had nearly all become great rolling stones. The country's youth and richness of spirit and energy kept people constantly on the go and brought into being more and more hotels.

All this, aided and abetted by the traditional free-handedness of the average American, accelerated the growth and development of the American hotel. And these conditions brought about the application of the stock-company idea to the financing of inn construction. Thus the first of the oversized inns, the City Hotel of New York, was built by a stock-company. Prior to that time Mine Host had converted his own, or someone else's, house into an inn. The stock-company idea took the inn off the one-horse basis and put it in the realm of big business. It made possible most of America's great hotels. The fact that our hotels were built by corporations, affording a field of investment similar to that afforded by railroads and industrial plants, was in itself a detail of American life that, in the days before the Civil War, astonished visiting Europeans.

The City Hotel was the first building erected expressly for hotel purposes in America, and though it was merely an overgrown inn, clinging closely to ancient traditions and practices, it set a new pace for size. It had seventy-three rooms — enough to cause visiting Europeans to call it " an immense establishment." When it opened, in the fall of 1794, New York was a boom town of about thirty thousand population, and the scalps that Iroquois warriors had been gathering from overbold white men who ventured into northwestern New York State were barely dry.[7]

The City Hotel, which stood on " the Broad-way " just below Trinity Church, has a conspicuous place in the history of the first two or three decades of nineteenth century New York. The old Knickerbockers thought it was quite a swell place and it quickly became the chief social center of the city. Here the gay New Yorkers, first to copy English and French fads and follies, danced the rigadoon, cotillion and *allemande,* and the " plain and fancy minuet," at weekly subscription dances given by " gentlemen of the town," who attended in knee-breeches, silk stockings, white dancing-gloves, London cocked hats and dress-swords. Here many important banquets were held and many other interesting events occurred.

Boston's first hotel, built as a hotel, was the Exchange Coffee House, opened in 1804;[8] and Philadelphia's first was the Mansion House, which opened under the name of Exchange Coffee House in 1807.[9] Baltimore's first real hotel building was the City Hotel, opened in 1826, and kept by David Barnum, who had been landlord of the Exchange in Boston. Barnum had been proprietor of the old Indian Queen Tavern in Baltimore, which started as a private dwelling and was enlarged several times. It was Baltimore's best prior to the opening of Barnum's new house.

And thus, with these as a starting-point, a crop of large-scale inns sprang up during the first quarter of the nineteenth century to meet the new conditions. New York's list, in addition to the City Hotel, included Washington Hall, opened in 1809; the Tammany Hotel, opened in 1810; Bunker's Mansion House, dating from 1821; and two or three others of lesser importance. Beyond the turn of the first quarter of the century came the National Hotel, opened in 1826, and the American Hotel, opened in 1827. New York's first skyscraper — for so it was regarded at the time — the six-story Adelphi Hotel, was also opened in 1827.

Boston had about as many of these overgrown inns as New York, for although but half the size of New York at the beginning of the century, Boston was still the hub of the most thickly settled and greatest industrial section of the country. Naturally New England was the section of heaviest travel, and there were perhaps more strangers on the streets of Boston at this time than on those of New York or Philadelphia, for, besides the great number of stages, the city's harbor was filled with vessels from overseas, and a steamer line, established in 1825, had cut the running time between Boston and New York to twenty-four hours.

All these overgrown inns, however, represented, at best, but a sort of secondary stratum of inn progress. They came, during a period of less than forty years, in between the twelve-thousand-year-old stratum of old inns and the present tertiary stratum, let us say, of palace hotels. They were, nevertheless, a vast improvement over the old-style inns. Dowdy and inadequate as they would be regarded now, they were impressive enough in a day when elegance was all but unknown in America. Indeed, it was to them, with their gaudy Long Rooms and bar-parlors, that the term " palaces of the people " was first applied.[10] They did, at least, take the first step, however feebly, toward the American hotel's showy ostentation. It was for home-town business. The traveler, here today and gone tomorrow, got nothing better than he had always been getting — except that he no longer was forced to put up with pot luck. The bountiful four-meals-a-day American plan came in during this period. It was the one great contribution of the overgrown inns to modern hotel-keeping, even though it was primarily a bid for the business of the " regular boarder."

CHAPTER I

YE BOWL AND PITCHER PERIOD

THE ENTIRE development of America's hotel system — indeed, the development of modern hotels throughout the whole world — had its origin in two historic hostelries, one of them the City Hotel in New York, the other the Tremont House in Boston. The City Hotel owes its distinction to the fact that it was the first building erected for hotel purposes in America, was remarkable for its size and was the first caravansary erected by a stock-company. The Tremont's distinction is that, by virtue of numerous superiorities, it was indisputably the first definitely recognized example of the modern first-class hotel — the true grandparent of all the swagger hostelries that dot the land today. It was so far in front of all its contemporaries, either in America or in Europe, that it stood alone, in a class by itself, and was universally conceded to be something entirely new in the realm of hotel-keeping. There were a multitude of details, great and small, that gave it its pre-eminence. As a building it was a national showpiece and was perhaps the largest structure in the country when it was opened. It was also one of the costliest. Its interior arrangement was radically different from that of all its predecessors. It was handsomely furnished and decorated throughout and fairly bulged with luxury. Numerous innovations for the pleasure and convenience of the guests were provided, and last, but not least, it started under a new and broader conception of management — the policy of giving the guest the utmost of comfort, luxury, and service. And by reason of all this it established definitely America's leadership in the art and science of hotel-keeping. Since its time this country has led the world in the number, size, and magnificence of its hotels, and the provisions made by them for the pleasure and convenience of their guests.

The Tremont House was so called in honor of the street on which it stood, commemorating the three hills on which Boston was built. It was opened on October 16, 1829, with a banquet at which Daniel Webster, Edward Everett, and more than a hundred other hand-picked Bostonians ate, drank, and made merry at one dollar per cover.[1] The event marked an unmistakable turning-point in twelve thousand years of innkeeping. The new hotel era was now positively on its way.

The cornerstone of the Tremont was laid, ceremoniously, on July 4, 1828, and soon thereafter staid Boston folks saw a massive building arising, its façade of white Quincy granite blocks. The building filled an entire square front on Tremont Street and was three stories and a half-basement high, with four-story wings on either end. Its architecture was chaste and simple, with massiveness and whiteness the outstanding characteristics. It was designed by Isaiah Rogers, who, like all other early American architects, drew his inspiration from Greek classicism. Rogers designed several other great hotels of America's past, among them the Astor House in New York, Cincinnati's famed Burnet House, the second St. Charles in New Orleans, the Battle House in Mobile, the Galt House in Louisville, and his masterpiece, the Charleston Hotel at Charleston, South Carolina. They were among the finest specimens of architecture in America during the first half of the nineteenth century. In all of them Rogers followed the same general style, with modifications and elaborations, and gave American hotels a standardized architectural character that persisted for many decades;

for other architects got their inspiration for hotel design from *A Description of the Tremont House, with Architectural Illustrations,* which Gray and Bowen of Boston published in 1830 in response to a general demand. This volume, indeed, was the standard text-book of hotel construction for the next fifty years. The interior arrangement of hotels today, in fact, follows much the same plan that Rogers worked out for the Tremont. All vestiges of Rogers's influence on exterior design have, in this age of skyscrapers, utterly disappeared, except that the Doric entrance may still occasionally be seen. It was all but universal for fifty years.

All America was proud of the Tremont, and Bostonians inordinately so. Whenever they showed distinguished visitors the sights of the town, they pointed first to the Bulfinch State House, hub of the solar system, and then to the Tremont, calling it " one of the proudest achievements of American genius." Thomas Hamilton, member of *Blackwood's* staff and author of *Cyril Thornton* and other best sellers, said that so many men of taste and talent extolled the architectural beauties of the Tremont to him that it got on his nerves, for he was not one of those who was swept off his feet by the building. But he was too well satisfied with the good living at the Tremont, he said, not to feel grieved " to be compelled to speak disparagingly of its architecture."

The interior lived up to the promise of the exterior. The ceilings were high; the floors of several of the public rooms were of marble mosaic; the decorations were in the latest French mode; the halls and guest-rooms were carpeted and there were curtains on the windows. Throughout the house there was carved walnut furniture, some of it imported and the rest the best product of New England craftsmen. The ten public rooms transcended those of all the Tremont's predecessors in number, grandeur, and size. Indeed, few hotels today, except some in the larger cities, give more space to public rooms than the Tremont did.

THE AMERICAN HOTEL

The first apartment the coming guest laid eyes on was, of course, the lobby. It must have made a powerful impression, aside from its marble floor and all its other finery, for it was the first hotel lobby in America that was not chiefly bar-room, and by this token it was the first to have clerks. The clerk theretofore had been a combination bar-tender, clerk, and porter, besides having to help Mine Host to carve meats, which latter duty the clerk continued to perform for many years after the Tremont's day. At that time the lobby was always called the office. It began to be called the lobby about 1850. Why the designation fastened itself on the office-lounge, rather than on the bar-room, which was even more popular as a rendezvous for politicians and lobbyists, is an etymological mystery. Another new characteristic of the Tremont's lobby was that, unlike its predecessors, there were no racks behind the desk, as there had been behind the bar, on which guests' hand-luggage was stored. There was a separate baggage-room, as there was a separate bar-room, and this bar-room was in itself an elegant place. Directly across from the old Tremont Theater, it was a popular rendezvous of all the noted actors who came to Boston, and of those who went to the theater to see their plays. Dickens says it was a large bar, with a stone floor, and was crowded all evening. "There," he wrote in *American Notes*, " the stranger is initiated into the mysteries of gin sling, sherry cobbler, mint julep, songaree, timber doodle and other rare drinks."

The passing of the bar-room is fresh in our memories, but there are few who remember another important room that has disappeared — the reading-room, once one of the chief drawing cards of every good hotel. It was the product of a time when there were no public libraries; only "mercantile" libraries, exclusively for shareholders. There were, however, at that time, reading-rooms that were a regular line of business, charging admission. The Tremont adopted this idea, stocking its room with newspapers from all the states and from overseas. Guests had free access, while Bostonians paid a small annual fee. The reading-rooms of many old hotels were run on this basis until about 1870.

The Tremont had a grand total of one hundred and seventy rooms and was the world's largest hotel at the time. Grandest of all its dozen public rooms was the main dining-room, seventy feet long and thirty-one feet wide and with a fourteen-foot ceiling. It was able to accommodate the then stupendous number of two hundred diners at a sitting and was decorated and furnished in a dazzlingly ornate manner, which threw the old Long Rooms into utter eclipse. It was warmed by two large open fireplaces with marble mantels, and by a direct furnace, out of which poured the heat from the kitchen fireplace and ovens. In the main section, with windows facing on Tremont Street, there were six rooms, each twenty by thirty feet, for private clubs and parties. Every pair of these rooms was connected by sliding doors, so that they could be doubled in size, if so needed. The south wing contained ten private parlors on the first and second floors, each with bedchamber attached. These were elegantly furnished and were for the permanent guests and distinguished travelers. On the first floor there was also a drawing-room and two smaller parlors.

When the Tremont was opened, the first time-honored inn tradition that it violated was that it did not have a swinging sign, nor any other sort of sign, outside the door.[2] The builders of the Tremont scorned to use such antique trademarks of the past, in the face of protests that such disregard of old custom was unthinkable. Colonial laws had required all inns to have signs, and those signs (following the style of the mother country) were wholly or half pictorial, because so many people did not know how to read. If strangers saw a white swan or a red horse painted on a signboard, or a goat wearing boots, or a pig playing a tin whistle, they knew they were at the door of an inn. Most of these signs were old-country adaptations. There was one notable exception, showing an Indian flapper in knee-length skirts — Pocahontas, emblematized into a signboard patroness of dozens of Indian Queen Taverns.

Likewise Bostonians looked in vain for the Tremont's stage and carriage entrance, for the old familiar horse-blocks out in front, and for the inn stables. All were missing. Every other house of call was well provided with these features. Ever since the traveler of ancient days had trudged along swampy trails leading his pack-horses, the innkeeper had attached as much importance to his equine guests as to his human guests. Many of the English inns of posting and coaching days — and some in America — were built with a hollow quadrangle in the center, with an entrance through a wide arch from the street. Stage-coaches, post-boys, and private chaises clattered into this cobble-stoned quadrangle, and there the horses were unharnessed and put in the stables on the ground floor. Above these stables were the guest-rooms, sometimes with a gallery overlooking the stable-yard — or, if you prefer a more pompous word, the courtyard. From this gallery the guests could be spectators of many exciting events. At times strolling players presented a play in the courtyard. Sometimes a group of acrobats, or a man with a monkey or a dancing bear, came along and put on a show. Or a felon was flogged, or an auction held. The builders of the Tremont, however, considered the courtyard and its stables things of the past for a hotel of the Tremont's class. There was a three-sided courtyard, but in it were rose-bushes and beds of other flowers, and the Greek portico out in front led only to the lobby. No strolling players or dancing bears ever got in, nor any vehicles.

One of the Tremont's distinguishing features was that it specialized in single and double rooms for guests. This, too, was something new. In the old inns it was the general

YE BOWL AND PITCHER PERIOD

rule that a traveler should share his bedroom and bed with one or more strange bedfellows. The fastidious person who wanted a room all to himself was exceptional and was generally considered a fool. The canons of travel etiquette did not demand such gentilities. This indifference to Morphean privacy was world-wide up to about the beginning of the nineteenth century, and it is doubtful if any one, in any country, ever got a private room at an inn much earlier than that time, or even so much as asked for one. In the old days even a king when he went traveling was not expected to sleep alone. Indeed, he, least of all, wanted to. The crowned head lay easier if there were a dozen or more trusted courtiers snoring near by. All inn beds in the olden days were extra large size and were of the trundle variety, and with or without the trundle pulled out could accommodate many sleepers. The innkeeper did not consider his house full until he had crowded as many people as possible into all parts of it, as well as into the beds. Thus we read of old European inns with accommodations for one or two hundred people. They were all packed into perhaps fewer than a dozen rooms, sleeping " spoon fashion " in the beds, on the floor, wherever there was space for one to lie down. One of the largest of the old inn beds was the Bed of Ware, which Shakspere mentions in *Twelfth Night*. It accommodated sixty-eight persons. In 1463 it was presented to King Edward of England by Jonas Fosbrooke, who spent thirty years of odd time carving it elaborately to make it worthy of its royal owner. After the King's death it was used in various London inns, including the Crown, the Bull, and the Saracen's Head.[3]

During the eighteenth century these omnibus beds went gradually out of use. It was perhaps the fastidious Englishman who first began demanding single beds and bedrooms. He demanded them vociferously in this country whenever he came over on a visit, and occasionally he got one. But here in America the traveling public was less finicky about single beds and bedrooms, and because of it the scorn and pity of supercilious travelers from abroad was poured on them. As it had been in the Old World but a few years before, mixed company made no difference.[4] It was not considered an act of turpitude for men and women to sleep in the same room. It must be remembered, however, that few women traveled unaccompanied by husband or parent. Only once in a blue moon was the taverner called upon to provide lodging for an unescorted woman. Often he refused to let one in. The redoubtable Sarah Knight, who made an arduous horseback trip from Boston to New York in 1704, to settle an estate, related such an experience in her famous diary.[5] A more amusing account is that related by Edward Allen Talbot, Esq., in a book describing a tour of America in 1823:

> On entering one of these taverns and asking for a single bed, you are told that your chance of getting one depends entirely on the number of travelers who may want accommodations for the night; and if you obtain possession of a bed by promising to receive a companion when required, it is impossible to say what sort of a companion may come; so that instead of hoping for the best, one is led into the commission of a sort of practical bull — to which, however, all who regard their own personal convenience are equally liable, whether they be English or Irish — by keeping awake for the purpose of receiving an intruder while no intruder comes to be received; and thus we are sometimes deprived of a night's rest, without any advantage.
>
> I remember once being compelled to take a bed on these conditions, because I could not otherwise procure it. I retired early to rest; and after contending a short time with my apprehensions of some ineligible bed-fellow, I dropped asleep. About midnight I was awakened by the chattering of five buxom girls, who had just entered the room and were beginning to undress themselves. Perceiving that there were only four beds in the apartment, each of which was already occupied by one person, I set it down as certain that I should have one, if not two, of these ladies. Under this impression I raised my head, and desired to be informed which of them intended me the honor of

YE BOWL AND PITCHER PERIOD

her company. " Don't be alarmed, Sir! " cried one of them. " We shall not trouble you nor your bed. A look is quite sufficient! "

I suppose I must have discovered some signs of fear, and probably looked horribly enough; for the idea of three in a bed was rather a formidable affair. This, however, was the first time in my life that I owed the luxury of a single-bed, or any other luxury, to my looks. . . . My prospect of good fortune was speedily confirmed by the sight of a large bed arranged on the floor, in which five young ladies had composed themselves to rest.[6]

The facetious Mr. Talbot was speaking, of course, of some inn in a remote district, for the writings of other travelers show that single beds were at least obtainable at the inns of the cities at that time. On the frontier and in undeveloped sections the entire upstairs of the inns was usually one room, filled with beds. For example, Captain Frederick Marryat, of *Midshipman Easy* fame, records that he slept in one inn room that contained twenty beds, two sleepers in each bed. This was somewhere east of the Mississippi in 1838.[7] Sleeping accommodations in the untamed districts were as they had been in colonial days, the days McMaster speaks of when he says: " The traveler . . . slept in the first bed he found empty, or, if all were taken, lay down on one beside its occupant without so much as asking leave, or caring who the sleeper might be." [8] William Tudor, a visitor in 1820, relates an anecdote that perhaps sheds further light on this interesting subject. Says he:

An individual in Connecticut, of great talents and respectable connections, who led a graceless, dissipated life, was traveling with a small party, the individuals of which were all known to each other. Among them was a very respectable matron, who, in the course of conversation, began to reproach the rake with the life he led. — She lamented that a man of his abilities, of such respectable family, should pursue such a course. Her zeal made her very eloquent, and the object of it began to wish to be rid of the discussion. He observed to her, that she was very severe; that people were very much the same;

that there was less difference between them than she supposed. O! no, she said; there was nobody as bad as he. — In a deprecating tone and manner he replied that most people would act alike, when put in the same situation; that his conduct and hers would be the same, if placed in similar circumstances. — She retorted that it was impossible; that they could never act alike in any case: he thought he could name one; — she defied him. — Suppose, then, madam, that in traveling you come to an inn, where all the beds were full except two, and in one of these was a man, and in the other a woman, which would you take? — Why, the woman's, to be sure. — Well, madam, said he, so would I.[9]

All this, however, was during the age of candles, but as late as 1830 in New York the temperamental Fanny Kemble, with her customary captiousness, wrote in her journal: "It seems to me that the people of this country have an aversion for solitude, whether eating, sleeping or under any circumstances,"[10] a criticism which was repeated forty years later (with far too much generality) by a writer in *Putnam's Magazine,* who declared guests liked to sleep in crowds " and may demand the same room and bed as others." Cowboys and hill-billies, yes, if there were a group of them traveling together; but not the general run of travelers. The single-room idea gained ground rapidly in this country from the time of the Tremont onward, and in all the first-class hotels travelers were required to " double up " with strangers only if they came at a time when all the single rooms were taken. The Tremont and other first-class hotels had emergency rooms with two or three beds in them, where new arrivals slept until the following day, when they were transferred to single rooms as fast as vacancies would permit.

Privacy was made doubly sure at the Tremont, for the hotel ushered in the novelty of a lock on the door of every room, no two of which could be opened with the same key. Ingenious patent locks became one of the wonders of the

YE BOWL AND PITCHER PERIOD

period, and the populace marveled over them perhaps more than we marvel over the mechanical wonders of today. Clever Yankees were inventing all sorts of them. In the *Family Magazine* they are mentioned as one of the marvels of the Astor House.[11] The Tremont's room keys were attached to iron bars, nearly half a foot long, an inch wide, and an eighth of an inch thick, so that guests would not be likely to carry them away in their pockets, a habit which guests still have and which has resulted in the only federal law applying directly and solely to hotels. It was enacted by Congress in 1926 and makes it possible for the guest to mail a room key back to a hotel, postage collect.

Keys for guest-rooms did not become universal until many years after the Tremont came on the scene. Dickens, on his first visit to the United States, in 1842, stopped at an inn in Ohio which had no locks on its doors. His room had two doors, opposite each other, both opening outdoors. The wind blew them open so often that he was forced to " blockade them with portmanteaus " to keep them closed.[12]

There were two other simple innovations at the Tremont that were considered luxurious. Every room had a bowl and pitcher, and every room had free soap — not the individual cake of scented soap of today, with its fancy wrapper, but a large piece of hard yellow soap that welcomed the coming and speeded the parting guest until it was all used up. A trifling matter it seems nowadays, but in 1829 even the cheapest soap was a costly luxury; until the latter 1840's practically every American family kept its own leach-tub for the manufacture of lye. Two or three times a year the family made a barrel of soap, for which soap-fat had been saved. Even today in the hotels of Europe, except a few in the principal cities, one does not get free soap. The bowl and pitcher, victims of low-comedy derision for these many years, were an innovation imported from London and Paris, where they had been introduced for the post-chaise trade about 1800. A few innkeepers prior to the Tremont's time had a supply of bowls and pitchers and would send one up to a guest's room, with a supply of water, on request, but it seems to have been a service grudgingly granted. In most of the inns of that period the guest could wash himself before breakfast and at other times in the bar-room, or, if at a country inn, he could wash in the kitchen or at the back-yard pump. Although the bowl and pitcher began to beat a retreat within a few years after the Tremont opened, they have not, to this day, given way entirely to hot and cold running water, as the jaded traveler frequently discovers when he puts up at some backward small-town hotel.

The Tremont began its career at a time when modern plumbing was so young that it was still strictly a first-floor matter, and no plumbing supplies were being manufactured in this country. The Tremont's plumbing, as up-to-date as possible, consisted of a group of eight water-closets — perhaps the first in America, except, possibly, a few in mansions — running cold water in the kitchen and laundry, and running cold water in the bath establishment. The Tremont's bath establishment had eight "bathing rooms," all in the basement "adjoining the housekeeper's apartments, the laundry and the larder." [13]

Gaslight was another novelty at the Tremont. Gas was in its infancy as an illuminant at that time. America's first commercial gas plant had been built in Baltimore in 1817 and it is probable (though not a matter of record) that Barnum's City Hotel had gaslight. The Tremont used gaslight only in its public rooms, and whale-oil lamps in the guest-rooms. Even these lamps were very uncommon. It is said that the old American House, still running in Boston, was the first hotel to have gaslight throughout the house. It opened in 1835. Until the latter 1840's, however, practically all hotels used gaslight only in the public rooms, per-

YE BOWL AND PITCHER PERIOD

haps because of installation costs or perhaps because Mine Host could not trust his guests with it. Sarcastic clerks are said to have instructed bellboys to "Show this gentleman to Room 248, and see that he doesn't blow out the gas," and gruff night-watchmen sometimes inquired: "What'd you leave your gas burning all night for?" The proverbial reply to this was: "Danged if I know, but there was a big sign on it that said: 'Don't Blow Out the Gas.'" Those were the days when "Another Gas Death in Hotel" was a common newspaper headline. It was Bill Nye who remarked that "The door of our room is full of holes where locks have been wrenched off in order to let the coroner in." There was a period in the existence of the old Grand Union Hotel in New York, along toward the end of its days, when an unusually large number of its guests committed suicide with gas. Simeon Ford, the landlord, explained that although he had never catered to this class of trade, the hotel seemed to be getting more than its share:

> We never have written letters to prospective suicides at other hotels inviting them to come with us at reduced rates [he wrote], and yet, when a man feels it is time for him to shuffle off this mortal coil, it seems perfectly natural for him to drift into our hotel, unostentatious though it may be. It is a comparatively easy class of trade to satisfy. They do not stop to inquire whether the plumbing is modern or antique. They do not ask whether their rooms are decorated in the style of the First Empire or the Seventh Ward. Give them a good six-foot gas-burner, about fifteen hundred feet of illuminating gas at $1 a thousand, and a few uninterrupted moments and they are content.
>
> Not long since I came into my office one morning and found a gentleman there simply boiling with rage. It seems he had just been married — indeed, had spent the first night of his marital career under our roof. On arising in the morning he had been told by some busybody that the room which he occupied had, on the previous day, been occupied by two persons who had committed suicide therein. He was very indignant. I endeavored to pacify him. I said: "My dear sir,

THE AMERICAN HOTEL

you would scarcely expect us to put a silver plate on the door, and silver handles, and consecrate the room to the memory of the dear departed. We are conducting a hotel, not a cemetery." [14]

Such were some of the physical characteristics of the old Tremont. The owners had spent three hundred thousand dollars to make it what it was, and although that is an insignificant figure as costs go in this day of forty-million-dollar hotels, it was a rather staggering sum one hundred years ago. It had taken the better part of ten years to get together enough money to build the hotel. The movement had started soon after the old Exchange Coffee House (which served very well in its day) went up in smoke, on November 3, 1818. But investors were afraid, perhaps because they had had a rather sad experience with the Exchange. It was a "community-owned" hotel and those who put their money into it were the forerunners of the legion of hotel stockholders today. They were stung badly by tricky financing and construction graft and, as one of them remarked, as he stood watching the building burn: "The Exchange was conceived in sin, brought forth in iniquity, and now is being purified by fire." [15] The Massachusetts legislature of 1824-5 authorized a company to build the Tremont at a cost of not more than five hundred thousand dollars and to raise the money by stock subscriptions.

But there were other things besides the superb building and its equipment that set the Tremont apart from all its predecessors. About the hotel there were many of those little intangible things that give a hotel quality. This, of course, was due to its managers, the Boyden family. There were three Boydens, whose ancestor had come from Ipswich, England, fourteen years after the arrival of the *Mayflower*. Simeon Boyden, the father, was a cloth-dresser and manufacturer of wool-cards in Orange, Massachusetts, prior to 1810, when he began keeping a tavern in Market Square,

YE BOWL AND PITCHER PERIOD

Boston, where the Plymouth stages started. Later he became landlord of the Indian Queen Tavern in Bromfield Lane (in 1818) and of the City Hotel on Brattle Street, Boston (in 1822). He was known as the "Prince of Landlords," and when he sold the City Hotel, he was paid a large bonus not to keep another hotel in Boston during a period of years. He had two sons. Frederick was running the New England Coffee House and was satisfied with it, and, as the father was barred from becoming proprietor of the Tremont, he suggested to the owners that they lease it to his other son, Dwight, who was then a clerk in a Boston counting-house. Thus Dwight Boyden became the titular head of the Tremont, assisted by his father in an unofficial capacity.[16]

Father and son assembled for the Tremont whatever innovations of service had been introduced elsewhere, and adapted and enlarged on them. To these they added numerous ideas of their own. They kept the hotel clean as a pin throughout, gathered together and trained a staff as it had never been done before, waited on their guests hand and foot, and gave them the best of everything, including French cuisine, introduced for the first time in a hotel. Theretofore *la cuisine française* had been confined to a few restaurants run by expatriate French chefs. The Tremont's "rotunda men" were the first bellboys, and Seth Fuller's newfangled annunciator — forerunner of the room telephone — was first installed at the Tremont. Self-service in American houses of call was at an end; the day of "the guest is always right" was just over the hill.

The Tremont was patrician from stem to stern and catered only to the upper stratum of European visitors and to those Americans who were getting on in the world — those rough and ready commoners who were becoming genteel and able to indulge their taste for luxury, pomp, and circumstance. There were more of them in Boston at that time than anywhere else. The Tremont made itself safe for upper-classdom by fixing a flat two-dollar-a-day rate. It had no fifty-cent or dollar accommodations for the *hoi polloi*, as the other hotels had in such profusion. Its management was the first to recognize, as a matter of policy, the fact that, in spite of all the shouting about liberty and equality — and there was a great deal of it then — there were upper, middle, and lower classes in America, and that the top layer was yearning for exclusiveness.

But, grand as it was in its day, it was but the beginning of modern hoteldom. It managed to round out its sixty-fifth birthday before it finally disappeared under the picks and crowbars of the wreckers, but twice in its career, in 1852 and again in 1889, it had to be closed for modernizing. Even then it was unable to keep step with the march of progress and in its last twenty years was lagging behind newer Boston hostelries. On the occasion of its first temporary closing the plumbing facilities were extended to all parts of the house, and other improvements made. On the second occasion the house was equipped with electric lights and other up-to-date features. But it hadn't long to go. The last guest moved out on December 3, 1894, and the first great representative of the bowl and pitcher age of hotel-keeping, the first to mark the full and recognized burgeoning of that remarkable institution known as the modern first-class hotel, became but a memory.

The opening of the Tremont had an almost immediate effect throughout the country. Every city in this nation of (then) twelve million population had unbounded faith in its future and wanted a hotel as good as the Tremont, or better, and got it as speedily as possible, whether there was business enough to justify it or not. Generally there was not, but American enterprise had accepted the theory that good hotels make much travel, and that no city amounts to anything unless it has one or more on which the community can

YE BOWL AND PITCHER PERIOD

lavish prodigal admiration and which will give visitors a favorable impression of the city's greatness, enterprise, and hospitality. This theory has prevailed since that time and is perhaps the chief reason (though not the only one) why America has so easily maintained her hotel leadership.[17]

Thus within a few years after the Tremont opened, a great many other fine hotels were built, and it lost rank as America's finest. Its first famous rival, the Astor House, was opened in New York on May 31, 1836. John Jacob Astor, accumulator of the first great American fortune, felt that if Boston could support a house like the Tremont, surely the metropolis could support one even finer, for New York was getting to be quite a city, even though the thrifty city fathers did continue to depend solely on moonbeams for street-lighting during half the month.

Then, as now, New York was the most cosmopolitan of American cities, and its travel was growing by leaps and bounds. A *Strangers' List* published in 1835, containing the names of all transient guests registered at the city's twenty-six hotels during a period of 207 days, from February 9 to September 4, listed 59,970 visitors to the city, or about 290 a day, in the period of heaviest stage and steamer travel. The editor of the *Sunday Morning News* called this " an almost incredible number," and Stephen B. Holt, landlord of the largest hostelry in the city, inserted a big advertisement explaining that the average stay of visitors was three days. Thus in six months at $1.50 a day this produced $270,000 in business for the hotels, "a very fair business for such establishments for six months," said Holt, "as the bill for board is generally the least item in the expenses incurred during a residence at a hotel." Therefore, he declared, he would not raise his prices, as some other hotels had done, but would keep them at $1.50 to $2 a day and $10 to $12 a week.[18] Holt and his hotel were in bankruptcy at the time.

Although Holt's Hotel was built four years after the

opening of the Tremont (Holt's was opened on January 3, 1833), it fell far short of the Tremont's standards. There was too much of the old inn about it, and as a building it was, as one writer said later, "a perfectly plain building, without the slightest pretension to architectural beauty, but it makes an imposing appearance from its magnitude." It was six stories high and had 225 rooms (at the beginning); its belvedere could be seen from Brooklyn Heights and by East River ferry passengers. The *Journal of Commerce* called it the "wonder of New York" and described its various features, especially the luxurious bedclothes, all made by Mrs. Mary Holt, who had spent six years with needle and thread (this was before the invention of the sewing-machine) stitching 1,500 towels, 400 pairs of sheets, 400 pairs of pillow-cases, "all ruffled and pointed," 250 bedticks and 300 patchwork bed-quilts of ample dimensions, several of them "composed of pieces no larger than a two-shilling bit."[19]

Holt's had other handicaps. One was its location, at Fulton, Water, and Pearl streets, near where Holt had made his money running a "one-shilling plate and two-shilling ordinary" at the Fulton Market. It was too far away from the main current of life on fashionable Broadway, and in a district distinctly seafaring and uninviting in character. Holt's always smacked of the sea, and its guests were mostly seafaring men — skippers and their mates, pursers and ships' doctors from all corners of the seven seas stretched their legs under its tables and drank its grog. On hot summer nights they could sit on the "captain's walk" on the roof and drink juleps. This walk, railed in with ornamental iron, was similar to those which at that time were more or less common on the square-built roofs of the more costly houses of the New England sea-coast towns. In more recent times it has been referred to as "New York's first roof garden."[20]

The old City Hotel continued to be cock of the walk despite all competition, as a social center, at least. It had been remodeled, enlarged, and improved and was being conducted in general in a style more nearly like that of the Tremont. Its only real rival was the American Hotel, at Broadway and Barclay Street, originally the town house of John C. Van den Heuvel, member of one of old New York's most exclusive families. His son-in-law, John C. Hamilton, enlarged it and changed it into a hotel, opened in 1827 under the management of William B. Cozzens, son-in-law of Abram (Brom) Martling, member of an old Knickerbocker family who had for many years run Martling's Tavern (torn down in 1814), where the Tammany Society was organized. In 1810 Tammany, which then had three thousand members, moved from Martling's Long Room, which Whigs called "The Pigpen," to the new Tammany Hotel, wherein was located the first Tammany Hall. Although the Tammany was small and tavern-like, the American was fitted up to make a direct bid for the same class of local business as that of the City Hotel. There was enough for both houses by that time.[21]

Thus it was fated that the famous old Astor House should be New York's first modern palace hotel. Just as the Tremont had overshadowed all its predecessors in Boston, the Astor relegated to the background all its predecessors in New York. Undisputed leadership passed to it at once. Although both were outdazzled within a few years, the Astor and the Tremont shared honors for two or three decades as the foremost symbols of luxury and extravagance. The Astor is perhaps the best remembered of all the old hotels of pre-Civil-War days, while many of the great New York hotels that outrivaled it in the nineteenth century are all but forgotten. Doubtless Horatio Alger, Jr., helped greatly to perpetuate the memory of it in the minds of Americans, for it figured largely in almost all of the hundred and nineteen books Alger wrote about the rise of fictional poor boys from rags to riches. It also figured in many other novels of the period.[22] There was the further fact that Thurlow Weed remained loyal to it, and because of this the Astor continued to be a great political center when it had fallen back as a hotel.

The Astor was at once a duplication and an elaboration of the Tremont, made of the same materials, designed by the same architect, Rogers, and run by the Boyden family. Dwight Boyden, whose reputation by this time was national, was the nominal manager, while his father and his brother Frederick had actual charge.[23] Fitz-Greene Halleck, the poet, who was John Jacob Astor's secretary, used to say that Astor copied all the features of the Tremont, even locating his hotel in a block adjacent to a cemetery, so that guests might have prospects beyond the grave. (The Astor was across the street from the St. Paul's churchyard on the Vesey Street side, while the Tremont was adjacent to the Old Granary burying-ground.) However, the Astor was a more impressive building than its Boston prototype. It was two stories higher, it had nearly twice as many rooms, and the architect had had afterthoughts which elaborated the exterior and interior. Astor, well past seventy when the cornerstone was laid, on July 4, 1834 (the same holiday that had marked the laying of the Tremont's cornerstone), had determined to astonish the world with his grand hotel, and, at an expenditure of four hundred thousand dollars, achieved his ambition.[24]

Every innovation that had distinguished the Tremont was adopted at the Astor. The public rooms of the Tremont were duplicated, but in larger size, and there were more parlor-and-bedroom suites. The Astor had its own gas plant. Although New York had had a gas plant for ten years, gaslight was still a novelty. The New York *Constellation* said, in its account on the opening of the hotel: "The house was lighted by this gas everybody is discussing; but the quantity consumed being greater than common, it gave out suddenly in the midst of a cotillion. Gas is a handsome light, but liable at all times to give the company the slip; and it is illy calculated for the ordinary use of the family."

The Astor had more plumbing and machine-age features in general than the Tremont. Plumbers by now were able to install water-closets and cold running water above the first floor. The Astor's bath establishment, in the basement, had seventeen "bathing rooms" and two showers. The Astor's steam-engine was a piece of machinery that everyone marveled over. It was capable, with the assistance of a force-pump, of "raising water to the several stories, allowing it to be drawn freely, whenever wanted." The water came from artesian wells. New York had no Croton water at that time. "The engine is also engaged in making itself generally useful in all culinary operations, in washing, supplying the baths, &c., &c.," said the *New Yorker*. "We believe it does not yet stipulate any assistance in bed-making, sweeping rooms, dusting furniture, attending on guests, &c., &c.; but in the onward march of improvement, we may expect all this to follow in good time." [25] The engine never got quite that far (it was a bit too early for Robots), but it did provide what may have been the first steam-heat ever used — not for general heating purposes, but to dry clothes in the laundry.

In the public rooms the furniture and decorations were showy and the transient rooms, as the *New Yorker* said, were "all fitted up and furnished in a style of unostentatious richness and severe simplicity, the sofas, bureaus, tables and chairs, from basement to attic, being uniformly of a beautiful black walnut, while the floors are as regularly overlaid with superior oilcloth of various tasteful patterns." There were 309 rooms, and in them, as one traveler relates, "they make up 500 beds regularly, but could make up 800."

According to this traveler the Astor's staff at this time, 1844, included about sixty waiters, five regular clerks, twenty-one washerwomen, five manglers and twelve cooks.

"Take it all in all," he said, "I ne'er shall see its like again. You never have occasion to ring the bell twice: they have twenty rotunda men who do nothing else but answer bells and carry out parcels. Dined at half past two. Three hundred sat down to dinner, everything that could tempt the appetite or please the epicure."[26] Another English traveler in that same year marvels over the fact that the bell on the fourth floor was answered in two minutes. "The waiters are drilled like a regiment of soldiers," he said. "We had a most sumptuous dinner, with literally 'all the delicacies of the season'; what is more astonishing is that you are allowed to take your meals at any hour you please, without extra charge; yet for board, lodging and attendance the price is only two dollars a day. It is to me quite incomprehensible."[27]

An amusing account of the Astor House was written by the sportive Jonathan Slick, Esq., in that humorous classic of early republican days *High Life in New York*.[28] In one of his letters to his father, Zaphariah Slick, Jonathan says:

> Look a here, par, did I ever tell you what a looking place that Astor House is? If I didn't, jest you suppose that all the stun walls in old Connecticut had been hewed down as smooth as glass, and heaped together, one a-top of t'other, over two acres of clearing, up, and up, half way to the sky, and a leetle over; suppose then the hull eternal great heap cut up into winders and doors, with almighty great slabs of stun piled up for steps, and pillars standing on eend, on the top, to hold them down — bigger than the highest oak tree you ever sot eyes on, and then you have some idee what a whopping consarn that Astor House is. At fust I felt a leetle skeery at going to board there, for thin, sez I, if they charge according to the size of the house, I guess it'll make my puss strings ache; but, think, sez I agin, the best

taverns, according to my experience, all'rs charge the leastest prices. I will give 'em a try anyhow.

You haint no idee how nation perlite this ere keeper of the Astor House is tu me! If he aint a born gentleman without help of a tailor, I never sot eyes on one. It would du your heart good tu see how he takes tu me, and how much time he gets to attend tu the hull regiment of boarders in this great stun house of his; and the minit he found out I was sick, up he cum, full chisel, to the room where I sot, and it raly would have tickled you and marm to see how awful perlite he was. I raly don't know when I've seen a feller that's took my notion so; he's a ginuine critter every inch of him. When I told him how peskily my tooth ached he went off and sent a nice nigger woman to take care of me. He sends me the newspapers every morning.

There was no prediction that the Astor House would fail because it was too big and ostentatious, but some timorous New Yorkers feared it might fail because it was "too far up-town." It fronted on the west side of City Hall Park, extending from Vesey to Barclay Streets, some distance north of the hotel center. North of it there was practically nothing but residences. In those days there were cornfields and trout streams long before one reached what is now Times Square, though imaginary streets had been surveyed and mapped as far north as One Hundred and Fifty-fifth Street, a fact which caused much hilarity, for it seemed to be carrying optimism to the point of absurdity. However, the American Hotel was just across the street and over on the other side of the park Jonathan Lovejoy's Hotel and the Tammany Hotel were prospering. But that side of the City Hall Park was already a busy business section, on the route of the stages that came down the Bowery from Westchester and New England. The section also was nearer the East River ferries. There were no transportation facilities in the immediate vicinity of the Astor, for the docks and the Hudson ferries to New Jersey were down nearer the Battery. But New York was growing and the Astor was soon in the center of things. Within two years after it opened, Joshua Walker started construction of the Carlton House at Broadway and Leonard Street, eight blocks northward, opening it in November 1840 for select transient and family trade.

Eventually the Astor's business began to ebb because it was too far down town — that coupled with the fact that it had become too old-fashioned to compete with more modern hostelries. Mayor Philip Hone in his famous diary called the Astor a "Palais Royal" which "for centuries to come will serve as a monument, as it is probably intended, to its wealthy proprietor."[29] But within thirty years the Astor had sunk to the rank of second class, and far short of its centenary it was dissolved in dust. It closed its doors on the first of June 1913, and workmen began tearing half of it down. The other half stood empty, its bleary windows facing the altitudinous Woolworth Tower for a few more years, and finally, in 1926, that, too, was torn down to make way for a skyscraper almost as tall as the Woolworth.

Before it reached the age of forty, the Astor had become so utterly antiquated that it had to close down, in 1875, for extensive remodeling and modernization, at which time it got its first private bathrooms. The management installed bathtubs in the parlors of the parlor-and-bedroom suites, for the suites had become a drug on the market. The neighborhood had become a noisy storm-center of business. Besides, one could get parlor, bedroom, and bath combinations in the fine new hotels of the aristocratic sections north of Union Square. And so the Astor ended its days with makeshift bathrooms that were about twice as large as many hotel bedrooms of today. The management made other improvements to prolong the life of the outmoded old house. Two elevators were installed, the rooms were piped with running hot water, and gaslight was extended to the upper floors.

YE BOWL AND PITCHER PERIOD

But it was hardly worth while. The Astor reopened on July 4, 1876, and was kept going, under various managements, with steadily diminishing success, until finally during its last years no hotel firm would touch it on a leasing basis. The Astor estate continued it in operation with a salaried manager in charge. With its bar and rotunda restaurant, which sometimes fed twenty-five hundred people a day, it continued as a taxpayer for a few more years.

But for ten or twelve years the Astor House enjoyed practically a monopoly of the cream of the commercial business, and for another ten or twelve years it went along on the momentum of its past. During that first quarter-century its register was a blue-book of most of the great and near-great who come to New York. Its decline after that period was rapid and even its architecture, once the pride of the country, was derided. The city's grime had smudged its chaste whiteness to a drab gray, and the new generation, in love with gingerbread, began to speak of it as "the prison-looking Astor." But it had its revenge on the mighty gingerbread palaces that robbed it of its popularity and elbowed it into the background. They are forgotten, while its fame goes marching on.

CHAPTER II

NEWFANGLED NOTIONS

INNUMERABLE things never dreamt of in the old-time innkeeper's philosophy have done their bit toward developing the modern hotel into its present fine flower within the last hundred years. This development, starting almost from scratch with the opening of the Tremont House in Boston in 1829, has moved forward along three outstanding lines — the increase in size, the increase in grandeur, and the adoption of every conceivable luxury-breeding gadget and form of service to outdo rivals and pamper the guest — who had never been pampered before to any appreciable extent.

Americans were duly impressed by the growing size of the country's caravansaries, but the thing that fascinated them was the elegance. There was little enough elegance in America in those days, and hotels gave the Average Man his first great eyeful of it. While landlords piled elegance on elegance, the Average Man looked on with wonder and approval. He liked it all the more because it was free-for-all elegance and just the thing needed to keep him stimulated to the spirit of the times. But, for that matter, even the lordliest Cæsar would have been struck with wonder by all this grandeur. American hotels had become, as one British writer said, " elysiums of grandeur," where even Queen Victoria, if she were to visit these shores, "need not fear the want of queenly accommodations, even in the everyday life of a first-class American hotel."

Or, as the editor of *Harper's Weekly* said: "Our hotels are monstrous palaces of gorgeous sloth and immoral ease."

Mine Host was the first business man in America to appreciate the advantage of glitter and ostentation. It was he who inaugurated the plate-glass age. From 1830 onward landlords did their utmost to outdo one another in impressiveness of architecture, in use of marble, mirrors, and gilt, velvet, satin, and plush. They spent money with a "sinfully extravagant" hand for carved mahogany, walnut, and rosewood, and for sumptuous furnishings and knicknacks of all sorts. They stocked their houses with the finest of linen, silverware, and porcelain. Standards of elegance mounted higher with the opening of each new hotel. The maximum of finery of one year became the second-rateness of the next. During the first thirty years of the modern first-class hotel, up to the time of the beginning of the Civil War, the rivalry in hotel elegance seemed to be a sort of game, like the annual blooming of new models of motor cars and radio sets. Within those thirty years the standard of elegance that prevails in our best hotels today — allowing for differences in taste — was attained.

In his mad scramble to put on all kinds of style Mine Host overlooked only one good item — the ornamental value of the uniform. It was not until 1877 that brass buttons and gold braid made their appearance in American caravansaries.[1] In that year James Breslin, of the old Gilsey House in New York, created a mild sensation by putting his bellboys, elevator men, and doormen into livery. "The idea is a good one and ought to be generally adopted," remarked the *Hotel Mail*, a trade journal. " The boys objected, but this will not interfere with the plan." And it didn't interfere. Within a few months every first-class hotel in the country had adopted the idea. Since then the idea has spread considerably, and today there are few institutions anywhere that can produce such a wondrous assortment of livery as awaits one at the doorways and in the lobbies, vestibules, and halls of the swagger hotels of America. Why American hotel-keepers were so slow in putting their

OLD GILSEY HOUSE, New York

flunkies into uniform is a bit of a puzzle. It surely could not have been because Mine Host feared that democratic America would not countenance so much pomp and circumstance. For many years prior to 1877 the leading hotels of London and Paris had glittered with fancy uniforms. It was

NEWFANGLED NOTIONS

one of the few particulars in which those hotels were able to steal a march on their American rivals.

The two inaugurators of hotellic splendor and luxury, the Tremont in Boston and the Astor in New York, were soon eclipsed in their respective cities by the super-grandeur of newer houses, and in other cities splendid new hotels were soon built. Older houses were remodeled and improved in service and appointments to come up to the new standard. Between 1830 and 1860 several hotels that equalled the

AMERICAN HOUSE, Boston, *last survivor of old nineteenth-century hotels in Boston*

Tremont were opened in Boston, notably the United States Hotel, which stood opposite Boston's first railway station and was opened by Holman and Clark on July 13, 1840; the American House, opened by Lewis Rice in 1835; the old Boylston Hotel, built by Charles Francis Adams; the Shawmut House, opened in 1837 by Gould and Rice, who boasted that it was the most elegant European-plan house in the country; the "new and beautiful" Adams House, which opened in the latter 1840's; the Revere House, which Paran Stevens opened on May 19, 1847; and the old Parker House, which Harvey Parker opened on October 8, 1856.[2]

In New York the supremacy of the Astor House was challenged first by the Howard Hotel, for many years

Horace Greeley's favorite, which Daniel D. and John P. Howard opened in 1839.[3] They were from Vermont, but had been running the old Exchange Hotel, on Broad Street near Wall, for several years and had taken rank as perhaps the most progressive and successful landlords in the city. But the Howard had cost somewhat less to build and lacked the Astor's architectural grandeur. Also it had about fifty fewer rooms. But it made up for these shortcomings in all other respects and easily shared the purse-proud business

REVERE HOUSE, Boston

with its slightly older rival. One of its frequent guests was John Tyler of Virginia, and after he became President of the United States, the hotel management put in his apartment the hotel's celebrated painting, a long-forgotten canvas called *Conrad and Medora*.[4] Jonathan Slick, the Connecticut Yankee whose letters to his " par " made all America laugh itself sick, gives us an excruciatingly humorous account of Tyler's parlor at the Howard:

> . . . In he went, right intu the harnsomest room that I ever sot eyes on in my hull life. Nothing that I ever see at the Astor House was a primin to it. The carpeting was all finefied off, and curlecued

with posies, and green leaves, and morning glory vines went a twistifying all over it as nat'ral as life, and all on 'em seemed kinder tangled up and trying to unsnarl all over the floor, till it raly seemed like treading on a patch of wild posies, with the moonshine a streamin over it; you would a'most smell the roses when a feller sot his foot on a bunch on 'em, they were pictured out so nat'ral and temptin.

A great round table stood in the room like an all-fired big toadstool, cut out of a solid tree, and fancified over with the heaviest kind of mahogany work; and a great big kind of a brass consarn stood on it, with a glass wash bowl on the top, all figgered off and chuck full and a drippin over with fire, that made the hull room look as light as day. You couldn't see the winders, for a hull dry-goods store of the finest sort of white shiny muslin fell all over 'em, tied up and streaked down with blue silk and tossels, and with great sticks of solid gold pinted off at the ends, stuck through the top on 'em and a shinin in the light.

Slick also described the Howard's settees and benches, "curlecued off" with cushions "all tosseled out in silk and covered with velvet, as soft as a young girl's heart and as blue as an old maid with too much larnin." Jonathan accepted the invitation of a pretty to sit beside her on one of these cushions.

The cushion give so that I sprung right up on eend agin, and when I see it rise up as shiny and smooth as ever, I looked at her, and sez I:
"Did you ever!"
"It's elastic," sez she, a puckering up her mouth.
"I don't know the name on it, but it gives like an old friend, so I'll try it again." [5]

The Howard took great pride in the excellence and prodigal abundance of its table, an all-important thing to take pride in in those days. It also scorned to employ French cooks and extolled the merits of "plain American cooking." Its marble-tiled dining-room was always crowded at meal hours and its ballroom, with imported mirrors reaching from the floor almost to the ceiling, with damask and Oriental tapestry between each two mirrors, was the scene of many notable soirées, as dinner dances were called in the 1840's.

Ten years was about the extent of the Howard's life as a social center and as a first-class house, though it continued in operation as a popular commercial house until 1868. It stood on the east side of Broadway, at the corner of Maiden Lane, and even as it was being built, the hotel center was moving uptown to City Hall Park and northward along Broadway. Half a mile north of the Astor House Joshua Walker was building the Carlton House, at Broadway and Leonard Street, completing it in the latter part of 1840; and two blocks north of the Astor, at 304 Broadway, just north of City Hall, a swagger little hotel called the Clarendon was flourishing, opened in 1837 or 1838 by John C. Warren. It had been named after London's leading hotel and was for ten years the favorite stopping-place of English visitors of the upper class. About 1850 a new Clarendon, well remembered by oldsters of the present generation, was opened at Fourth Avenue and Eighteenth Street, east of Union Square.

The second real challenge to the Astor's leadership came in 1844, when the aristocratic New York Hotel opened on November 20 of that year. Superior to the Astor in many respects, the New York began its career chiefly as a family hotel, for it was too far north along Broadway, during the first few years, to make much of a bid for transient business. It stood at the corner of Waverly Place, with its back to Washington Square, the city's most fashionable residence center at the time. The caustic William M. Bobo, up from Charleston on a visit, called it "the acme of high-flung hotels," giving " too much pork for a shilling."

The Astor was definitely elbowed out of first rank by the old Irving House, which opened on September 20, 1848.

NEWFANGLED NOTIONS

Four other remarkable hotels of Broadway's past came on the scene about four years later—the Metropolitan, opened on September 1, 1852; the St. Nicholas, opened on January 6, 1853; Taylor's International Hotel and Saloon, opened in the spring of 1853; and the choice old Prescott House, named after the historian, which was opened on July 28, 1853. These were the outstanding hotel "dazzlers" of New York during the first quarter-century of the modern hotel era. Just beyond this period there arose another hotel of surpassing size and excellence, the famous old Fifth Avenue Hotel, which was opened on August 23, 1859.

Between 1850 and 1855 an unusually large number of new hotels, of varying sizes and types, were built in New York, for it was expected that great crowds would come to the city to see the Crystal Palace, America's first "World's Fair." President Franklin Pierce came to New York to open this exposition and he and several members of his Cabinet were guests of honor at a grand banquet at the new Metropolitan Hotel on the night of July 15, 1853. As a drawing card the Crystal Palace did not quite live up to expectations at first, but toward the end of the year the crowds began to come, and, with additional exhibits from year to year, it kept running until the building burned down on the night of October 5, 1858. The hotels of lesser note that were built for these crowds, although smaller and sometimes less ornate, all had their special points of excellence. The list included the St. Denis, opened in 1852; the second Clarendon; the Gramercy Hotel; and the Cosmopolitan, the oldest existing New York hotel, opened in 1850. Another of this group of old hotels was the La Farge House, at Broadway and Bond Street. A white-marble-fronted palace of about two hundred rooms, it was rushed to completion to help skim the cream of the second year's Crystal Palace business, but on its opening night, January 8, 1854, it burned to the ground. It was rebuilt and reopened in the spring of 1856 under the management of Henry Wheeler and for the next dozen years was one of New York's leading hotels. The Brevoort Hotel, Fifth Avenue's first caravansary, was also one of this crop of hotels, opened on September 7, 1854 and still going strong.

LA FARGE HOUSE, New York

Other cities built hotels fully as elegant, fully as up to date, as those of New York, though fewer of them. New Orleans had its St. Louis and St. Charles hotels, both opened soon after the opening of the Astor House in New York. The Verandah and Exchange hotels were two other fine houses in the Crescent City. Philadelphia had the American House, opened in 1844, and H. J. Hartwell's Washington House, opened in 1845. Then came the Girard House, opened on January 26, 1852, under the proprietorship of

Presbury and Billings, and the La Pierre Hotel, later known as the Lafayette, opened in 1853. Outclassing these was the old Continental Hotel, opened on February 16, 1860, which was torn down in 1923 to make way for Philadelphia's present largest, the Benjamin Franklin Hotel. Baltimore, fourth largest city of the Atlantic seaboard, could boast of its enlarged and modernized City Hotel, better known as Bar-

THE SECOND ST. CHARLES HOTEL, New Orleans

num's Hotel, which was opened on September 27, 1826, and survived until April 4, 1889. Its first proprietor, David Barnum, was a nationally known Boniface, who gave his house a wide fame in the 1830's and 1840's. His chief rival in Baltimore was the Eutaw House, which William Hussey opened in July 1835. The Gilmore House with grilled balconies up to the third floor of the Monument Square frontage, was another notable Baltimore hotel of the old days. It was opened in 1856. One of the finest of them all was the old American Hotel in Buffalo, opened in the same year as the Astor House in New York, and by many travelers said to be fully as elegant and as well conducted as the Astor. It burned down on March 10, 1850, was rebuilt, and again burned down on January 25, 1865.

Westward the course of hoteldom made its way rapidly. Pittsburgh had its old Monongahela House, Cincinnati its Burnet and Spencer houses, and Louisville its Galt House, The booming little city of St. Louis was justly proud of its Planters Hotel, opened in 1841; and a score of years later, with other fine houses, was so sure of its position as the metropolis of the Middle West that it was scarcely mindful of the vigorous young city of Chicago, which, although less than thirty years old, was growing like a weed and was already making a good beginning as a city of grand hotels.

These were some of the caravansaries that during the thirty years preceding the Civil War made Americans gape with wonder and overtaxed Europe's credulity. It was a period of hotel construction and development which E. L. Godkin, editor of the *Nation,* called "extraordinary and precocious," a period when the art of hotel-keeping in America "shot far ahead of anything of the kind known in Europe."[6] American hotels were, as Godkin said, "the wonder of the Old World and formed a prominent feature in the tales of all travelers who had crossed the Atlantic. Their size, the perfection of their organization, the lavishness and excellence of their table were constant subjects of admiration in European newspapers. In fact, they were so much talked about that at least the belief was spread in England, and is firmly held in England by large numbers of people to this day, that all Americans lived in hotels, and that home life in a house was almost unknown on this side of the Atlantic. There was nothing in England, or in France or Switzerland either, except a very few expensive hotels, at which great personages on their travels took 'suites of apartments,' and which no man of moderate means dared to

48

enter." Both at home and abroad American hotels were regarded as skyscrapers are said to be now, as "the most distinctively American thing in the world." [7]

George Augustus Sala, a popular London journalist, was one of the most enthusiastic admirers of America's hotels. "The American hotel," he said, "is to an English hotel what an elephant is to a periwinkle, to borrow a simile from Tupper's Ode to Chaos. . . . An American hotel is (in the chief cities) as roomy as Buckingham Palace, and is not much inferior to a palace in its internal fittings. It has ranges of drawing rooms, suites of private rooms, vast staircases and interminable layers of bedchambers." [8]

All through this precocious period the opening of each new palace hotel was quite a notable event and was widely heralded. Editors, in detailed descriptions studded with superlatives, expressed their amazement in italics and exclamation points, especially when quoting the cost of buildings and furnishings. The zeal for making and acclaiming new records of achievement was already in the American blood. The native walnut furniture of the Astor House had cost *seventy thousand dollars* and its silver and china had cost *twenty thousand dollars!* The hotel had Brussels carpets, marble-topped tables, blue and white "mosaik work" on its vestibule and office floors! Its men's dining-room was *one hundred* feet long and *forty* feet wide, and had a frescoed ceiling *nineteen and a half* feet high! All told, the Astor had cost more than *three hundred and fifty thousand dollars!*

Eight years later there was another gasp of italicized astonishment when the New York Hotel opened, for it had cost more than *five hundred thousand dollars* for building and equipment. And when the Astor House had reached the ripe old age of twelve, the Irving House was opened, a half-million-dollar building with more than a hundred and fifty thousand dollars' worth of furniture! Its prodigal owners had spent thousands of dollars for marble mosaic floors in practically all of the public rooms and had squandered no less than a thousand dollars on a marble washstand in the hotel's "dressing room," which was presided over by "the inestimable Charles Ridgway, the unrivalled haircutter, wig-maker, etc." "Nobody but a *Howard*—a Philanthropist—could have thrown under one roof so many comforts for poor vagabond humanity," said Greeley's *Tribune*.[9]

The Irving had been built by Captain Dan Howard, who had sold the Howard Hotel a few years earlier at a handsome profit. Captain Dan, perhaps the first Boniface to acquire any sizable sort of bank-roll, was for thirty years or more one of New York's most prominent citizens. His last hotel venture was the old Hoffman House, completed in the fall of 1864. Read, Wall and Company was the title of the proprietors, and Howard was the principal member of the firm—the "& Co." It was the style of those days.

The Irving House occupied the block front on Broadway from Chambers to Reade streets, on the "fifty-cent side" of the street. Opposite, on the "shilling side," stood Stewart's department store. The "fifty-cent side" of Broadway in those days had all of New York's choicest shops and for many years was a popular afternoon promenade for the belles and dandies of the town.

Although the Irving had but a short career, despite its elegance, it was one of the most notable hostelries of nineteenth-century New York and takes its place as the introducer of several important innovations of hotel operation and construction. It was the Irving House that introduced that showy falderal of modern hotel-keeping, the bridal chamber. The Irving had a number of these fairy-like boudoirs, which the enraptured reporter of the *Tribune* declared were love bowers "where Eve might have whispered love to Adam after she was expelled from Paradise without regretting the change." The *Evening Post's* reporter, al-

NEWFANGLED NOTIONS

though admitting the sumptuousness of these chambers, was horrified at the thought that they were known by such a vulgar term as "bridal chambers." There is no record of how the Irving's bridal chambers were furnished and decorated, for the reporters had too many other marvels to write about, but those of the St. Nicholas Hotel of 1853 were "lined and ornamented throughout with the purest of white satin — with an exquisite canopy of white satin gathered in heavy folds at each corner, falling over a bed of lace and white satin, which is also surrounded by cushions of white satin." [10] It appears there was no dearth of white satin. The management boasted that it had used five hundred dollars' worth in the principal suite. Carved woodwork, gold-leaf, four chandeliers sparkling with a multitude of crystals, a massive carved four-poster bed — these were some of the features of the marvelous chamber. As a writer in *Putnam's Magazine* said, "Its bridal chambers are scandalously splendid, and timid brides are said to shrink aghast at its marvels of white satin and silver brocade." [11] All palace hotels had bridal chambers for two or three decades thereafter, until practical jokers and irrepressible newspaper humorists of the Philander C. Doesticks school laughed them out of existence, and the time came when not all the king's horses and all the king's men could have dragged a pair of honeymooning newly-weds into a bridal chamber. Such chambers then became known as the governor's suite, or the presidential suite. When Mayor Abner Kirby of Milwaukee opened the second Kirby House in that city, about 1860, he gave each of the one hundred and thirty-six rooms names instead of numbers. Faded newspaper clippings tell of his sending newly-weds to "Paradise," the bridal suite, and drunks to the room called "Hell."

The bridal chamber of the St. Nicholas was typical of that hotel's general grandeur. Undoubtedly the St. Nicholas was the outstanding representative of hoteldom's super-elegance during the period before the Civil War, fully meriting Dickens's declaration that it was "the lordliest caravanserai in the world." [12] The St. Nicholas was a six-story white marble treasure-house of fine, expensive things, such as window-curtains costing $700 apiece, gold embroidered draperies costing $1,000, a grand piano valued at $1,500. On all sides in the public rooms, with their twenty-two-foot ceilings, there was paneled mahogany and walnut, carved richly in scroll and figure designs. Every room, public or private, was crowded with rosewood and mahogany furniture, and the chairs and sofas were upholstered in Flemish tapestry. Turkish rugs and thick Brussels carpets silenced the footfalls in hallways and rooms, and window-hangings of damask and figured silks hung at windows and between beveled French pier-glasses in ornate gilt frames. Mirrors and mirrors and mirrors — they were everywhere, in public and private rooms, in vestibules and halls, with the gaslight from huge fancy chandeliers blazing down through a riot of colored prisms on their highly polished surfaces. And everywhere, it seemed, there was gold paint. The St. Nicholas laid its gold-leaf on with such lavishness that it gave rise to a popular joke of the day. It is related that an English comedian declined to put his shoes outside the door to be shined, for fear the management would gild them.

In this day of *modernistic* furniture and decorations and contempt for the past we may all be expected to smile — or sneer — at the bad taste of the St. Nicholas, like the lady in the hobble skirt laughing at a lady in a crinoline (as Professor Walter Raleigh said). Even in its own day reporters described the St. Nicholas as "a display of barbaric splendor, rather than art or true refinement," but admitted that it went no further in offending good taste than did the expensive mansions of the nabobs of society. Thus it seems to have been merely representative of its time, and although the hotels of later days may have been an improvement in the matter of good taste, it is doubtful if any have surpassed it in mere richness and grandeur. The *Tribune* called it an unparalleled establishment, " the *ne plus ultra* of expense, of richness, of luxury," and declared that palaces were not more sumptuous. " Whatever of splendor and gorgeousness in this way money could procure seems to have been obtained for this hotel with a view to outdo every other in elegance and splendor," said the *Tribune*. " It is evident that a new era has begun for these great metropolitan caravansaries. Henceforth they must be furnished without regard to cost; the days have gone by when quiet comfort, mere neatness and a good table were sufficient." [13]

The St. Nicholas was the costliest hotel of its time, the first to go beyond the million-dollar mark. As it stood, with a small addition built in 1856, it represented an outlay for building, equipment, and site of approximately two million dollars, an insignificant figure as hotel costs go nowadays, when there are hotels having an assessed value of thirty to forty million dollars for building and site.[14] The St. Nicholas also was the largest hotel of its time. The addition of 1856 gave it five hundred guest-rooms, but the old Fifth Avenue Hotel of " Amen Corner " fame opened up in 1859 with five hundred and thirty rooms and held the distinction of being the world's largest for about fifteen years. Five hundred rooms was about the limit in size — although there were a few a little larger — until modern steel construction and other mechanisms made taller buildings possible. Even for many years after the elevator came into use, five or six stories was the limit of height. Hotels like the St. Nicholas sprawled over much more ground space than is required for a hotel three or four times its size today. Another architectural feature of those old hotels was that their rooms were much larger than those of today, two or three times as large, and there was a corresponding prodigal waste of space in hallways and throughout the house.

As for the maximum size, few hotels, then as now, attained it. Most of the hotels built before the 1870's were houses of a hundred to three hundred rooms. For example, the Hoffman House started with only 212 rooms and the Brevoort with 103. Even the old Metropolitan Hotel, occupying a full block front, had only 353 rooms.[15]

The superiority of the hotels of today over the old St. Nicholas and its contemporaries lies, not in their elegance, but in their architecture and construction and their use of all the latest machine-age devices. The St. Nicholas lasted little more than thirty years, closing in 1884.[16] Many of the old hotels have lingered on into an old age of decrepit shabbiness. Others have become office buildings, loft buildings, even warehouses.

Mine Host has been only slightly responsible for the high death-rate of American hotels. His responsibility lay in the fact that he was among the most enterprisingly daring of America's early business men. None was more eager than he to build ever larger and finer and keep strictly up to date. He was perhaps the most eager of all to recognize the machine age and adopt its products. Like most Americans throughout the nineteenth century, Mine Host was obsessed with what Carl Russell Fish has called " the spiritual urge to try new things," and welcomed the conquests of Yankee ingenuity with open arms. It created for him a sort of Frankenstein monster, known as Service. He set a new pace for the world in luxury and service, covering all aspects of hotel operation, including mechanistic things. Once started, there was no stopping. The spirit of the age and the spur of competition saw to that.

And so the rapidity of mechanical and structural development made the average hotel a hopeless back number

NEWFANGLED NOTIONS

within a few years. Each new house had something the older houses did not have, and ten or twenty years made all the difference in the world in the status of a house. New hotels today are not suffering so much in this respect, but improvements structural and mechanical are still going on and the future is hard to foretell. It would be risky to predict the fate of today's hotels fifty years from now.

A bulky catalogue would be needed if one were to list and describe all the thousand and one " newfangled notions " that hotel men have experimented with, successfully and unsuccessfully, since the 1830's, when machine-age economy began its advance in hotels. There has been a wide range of innovations of all sorts, mechanical and otherwise. Some of them have been of such paramount importance that they have " revolutionized " the hotel business three or four times within the past century.

One of the first and most important innovations of modern hotel-keeping was modern plumbing and its bright particular jewel the modern bathroom. Our hotels were the chief beneficiaries of modern plumbing throughout most of the nineteenth century. They gave two generations of Americans an opportunity to scrape their first acquaintance with bathtubs, hot and cold running water, water-closets, and steam-heat. It has been said that today the American public worships the bathroom. If that be so, the birth of that worship was in America's hotels in the 1840's and 1850's. Of all the many ways in which American domestic life has been influenced by hotels, the influence of the hotel bathroom stands pre-eminent.

" Every room with a bath " has been the proud boast of a great many American hotels since the 1890's, but men still living were born at a time when no hotels had rooms with baths, nor even so much as a bathroom " down the hall." The only baths in hotels prior to the middle 1840's were public bath establishments. Some of these were in the basements of hotels. Others were located near hotels. Perhaps the first bath establishment in America was opened early in the summer of 1794, in New York, " at the bottom of Liberty Street, lately Crown Street, on the North River." James Knox was the proprietor. He advertised the opening of a " new and elegant bathing house, for long desired by the ladies and gentlemen of New York," and announced that cold baths would be one shilling, " either outside or under cover," and warm baths four shillings. " Caps, towels and refreshments " also were provided.[17]

Within the next few years quite a number of similar bath-houses were opened in New York, Boston, Philadelphia, and elsewhere. The first hotel to have such an establishment in its basement was Barnum's City Hotel in Baltimore, which was opened three years earlier than the Tremont and was, by the way, the nearest approach to a first-class hotel of all the Tremont's predecessors. Barnum's Hotel was also the first to have a barber-shop in connection.

The hall bathroom and the private bath as a fixed part of hotel service first appeared in 1844, when the aristocratic New York Hotel was opened. Before that time, however, it had evidently been possible for a guest to take a bath in his room, for Lieutenant R. D. White of the British Navy, who was a guest at the old Astor House in 1839, records in his diary that when he arrived at the hotel, early in the morning of a hot July day, he ascended to his room, " up numerous flights of stairs," took a refreshing bath, and then descended to the men's ordinary for breakfast.[18] But the Astor House had no hall bathrooms nor private bathrooms, until after the Civil War, when, as was said in the preceding chapter, it began using a few bedrooms as bathrooms, connected with other bedrooms that had formerly been parlors in the days when the Astor had had swagger permanent guests. Like the Tremont and Barnum's, the Astor had a basement bath establishment, run by "Dr." Henry C. Rabineau, hydropath specialist. Lieutenant White probably took his bath in one of those newfangled portable bathtubs on wheels, and the water for it probably was hauled to his floor on the Astor's marvelous steam dumb-waiter.

A legend which has found its way into print many times within the past dozen years has perhaps given the reading public of today a misconception of the real history of baths and bathing in America in the early days of the republic. Like all legends, this one is far from the truth. It makes out that baths and bathing had a hard struggle to win their way to popular favor and met with much official opposition, including the passage of an ordinance by the Boston common council in 1845 making bathing unlawful except on medical advice; and the failure of passage, by only two votes, of an ordinance before the Philadelphia common council, in 1843, to prohibit bathing between November 1 and March 15. There may have been some agitation by busybodies for bathing-laws of one sort or another, in the interest of health, for one must remember that taking a bath in pre-plumbing days was not the pleasure it is now. It was an ordeal in cold weather, except under the best possible conditions. The poor wretches of those days laid themselves wide open to heavy colds, pneumonia, lumbago, and an assortment of other ailments if they took a bath except during what used to be called "the heated term."

But there was no opposition to bathing because our great grandparents preferred to go about dirty, or considered bathing indecorous, or had religious objections to it. On the contrary, bathing was in great vogue throughout the first half of the nineteenth century; it reached the proportions of a craze. There were a great many bath establishments in all cities and they did a rushing business. Many of them were water-cure "sanitariums" run by hydropathic quacks. Hydropathy, attaining its first vogue at European spas some four hundred years ago, was at the height of its popularity in this country in the 1840's and 1850's. The cult grew to such proportions that it supported for several decades a bi-weekly journal, the *Water Cure Journal and Teacher of Health*, edited by Dr. Joel Shew, author of a book on hydrotherapy that was one of the best sellers of the day.[19] Baths and their curative properties were a favorite topic of conversation in those days, and sometimes of heated argument. In New York the bath establishments were overrun until even the outlandish hour of midnight, according to the diary of a Broadway dandy in 1852, and were an important feature of the city's night life.[20] One could get mint juleps to drink while sitting in a bathtub, and the bath establishments also sold " aromatic Seidlitz powders, fragrant tooth paste, the Shaker's concentrated syrup of sarsaparilla, Liverwort and cohash." To keep the craze going all sorts of baths were invented and patented — compressed air baths, immersion baths, medicated shampoo baths, steam and vapor baths, mineral baths, sitz baths, mud baths, photographic baths, galvanic baths, and baths of all nationalities, creeds, and previous conditions of servitude.[21] The Turkish, Swedish, and Russian baths and several others survive in the bath emporiums of today. Hydropaths advocated bathing as a sure cure for almost every ailment and were among the most liberal and clever advertisers of the period. The Fountain Baths of New York advertised:

> Go, in this changing weather, take a bath!
> It soothes the mind, the body gives relief;
> Comforts the system, drives away all wrath —
> A perfect antidote for toil and grief.[22]

Descending from poesy to prose, the management declared that " a warm bath to a healthy man is refreshing, to an invalid the best medicine in the world. Any candid physician will tell you this."

NEWFANGLED NOTIONS

The bath establishments in the hotels of that time were among the best, but there were others just as good in rather handsome buildings of their own. They were elaborately fitted up and prided themselves on their elegance. This generation doubtless would have considered them crude in their bathing-facilities, for the blessings of modern plumbing had not yet descended on the world to any great extent. But even as far back as Knox's original bath establishment in New York there was some sort of system of piping hot and cold water into the tubs, for Knox in his advertisements said: "The private apartments for the warm bath, which are kept supplied by a constant stream of water, tempered to such a degree of heat as may be agreeable to the bather, will be found equally useful and commodious." There is also, among other clues, the account given by Robert Sutcliff, an Englishman, of his visit to a bath establishment in New York in 1804:

> This morning I was conducted by my companions to one of the Public Baths kept in the city of New York. These Baths are upon a plan I had not seen before. On each side of a long and spacious passage, is a range of small rooms, in each of which is a bath sufficient to accommodate one person; with suitable conveniences for dressing and undressing. On the side of each bath are two brass cocks, the one furnishing warm and the other cold water; so that the bather may have the water at what temperature he pleases. There is also a valve, by means of which, if there is more water than is pleasing, he may let part of it out. Some of these baths are made of white marble; and are so constructed that a person may lie down or sit in them. So grateful it is to remain a considerable time in them, in the warm season of the year, that it is a common practice for bathers to take books with them to read while they indulge themselves in the Bath. There are also baths in a different part of the house set apart for females.[23]

Warm baths in those days were often prepared in a tub with a cover on it, to conserve the heat. There were various sorts of these covered tubs. One of them is said to have been designed by Benjamin Franklin, who modeled it somewhat in the shape of a shoe. It was in a tub somewhat similar that Marat was sitting when he was stabbed to death by Charlotte Corday. Ordinarily the tubs were oak or pine boxes lined with copper, lead, or zinc, made to order by carpenters and tinsmiths. One can still find such tubs in old mansions gone to seed, principally in Eastern cities. The old St. Nicholas Hotel, in keeping with its general magnificence, had some bathtubs that were boxed in with carved

THIS IS NOT A COFFIN. IT'S A BATHTUB, VINTAGE 1870's

walnut, and the bathroom walls were similarly elaborated. The old Prescott House in New York also is said to have had some bathrooms of this type, and perhaps there were others in other swagger hotels. Carved walnut was the first fashion in elegant bathroom decoration in New York. The ancestor of the glistening enameled tubs of seamless pressed steel in vogue today was patented by J. L. Mott of New York in 1853, but these old-fashioned cast-iron tubs were not exactly things of beauty. They, too, were boxed in for many years. White paint and enamel began to come in a little while before the dawn of the gay nineties.

All the crop of hotels built for the Crystal Palace business in New York had private bathrooms, and no doubt many were elaborately fitted up. A writer in *Putnam's Magazine* at the time speaks of " the unlimited number of baths, which are now matters of course in our hotels." [24] Doubtless all the better class of hotels after the opening of the New York Hotel had private bathrooms and hall bath-

SWAGGER BATHROOM INTERIOR OF SIXTY YEARS AGO

rooms. In the following year, 1845, Hartwell's Washington House in Philadelphia boasted of its private baths in " fine apartments for ladies and gentlemen," and a little later the old Coolidge House in Boston opened with private baths for guests.[25] It was many, many years, however, before a hotel could boast of " every room with bath." The first hotel to make this boast appears to have been the Victoria Hotel in Kansas City, built by George Holmes on Ninth Street between McGee and Oak streets and opened on May

14, 1888.[26] The Victoria had two hundred and forty rooms, all parlor and bedroom suites, with a bath for each suite. A smaller hotel, the Castle Square in Boston, later called the Arlington, advertised itself when it opened, in 1894, as being the first hotel to have every room with bath. But it, too, was a family hotel, with parlor and bedroom suites throughout. The late Ellsworth M. Statler seems to have been the pioneer of "every room with bath" in transient hotels, the original Hotel Statler, which opened in Buffalo in 1907, being thus equipped.

Plumbing in its early days was a vexatious and expensive problem for hotels, as it was everywhere. It was noisy and smelly and otherwise faulty; drains clogged with exasperating frequency. The first step in modern plumbing in hotels was, of course, the simple cold-water faucet in the kitchen or basement. The trade of plumbing was quite a different thing from what it is today. George Youle, New York's pioneer plumber, back in 1794, was a pewterer as well. His chief work was making house leads and scuppers, gutters, cistern linings, etc. The etc. included the manufacture of pewter distilling-worms, "suitable for stills of from 10 to 30,000 gallons," also the manufacture of spoons and candle molds.[27] Plumbers make hardly any of those things nowadays; if they do, they don't advertise the fact. When the Tremont House was opened, plumbing seems to have still been strictly confined to the first floor and basement, but within three or four years plumbers had begun piping water to upstairs rooms, and in 1833 the New England Coffee House was able to advertise that it had running water on the top floor, "by hydraulic pressure."[28] It evidently took another ten years to get plumbing to the point where private bathrooms were possible.

Another branch of plumbing, the installation of heating systems, was also in its beginning at this period. Experiments with steam and hot-water heating plants had begun

NEWFANGLED NOTIONS

in the early 1830's, and in 1839 Niblo's Conservatory in New York was successfully heated by hot-water pipes. In 1840 a plumber began advertising in New York newspapers that he was prepared to install hot-water heating systems. So far as is known, no hotels took advantage of this offer. First-class hotels had either fireplaces or little parlor stoves in suites and bedrooms. But it is said that heated bedrooms were none too common in the one-towel houses. Warming-pans were used, as they had been in some of the old inns, to take the chill and dampness out of sheets at bedtime. But at least as far back as the eighteenth century Americans had developed a fondness for plenty of heat, as is indicated by the comments of various European travelers. Like food, fuel was plentiful and cheap.[29]

Perhaps the earliest use of steam-heat, as said before, was at the old Astor House for the drying of clothes in the laundry. " The drying process is accomplished in five minutes, by spreading the clothes on wooden horses running on railroads, and leading them into a large close apartment heated to a very high temperature by steam," said a writer of 1843.[30] The hotel may not have had this feature at the beginning of its career. By 1846 the problem had been worked out sufficiently to make steam-heat an actuality. In that year the Eastern Exchange Hotel in Boston had the distinction of being the first public building in America heated by steam.[31] Small wrought-iron pipes conveyed the steam, and the heat was diffused by coils of pipes. Radiators came in later. The first was patented in 1855 by A. D. Pelton of Clifton, Connecticut, whose " radiator of steam heat apparatus " was the pioneer of thirty other radiator patents within the next twenty years.[32] One of the glories of the Metropolitan, St. Nicholas, Prescott, and other hotels of that period was that they had steam-heat on all floors. But they had it only in the public rooms and the hallways of bedroom floors. The guest-rooms still had parlor stoves and fireplaces. George Augustus Sala was much amused by the stoves. It seemed ridiculous to him that anyone should want heat in a bedroom.

It was not until the 1870's that steam-heat and all other facilities of modern plumbing came into widespread use, and although hotels led in adoption of these innovations, even in them plumbing and steam-heating were not at all universal during the first fifty years. For example, as late as 1877 the American House in Boston was able to advertise that it was "the only transient house in Boston with water fonts in every chamber."[33]

The one great invention conceived almost chiefly as a result of the demand for it in first-class hotels was the "vertical railway," that useful contrivance which we know today as the elevator, without which our skyscrapers would be impossible. The first elevators were installed in the old Fifth Avenue Hotel in New York in 1859, but the elevator idea had been in the minds of several inventors for a score of years or more before that time. As early as 1833 Holt's Hotel in New York had been equipped with a crude steam-power hoisting apparatus, used to carry baggage to upper floors. It is not improbable that this crude lift sometimes carried a passenger, as is more than intimated by Asa Green, who wrote a satirical volume in burlesque imitation of the travel books written by visiting foreigners. Green mentions the hoist at Holt's, saying it was used to haul baggage and passengers to upper floors; which may have been an exaggeration, as was Green's statement that Holt's was eleven stories high and "looks down on surrounding buildings in the same manner as our most gracious English nobility look down upon the peasants beneath them."[34]

The need for elevators was often discussed. "Baggage is hauled up, but the guest must trudge up the stairways," lamented the *Tribune,* in its account of the opening of the

Metropolitan Hotel in 1852.[35] Again, a few months later, when the St. Nicholas Hotel opened, the same newspaper deplored the lack of elevators, saying: " In a six-story hotel it is five weary flights of stairs to the top. This is an awful toll for human legs, and unnecessary. There is steam power at hand and there are ingenious brains enough to

HOTELS WERE THE FIRST TO INSTALL ELEVATORS

invent an elegant and convenient apparatus to convey skyward the upward-bound and earthward the descending, without such excessive labor of mortal muscle." [36] In that same year a model for a passenger elevator was exhibited at the Crystal Palace. It was an elevator similar to this model that was installed at the Fifth Avenue Hotel five years later. The Fifth Avenue had three elevators, but only one was for passengers. It was near the main entrance and grand staircase, at the end of that long, wide corridor that led from the street entrance to the desk. " For the benefit of those who are desirous of sparing their ambulators any extra trouble, this will be found very advantageous," said *Leslie's Weekly;* [37] and the *Tribune,* triumphant at last in its campaign, felt certain that anything that would save women the " debilitating labor" of climbing up and down stairs would be popular. But the women were not the only ones who appreciated the benefits of the elevator. It made an equally big hit with the he-men of the day.

Compared with the swift, smooth-running elevators of today, the Fifth Avenue's pioneer lift was a slow, crude affair, though the car had plenty of carved mahogany and nice plush seats. The chief value of the elevator from the hotel management's point of view was that it made the guest-rooms on the upper floors as desirable as those lower down. Heretofore the top floors had always been cheaper than the rest in the six-story houses, but now that flights of stairs no longer held any terrors for the guest, upper rooms could be sold as easily as those nearer *terra firma,* and at corresponding prices.

After the elevator the next great innovation in hotels was electric light, successor of the flickering, treacherous, and smelly gaslight which had been a novelty a few years earlier. On the morning of October 21, 1879 Thomas A. Edison pronounced his incandescent lamp a feasible commercial invention, and early in 1882 the old Hotel Everett, run by Samuel H. Everett at 84–90 Chatham Street (Park Row), New York, blazed forth with one hundred and one of Edison's incandescents in its main dining-room, lobby, reading-room, and parlors. This was the first hotel lighted by electricty.[38] This Hotel Everett was in no way affiliated with the old Everett House on the north side of Union Square, which most old-timers remember perhaps better

NEWFANGLED NOTIONS

than they do the Park Row Everett. But all its former glory has departed; only the worn shreds of its olden grandeur remain. It stands about two blocks northeastward from City Hall Square, and the trains of the East Side L go thundering past its windows. Even at the time the electric lights were installed, the Everett Hotel had seen much better days, despite the fact that Everett announced in advertisements that " the grandeur displayed within the marble walls of these establishments [referring also to another hotel that he owned] is unsurpassed and the cuisine has no superior, both in edibles and service." It was far from the hotel center, which had moved far northward along Broadway by that time.

Samuel H. Everett and his brother, C. E. Everett, had for several years been running a very popular restaurant on Vesey Street, down near the Washington Market and Jersey ferries. In 1872–3 they built a two-hundred-room hotel on the restaurant site, 102–106 Vesey Street, with a wing running through to Barclay Street. This was opened in 1874 and was known as Everett's Hotel and Grand Dining Room. Everett continued to operate this hotel after he had become proprietor of Crook's Hotel. He installed electric lights in both, long before any other New York hotels adopted the new form of illumination. Everett's enthusiasm for electric lights knew no bounds, perhaps because he had for many years been a friend of Edison. He was also a close friend of the Rev. T. De Witt Talmage, a Brooklyn divine who attained a fame almost equal to that of the Rev. Henry Ward Beecher. The Hotel Everett started with one hundred and one lights, forty-four of them in the dining-room, the rest in the office, reading-room, and parlors on the second floor. The little house organ which the Edison company published mentions that " the chandeliers for the lights are unusually expensive and present a beautiful appearance." A few months later Everett had a larger plant installed in his

Vesey Street hotel, the second in New York to be so equipped. When Edison installed this plant, two lamp-posts were erected at the curb, with the name of the hotel painted on the glass. These two lamp-posts were illuminated with clusters of thirty-two-candle bulbs and constituted New York's first electric sign — the first bright glow of the Great White Way.[39]

The second hotel to have electric lights was the Palmer House in Chicago. The enterprising Potter Palmer installed a small plant in his hotel in the spring of 1882. It provided ninety-six lamps for two dining-rooms. The Vendome Hotel in Boston, then operated by J. W. Wolcott, was the third, in June 1882, with a plant that provided fifty lamps for the main dining-room and ten in the front office. During the first four or five years of the electric-light age hotels used the new illuminant only in public rooms and continued using gas in guest-rooms. There were a few exceptions. The first hotel with electric lights in all its guest-rooms was the Sagamore Hotel at Green Island, Lake George, New York, a summer-resort house, which began its 1883 season, under the management of M. O. Brown, with a plant of 350-light capacity, including one in each of the 172 guest-rooms. The Edison company laid stress from the beginning on the advantages of electric lights in hotels, but hotel men, in common with business men in general, held out against it as long as possible. For example, such a notable hotel as the old Fifth Avenue in New York did not install electricity until 1891.[40] Out of 123 Edison light-plants in the country in October 1882, only five were in hotels.[41] But before the end of the decade, hotels almost everywhere had electric lights, and no hotel could call itself first class that did not have them. Perhaps the first hotel to go in for electric lighting on a grand scale was the Ponce de Leon at St. Augustine, Florida, which in 1887 had a plant supplying current for 4,100 lights.

NEWFANGLED NOTIONS

The telephone, which came into use about the same time as electric lights, necessitated another radical and expensive readjustment in hotels, for in the course of a few years it routed the " electro-magnetic annunciator " out of all the real swagger hostelries and substituted room phones in its stead. Any middle-aged hotel guest today should be able to hark back to the time when very few hotels had room telephones — none prior to 1894 — but used, instead, an annunciator system. " One ring for ice-water, two for bellboy, three for porter, four for chambermaid, and not a darned one of them will come,"as a wisecracker of the gay nineties said. The annunciator had been doing noble service in hotels ever since the days of the Tremont House, which began with a system invented by Seth Fuller, the first machine-age contraption patented solely for use in hotels. A few of the old inns of the better sort had put ordinary handbells in the rooms. This plan was in use in some of the older, less pretentious houses as late as the 1850's. The introduction of the annunciator must have been a real gift from heaven to landlord and guest alike, for it muffled the dingdong of the hand-bells and enabled the guest to press a pushbutton — America's first — in his room whenever he wanted to ring for ice-water or call a bellboy. A tinkle or buzz in the office and the dropping of a metal disk which revealed a room number was all the noise it made.[42] Various types of annunciators were invented in subsequent years. The old Holland House in New York when it was opened, in 1889, had one with a dial in each room. A list of a hundred and forty articles was printed on the dial. The guest turned the dial to the article he wanted and pressed a button. The bellboys and clerks did the rest. The famous old Grand Union Hotel, which stood opposite the Grand Central Terminal in New York, used annunciators until it closed. Simeon Ford, whose after-dinner speeches sent many a gathering into convulsions of laughter, closed the Grand Union in 1914, and when wreckers demolished its 842 rooms — all at a dollar, and a dollar and a half — the last great stand of the old annunciator disappeared. It is said to be still in use in a few old hotels on back streets in cities and in the smaller communities.

The annunciator had obvious limitations, and as early as 1877, when the telephone was still a "scientific curio," the *Hotel Mail* predicted that room telephones and telephone clerks would soon be standard features of hotels.[43] It took the telephone about fifteen years, however, to reach that stage of development. The first commercial switchboard began operating in New Haven in 1878, and New York's first exchange was opened in 1879. Several New York hotels were among the original "numbers" on that exchange. They had office telephone connections and a few permanent guests in family hotels had private phones, but that was as far as the use of telephones in hotels went until 1894, when the Hotel Netherland reopened, after having been closed several months for alterations. It was the first hotel to have room phones and a hotel switchboard for them.[44] In those days electricians had to work out their own plans for installation of room phone systems, this perhaps being the chief reason why hotels generally were so tardy in fulfilling the *Hotel Mail's* prediction. Even such a notable caravansary as the Waldorf, opened in 1896, used annunciator's until 1902, when room phones were substituted, eight years after many other hotels had installed them.[45]

Such were some of the major machine-age innovations that kept Mine Host in a continual hop, skip, and jump of readjustment from 1830 on through the rest of the century. There were many minor innovations that helped to widen the gap between the old-time inns and the modern first-class hotels. As, for example, spring beds. When the first modern hotel, the Tremont House, was opened, there was no such

NEWFANGLED NOTIONS

thing as a spring bed. The first bedspring was patented in 1831 by J. French, of Ware, Massachusetts, and within the next dozen years a few first-class hotels probably introduced French's invention. The St. Nicholas and Metropolitan hotels in New York had them in every chamber, but they were enough of a novelty at that time, 1853, to warrant special mention in the newspapers. "The beds consist of a *sommier elastique* or spring mattress, with a heavy hair mattress upon it — better could not be," said the *Tribune* in its account of the St. Nicholas.[46] Meanwhile the average American continued for forty years, when at home, to sleep on the old-style corded beds or on slats covered with a mattress stuffed with hair, felt, or what have you, for quantity production of bedsprings was not possible until a machine had been invented for their manufacture. Thus they remained a costly luxury. Until 1871 springs were all made by hand, generally in little factories that devoted most of their time to supplying ladies with duplex elliptic frames whereon to drape their hoop skirts.[47]

Another minor hotel innovation gave rise to a separate line of business that flourishes throughout the country. One day in 1866 Francis H. Jenks, a New York bank official, made a business trip to Boston and stopped at the old New England Hotel, which Lambert Maynard had been running since 1848. A good many cattle-drovers from Maine, Vermont, and New Hampshire used to stop at the New England in the 1850's, and after they had sold their live-stock, had fat wallets, which they did not care to carry about town with them. Maynard bought at auction one of those sheet-iron Salamander safes that a New Englander had invented in the 1820's and had a carpenter put compartments in it, with individual locks. He rented these by the day or week to drovers, market gardeners, and other guests. The plan was a big success. It gave Banker Jenks an idea, and upon his return to New York he began to organize the first

71

stock-company for the conduct of a safety-deposit-box business. The company was called the Safe Deposit Company, and its vaults and boxes occupied the basement floor of the Mutual Life Insurance Building, at Broadway and Liberty Street. A similar company was organized soon after in Philadelphia; the first in Boston, the Union Safe Deposit Company, was organized in 1868.[48] The idea also spread among hotels after the Civil War, and a safety-deposit-box service for temporary care of valuables is still a feature of first-class hotel-keeping.

And so the introduction of new conveniences, great and small, has gone on in all departments of the hotel, and is still going on. The big basic forms of mechanical service, such as plumbing and heating, elevators, lighting, telephones, ventilation, are now all thoroughly developed and perfected and perhaps will no longer have a share in making hotels obsolete — though one cannot be certain about that. Skyscraper architecture also seems to have reached a stage of development that will remain fixed for a while, at least, though one reads many startling predictions for the future. Locations in most American cities have, by this time, become fairly stabilized, but may have to be readjusted if travel by air supersedes all present modes of travel. Just at present it is frills of service of a minor nature, things that are still in the pure luxury class, that are receiving Mine Host's attention. He is manifesting toward these the same progressive spirit that he manifested a hundred years ago when the first modern hotel came on the scene with so many of them. The most recent mechanical innovation in hotels is room radios. Mine Host expects the next perhaps will be television.

CHAPTER III

WESTWARD HO

TAVERNS as primitive as those of colonial days were practically universal west of the Alleghenies at a time when the evolution of the modern hotel was in full swing in the cities of the Atlantic seaboard and in New Orleans on the Gulf coast. During the first quarter of the nineteenth century there were no cities in what is now our Middle West in which to build pretentious hotels. But many cities were getting a start, and when Cincinnati, Pittsburgh, Louisville, Chicago, St. Louis, and other places began to grow, their hotels grew with them; indeed, ahead of them. The characteristic tendency of all America to go the limit in hotel elegance and size manifested itself even more in the West than it had in the East. Whereas the smaller cities of the East were often content to get along with old inns remodeled and enlarged, the vigorous young cities of the Middle West, though much smaller, built palaces for the wayfarer. By 1850 many a booming little city of the plains had at least one hotel nearly or quite up to the standard of those of Boston and New York.

When the Tremont House opened in Boston in 1829, Chicago was a frontier outpost of some two or three hundred people; and in 1836, when the Astor House was opened in New York, Chicago had about three thousand people. San Francisco and Los Angeles were somnolent Mexican villages, each with only a handful of people. Cincinnati, center of a great river traffic, and growing like a weed, was the metropolis of the Middle West. It had a population of twenty-five thousand in 1830 and boasted nearly fifty thousand ten years later. Farther west on the Ohio, Louisville was booming; farther north Pittsburgh, Buffalo, Cleveland, and Detroit were the only places of consequence. Detroit had a population of ten thousand, and Buffalo of eight thousand. New Orleans was the biggest boom town of the lot at that time, but New Orleans was a seaport and in the Far South, and there were special conditions that caused her growth.

Practically every foot of United States territory west of the Mississippi and vast tracts east of the river were still Indian country. The government was selling choice farm land in Ohio, Indiana, Michigan, Illinois, and other states at a dollar and a quarter an acre, and settlers were swarming westward. Other myriads were coming from western Europe. By 1850 they had filled up the region east of the Mississippi and were pushing the frontier westward across Iowa and Missouri and into Nebraska, Kansas, and other trans-Mississippi states.

During this period village and wayside taverns sprang up everywhere, and the unending procession of emigrant wagons that toiled along every westward trail from daybreak to sundown filled them to overflowing. The accommodations of these taverns were of the roughest, often the dirtiest, sort. Some were log houses, some frame, but all were of the same rough-and-tumble character. This was all a part of the business of pioneering, which necessitated a reversion to primitive living. Life had to be lived at its roughest, and the luxuries and softening influences of civilization were not to be had. As the frontier moved westward across the Alleghenies and onward toward the Mississippi and the Pacific, the conditions of early colonial days were repeated. In the immature West a man and family with a wagon-load of household goods, including a barrel of flour, a bag of salt, and a barrel of whisky, could come along and pick out a likely site, chop down a few trees, put up a log hut, and hang out a sign: " Tavern." That was about all there was to it, except that Mine Host then had to go out in the back yard and shoot a deer or a wild turkey to stock his larder.

Charles Cleaver, a Chicago pioneer, gives an excellent description of a tavern at Michigan City, Indiana, at which he and his family and friends stopped overnight during their covered-wagon trip from New York to Chicago in 1833.

> It will answer [he wrote] for nineteen out of twenty of all we have stopped at during our journey. The outer door opens into a large, dirty room full of smoke, used as a sitting room for men folks, and also as a bar room, for in one corner, generally in the angle, you will see a cupboard, with two or three shelves, on which are arranged in bottles the different colored liquors. I suppose the color is about the only difference you could have found in them; the brandy, gin and whisky generally come from one distillery, in Ohio, with the addition of burnt sugar and juniper berries to suit the taste of their customers.
>
> From this room you would enter the family sitting room, also used as a dining room for travelers, and out of that usually a kitchen and small family bedroom. The upper story, although sometimes divided into two rooms, was often left in one, with beds arranged along the sides. Once in awhile you might find a curtain drawn across the further end of the room, affording a little privacy for the female part of the occupants, but not often even that, the beds being occupied promiscuously on the first-come-first-served principle. As for the table they set — well, I suppose they did the best they could, for certainly there were few dainties to be purchased that winter for love or money, and the appliances for cooking were far from what they are now. In many, a pot hung over the woodfire, a frying pan and a baking pot being about all they had for culinary purposes in those days.
>
> Meals usually consisted of bread, butter, potatoes and fried pork; now and then you might get a few eggs, but not as far west as

Michigan City. Such were the accommodations travelers had to put up with in those early days. If they could find a tin wash basin and clean towel for the whole party to use, generally used standing on a bench outside the back door, they considered themselves fortunate. Nine times out of ten the beds were all occupied, or at least bespoken, but our travelers were well prepared for such occurrences, as the one-horse wagon was filled with mattresses, blankets, pillows, cloaks and other articles to make a comfortable bed on the floor, which was done according to circumstances, sometimes in the bar room, sometimes in the dining room.[1]

This first-line brood of taverns was short-lived. The villages of the region grew rapidly. Within a few years some of them were cities. Capitols, courthouses, schools, churches, colleges, and mansions were built and Main Streets were lined with business houses, large and small. Invariably a fine hotel graced a prominent corner and was the pride of the city. In those cities destined to major greatness, particularly Chicago, St. Louis, and San Francisco, hotels were built during the 1860's and 1870's that set a pace even for New York. That is not to say that those cities were superseding New York as the greatest hotel city in the world, but that individual hostelries larger and finer than any in the metropolis were arising, built by local capital and managed by landlords (generally graduates of the Boston and New York school) who vied with the metropolitian managers in the adoption of the numerous progressive ideas that have improved American hotel-keeping within the past hundred years. For example, San Francisco's old Palace Hotel was the world's largest and costliest caravansary when it was opened, in 1875. Four million dollars had been lavished on the building and another half million on the furnishings. It was a new high mark to shoot at and remained so for several years.[2]

In Chicago the great fire of October 9, 1871 wiped out of existence practically all of Chicago's early-day hostelries, and the city started life anew with a fresh crop of magnificent houses, all of them up to the minute in everything that then appertained to first-class hotel-keeping. Especially was this true of the "Big Four" — the Tremont House, the Sherman House, John B. Drake's Grand Pacific Hotel, and Potter Palmer's Palmer House. These elaborate caravansaries raised the standard of comfort and luxury beyond anything New York had to offer.

The history of hotel-keeping in all the cities of the Middle West and Far West follows pretty much the same general outline: first the crude, makeshift taverns of early pioneer days, run by a landlord and his family; then the small hotels with something of the luxuries and comforts of the hotels of the East. These were enlarged and improved from time to time as the city grew. Finally, a grand hotel of the New York palace pattern, often the largest and most expensive building in the town. Every city had one and treasures the memory of these fine old hostelries of a bygone day where presidents, stray royalty, and other great folks were hospitably entertained.

Chicago's hotel development is typical of what happened in many cities, though it happened on a larger scale in Chicago than elsewhere. The first little log tavern in Chicago was built by James Kinzie, "Father of Chicago," in 1828, on a fork of the Chicago River, at a point known as Wolf's Point. Archibald Caldwell was its first landlord. His certificate as a tavern-keeper, issued by the Commissioners of Peoria County, is dated December 8, 1828.[3] Caldwell ran the tavern for a year or so and then decided to move on to the busy little fur-trading post of Green Bay, Wisconsin. He felt sure that Green Bay had a greater future than Chicago. His successor was Elijah Wentworth, a Maine man, who had come to the banks of the Wabash in October 1829, with his wife, two sons, and two daughters, headed west in two prairie schooners pulled over the villainous roads by three yoke of oxen. Bad weather forced Wentworth to tarry in Chicago, and when Caldwell deserted the Fork Tavern, as it was then called, Wentworth decided to take charge, at a rental of three hundred dollars a year.

The trickle of settlers from the East was growing and within a few months the Fork, which Wentworth had renamed the Wolf Tavern, had competition. Sam and Hank Miller built a tavern on the other side of the river, and Mark Beaubein, a jolly French-Canadian ferryman from Detroit, began to provide lodging and food for the humbler travelers in his log house at the point where the south branch of the Chicago River turned into the main stream. This was destined to flower into the Sauganash Tavern, perhaps the most famous of Chicago's early hotels.

Beaubein, who died in 1882, built the Sauganash in 1831. It was, he averred, the first frame building in Chicago. The little frontier outpost then had about three hundred inhabitants, a good half of them newcomers. Most of this population lived either in the taverns or above the stores. The Sauganash prospered mightily, perhaps because Beaubein had a natural talent for tavern-keeping; more likely because he played the fiddle every night so that his guests might dance. It made the Sauganash the chief social center of the town and gave it a popularity which it retained long after more comfortable hostelries had been built. The Sauganash had, however, outlived its popularity and usefulness by March 1851, when it went up in smoke, a fate that overtakes many landmark hostelries.

Four years after the Sauganash was built, Chicago could — and did — boast of its first brick hotel, the Lake House, at Kinzie and Rush streets, opened in 1835. J. S. Buckingham, a British visitor who stopped in Chicago in 1840, when the town had a population of six thousand, was surprised at the large crowds on the streets and the general bustle and activity. "There are four hotels, all good," he said, "and the Lake House is very superior."[4] In 1837, two years after the Lake House was opened, Chicago, which then had a population of 4,170, was incorporated as a city. The Hon. F. C. Sherman, later mayor of the city, celebrated the event by opening the first Sherman House, then called the City Hotel, under which name it went until 1844, when it was remodeled and enlarged to five stories. Jacob Russell, who had been proprietor of the Lake House, was its lessee and proprietor. The Sherman House and the Lake House shared honors as Chicago's leading hostelries until 1850, when the Couch brothers, Ira and James, built the third Tremont House. The first two Tremonts, both burned, had not been of the first-class type. The first, built by Alanson Sweet in 1835, was destroyed by fire on October 27, 1839; and the second, a three-story frame structure, was opened in May 1840, and burned on July 21, 1849. A guide-book of the year before gave precedence to the Lake House, affording " accommodations equal to any Eastern hotel," at a dollar and a quarter a day, and the Sherman House, " where a splendid table is set." Others mentioned included the Tremont House, the Mansion House, the Western Hotel, and the American Temperance House.[5] The Couch brothers had prospered mightily during thirteen years of hotel-keeping in Chicago and were firm believers in the future of the city, which by 1850 had grown to a population of twenty-eight thousand. When the second Tremont burned down, they bought additional lots and covered the entire site, at the northwest corner of Lake and Dearborn streets, with a five-and-a-half-story structure, designed by J. M. Van Osdel. It cost seventy-five thousand dollars, for which seemingly insignificant amount one could get quite an impressive building in 1850, in Chicago. The Couches got such a palatial place, in fact, and fitted it up so elegantly, that skeptical Chicagoans, according to an early historian of the city, chuckled to one another, calling it "Couch's Folly." It was, they contended, "wholly uncalled for by the demand of the times."⁶ But though Chicagoans may have doubted the wisdom of erecting such a pretentious structure, they were none the less proud of it, and the editor of the *Gem of the Prairies* went so far as to say: "There is perhaps no hotel in the Union superior to it in any respect. Its internal arrangements, including furniture and decorations, are all in the highest style of art, and of the class denominated princely."

The new Tremont was opened on May 29, 1850 and was a success almost from the start. Its guests came mostly from the East, by wagon, stage-coach, and lake steamer, for Chicago then had only one railroad, the Chicago and Galena, which had been completed two years before. About the time the Tremont was opened, Frank Parmalee established his famous bus line, and within another two years he was hauling passengers to and from the hotels and three railway stations, for in 1852 the Michigan Southern and the Michigan Central railways both reached Chicago from the East. It was now possible, if trains ran on time, to make a trip between New York and Chicago in forty-eight hours, "all railroad except a fine steamboat ride midway on Lake Erie."⁷ The part of the trip made by steamer was between Dunkirk, New York, and Toledo, Ohio. The coming of the two new railroads gave the city's growth such momentum that within the next decade its population had risen to approximately a hundred and ten thousand.⁸

The result of all this was that "Couch's Folly" was enlarged twice within the next eighteen years, and in 1868 had nearly three hundred rooms. It boasted a "Ladies' Parlor" furnished at an expense of ten thousand dollars, had installed "Atwood's celebrated improved passenger elevator," and was proud of its cuisine, "unsurpassed in bounty and elegance."

Chicago's second notable hotel of metropolitan proportions, the Briggs House, built by William Briggs at Randolph and Wells streets, was opened about a year after the Tremont was completed. It boasted that it was the largest hotel west of the Alleghenies, though that was not quite the fact. But in grandeur it equalled the Tremont and during its long career provided shelter for many noted guests. It was, in the 1850's, Abraham Lincoln's favorite hotel and he made it his campaign headquarters during his first candidacy for the Presidency.

The success of the Tremont and the Briggs House, together with the coming of the railroads, started Chicago on its way as a great hotel center. The future of the city was now assured, and what had happened in New York in the 1840's and 1850's in hotel construction happened all over again in Chicago in the 1850's and 1860's. One fine hotel after another was built, and by 1860 the city had enough first-class accommodations to take good care of the second Republican national convention, held on May 16–19 of that year. It was the convention that nominated Lincoln.

Fast as the city grew, the demand for hotel accommodations grew even faster, for the entire West was growing at breakneck speed, and Chicago had become its main gateway and its chief distributing point. A guide-book of 1869 listed twenty leading hotels, and there were, of course, many of less elegant type.[9] By the time of the big fire Chicago had become a city of more than three hundred thousand people, had eleven passenger stations for as many railroad lines, and was rightfully claiming the distinction of being the greatest railroad center in the world.[10]

The fire, on the fateful night of October 8, 1871 and the next day, wiped out practically all of Chicago's fine hotels. One of the first to go was the original Palmer House, which had been opened only since October 1, 1870 and which had proudly been advertised as "the only fireproof hotel in the world." It had been built by Potter Palmer, Chicago's merchant prince, at a cost that made the cost of "Couch's Folly" seem like pin-money by comparison.[11] The new Grand Pacific Hotel, which had been completed and opened but a few days, also was wiped out of existence. Along with them went the Tremont and the Briggs House, the Adams House, the Massasoit, the Garden City and Revere houses, the Sherman House, the Laclede and St. James hotels, and all the rest of the biggest and best. Chicago was left practically without hotels. But that did not stop travelers from pouring into the city, nor did the fire stop the city from growing. Strangers were accommodated in all sorts of makeshift hostelries, and then, within less than two years after the conflagration, the city welcomed wayfarers with a brand-new set of hostelries, that were unsurpassed anywhere. Edwards's Chicago directory of 1872 listed eighty-two hotels of all grades. Most of these, of course, were of the cheaper, smaller sort. But all the old leaders were quickly and magnificently rebuilt, and within six years after the fire Chicago had sixteen hotels of the first grade, each accommodating two hundred to eight hundred guests, and there were also about a hundred and forty of lesser rank. The leaders were the last word in fireproof construction as it was understood at that time, and few hotels anywhere equalled them in this respect. They were, too, right up to the minute in every conceivable device that their progressive landlords could think of, and fairly teemed with innovations that, for the time being, put New York hostelries completely in the shade. A guide-book of 1873 said that Chicago had built about twenty first-class hotels since the fire, at a cost of eight and a half million dollars, including the Palmer House (not then quite finished), the Grand Pacific, Tremont, Sherman, Briggs, Gardner, Matteson, Commercial, and Clifton houses, all on the American plan, and Burke's and Kuhn's, European plan. A large number of small houses, of varying quality, also had been built.[12]

The Grand Pacific, the Palmer House, the Tremont, and the Sherman House were known as the "Big Four," and of all the magnificence which these hotels displayed, the one feature that captured the imagination of the country and is perhaps best remembered today was the fact that two hundred and twenty-five silver dollars were imbedded in the checkerboard tile floor of the barber-shop of the Palmer House. Mere hotellic magnificence was taken as a matter of course, but silver dollars in the floor of a "tonsorial parlor" was indeed a novelty of extravagance, and something to talk about. It had the same effect that Coal Oil Johnny produced when he lit his cigars with five-dollar bills. The idea gave the Palmer House more publicity than any other one thing, but the novelty of silver-dollar flooring soon wore off, for within a few years pretty nearly every live-wire town in the country had its "Silver Dollar Saloon." Incidentally, the silver dollars in the Palmer House barber-shop were not put there by Potter Palmer, but by William S. Eaton, lessee of the shop, who cashed in on the idea handsomely within the next few years. Everyone wanted to see that floor out of sheer curiosity, or to verify the reports that a fool could thus waste his money.

Chicago's swift rise to the forefront as a city noted for the number, size, and quality of its hotels was paralleled by a similar and even more spectacular advance in San Francisco.

Before the world learned that Johann Sutter's boss carpenter, "Mr. Marshall of New Jersey," had, by a chance blow of his pick, discovered gold in the California hills, in January 1848, San Francisco had one little tavern, one and a half stories high, fronting on the plaza. An American had built it in 1847 and called it the City Hotel.[13] California was still Mexican territory, officially, but was already flying the Grizzly Bear flag and becoming rapidly Americanized. The little old City Hotel was quite sufficient to handle all the business that came its way, until the summer of 1848, when news of Marshall's discovery began to be noised about. Then began the great stampede of gold-seekers and adventurers, and the meteoric rise of the city. "Of all the marvelous phases of the history of the present," prophetically wrote Bayard Taylor, who arrived at the Golden Gate in December 1848, " the growth of San Francisco is the one which will most tax the belief of the future." [14]

He was pretty nearly right. The annals of San Francisco during the gold-rush days read like a fairy-tale. The swift rise of the city's hotels is an interesting part of the fairy-tale. Within twenty-five years after the rush began, San Francisco's population had increased to 160,000, and besides being graced by the largest, costliest, and grandest of all hotels anywhere in the world, the city had several others that would have been ornaments to Broadway. Samuel Bowles, editor of the Springfield, Massachusetts, *Republican,* visiting San Francisco in 1868, pronounced them the equals of the very best hotels of the East. The boosters were perhaps justified in announcing vociferously that San Francisco was the greatest hotel city in the world.

When the mad rush to the new El Dorado began, thousands of sailors deserted their ships, lying at anchor in San Francisco Bay, and scurried away to the hills in search of " color." All of a sudden there was urgent need for hotels, but there was no one to build them. Instead, some of the deserted clippers were dragged ashore, wedged between posts, and converted into stores and hotels.[15] One of these was the famous old clipper ship *Niantic,* which burned in a general conflagration in 1851. The Niantic Hotel was built on the ship.[16] They were the only "hotels," other than the little City Hotel, that San Francisco had for a few months, and then a number of jerry-built bunk-houses, ironically called Astor House, Irving House, Tremont House, and so on, sprang up. In these places scores of guests slept in one room, in bunks, on cots, and on the floor.[17] There was usually a double row of three tiers of bunks the full length of the second floor of the building, with a narrow passageway between. There was not enough height in the bunks for a guest to sit upright, and those who forgot this fact when they awoke got a severe bump on the head.

Successive crops of these wooden shell hostelries, with gambling-halls and restaurants on the first floor, were wiped out by the six fires that swept the embryo city during the first three years of the gold-rush. Each time the new buildings were an improvement over the old. After a few months in the hills Bayard Taylor came back and found several large hotels which were " equal in almost every respect to the second-class houses in Atlantic cities." One was the Graham House, which had been brought almost bodily from Baltimore, and another was the original St. Francis Hotel, with rooms " furnished with comfort and even with luxury, its table lacking few of the essentials of good living, according to a ' home taste.' " Best known of the San Francisco hotels of the early gold-rush days was the Parker House, built in 1849 by Robert Parker of Boston. This was a two-story building about sixty feet long, boarded on the outside and ceiled with the cotton cloth that was so popular a feature of the city's construction at that period. It fronted on the Plaza (the present Portsmouth Square) and was opposite the City Hotel. The customary gambling-hall, bar-room, and restaurant were on the first floor, and offices and bunks above. It disappeared in San Francisco's first fire, on December 24, 1849, and a new Parker House with a gaudy veranda was built.

Already San Francisco had begun to boast of its fine hotels, even though they were still being built of pine boards and cotton cloth. Listen to the grandiloquent editor of the *Alta Californian,* reporting the Parker House opening:

> The ballroom, the most magnificent and spacious in the country, was graced with the loveliness of many lands. The staid and quiet matrons of our Atlantic States, the gay daughters of Erin, the gazelle-eyed maidens of Alta California, mingled with the gay uniforms of the army and navy, shone conspicuously in the brilliantly lighted room. Not until the early finger of morn had dispersed the purple mantle of night did the votaries of Terpsichore return home.[18]

Rich as the pickings were (sometimes) in the gold-fields, they were not any richer than the business of running a hotel during those first few years of the gold-fever, as the journals of many of the Argonauts show. Stewart Edward White in his novel *Gold* touches upon this situation, presenting a fictional conversation between the proprietor of the Parker House and a group of his guests, who were not prepared to pay the prices asked:

> " I know how you boys feel," the proprietor said. " There's lots in your fix. You'd better stick here tonight and then get organized to camp out, if you're going to be here long. I suppose, though, you are going to the mines? "
> " There's plenty of gold? " ventured Johnny.
> " Bushels."
> " I should think you'd be up there."
> " I don't want any better gold mine than the old Parker House," he said comfortably.

The proprietor of the Parker House was running a two-story frame hotel, bar-room and gambling-hall that had cost $30,000 to build, at San Francisco prices, and that rented for $15,000 a month, according to one authority,[19] and according to another authority rented for $110,000 a year, plus $60,000 a year paid by the professional gamblers.[20] Rents on this scale were the rule for several years.

The price for a little cigar-stand at the entrance of the Union Hotel in 1854 was, so one chronicler states, $4,000 a month. The stand was small, "just large enough for one man to stand in," but it paid its way. The Union at this time was the political headquarters of the city and was the favorite hotel, for the time being, of the Army and the Navy.[21] A single bowling-alley in the basement of the Ward House, which was built on the Plaza in 1850, rented for $5,000 a month, cash in advance, while guests upstairs paid Mine Host at the rate of $250 a month for a miserable little room. At the St. Francis in 1850 one could get what Bayard Taylor called the best board and room in the city at the "unusually cheap" price of $150 a month.[22] The Rev. William Taylor of Baltimore, who went to California in 1849, reported that a bunk cost $30 a week, and the proprietor made no extra charge for "the third plague of Egypt, accompanied by a Lilliputian host of the flea tribe."[23] It was possible, however, according to one authority, to get a bunk in a room with fifty other men for as low as six dollars a week. The sleepers lay on straw ticks, each covered with a single blanket. If there were no blankets left for late comers, Mine Host took them from guests already asleep.[24]

But all this passed away after about six or eight years, by which time San Francisco had begun to emerge out of the mining-camp stage. Meanwhile several hotels providing plenty of comfort and privacy had been established. It has been said that the best hotel during the first ten years was the Oriental, a four-story frame structure, opened in 1851.[25] In that same year, or the next, San Francisco got its first brick hotel, the International. Among others of note was Wilson's Exchange Hotel, later called the American Exchange, which was opened in 1854 and, although frame, was advertised as being fireproof. It was, at least, the largest at the time, with a hundred and thirty rooms.

Within ten years after the gold-rush was started, San

Francisco was a city of well on toward a hundred thousand people and was shedding its mining-camp characteristics. The city's future was assured, and a great building boom began. It was then that San Francisco got its first real metropolitan hotels of pretension, built, equipped, and operated in the style of the best hotels of the East. First on the list was the Cosmopolitan, opened in 1859, followed by the Occidental, a house of four hundred rooms, built by James A. Donahoe, pioneer banker. It was opened early in 1861, and a little later a third pretentious hotel, the Lick House, was opened. Then in 1862 the heirs of J. C. Christian Russ completed the Russ House, which stood on the site of the present Russ Building, San Francisco's tallest skyscraper. Christian Russ was a fellow-countryman of Johann Sutter and had brought his family of twelve to America from Switzerland in 1847 to help colonize Sutter's "New Helvetia." He bought land in and around San Francisco at a few dollars an acre, and although he died in 1857,[26] he lived to see it increase in value more than a thousandfold. Russ was one of those who, when the gold-rush began, was content to remain in San Francisco and let others bring back the gold from the hills. He established Russ's Garden and in 1850 built a hotel called the American.

The Russ House was solely for transients, while the Lick, the Occidental, and the Cosmopolitan had many sumptuously furnished suites, occupied by the aristocracy of the town, forming three different social groups, known as the "Lick House set," the "Occidental set," and the "Cosmopolitan set," the latter composed of Virginia City bonanza kings and their wives.[27] Another fine hotel, the Grand, came on the scene in 1869. Although it had but two hundred rooms, it cost more than a million dollars to build, and it excelled in splendor any other hotel in the world. Thus within twenty years after the discovery of gold San Francisco had five grade-A hotels, as magnificent as one could find anywhere, with accommodations for two thousand guests and representing an investment of more than five million dollars. They were doing a gross business of three million dollars a year and were gilt-edged investments.[28] Contemporaneous with these five resplendent leaders, there were sixty or seventy others, " any one of which in its grade cannot be excelled, if equalled, in any city in the civilized world," as one enthusiast said.[29] There were such excellent houses as the Brooklyn, the Commercial, the International, and the American Exchange — and there was also that famous old haven of roistering and rest for the " honest miner " the What Cheer House.

Many of San Francisco's cheaper hotels (none of them by now in the bunk-house class) were rendezvous of the " honest miner," as Bret Harte called him. Whenever the honest miner came down from the hills — twice a year if lucky; once in two or three years if not — he preferred some one of the humbler hostelries, no matter how much gold-dust he carried, where he could be himself. He did not believe in squandering his nuggets for expensive hotel accommodations in surroundings into which he did not fit. Instead he liked to spend it spectacularly over the bar, at the faro table, and in the brothels of the Barbary Coast, playing Coal Oil Johnny where it would have the most gratifying effect.

The What Cheer House, which began its career in the middle 1850's, was the miners' prime favorite. It was a five-story brick hotel " for men only." Although San Francisco was distinctly a man's town, women had begun to flock in from everywhere — and the " gazelle-eyed maidens of Alta California " were already on the job. Mine Host R. B. Woodward wanted none of them at the What Cheer and so from the first prescribed rules which rigidly excluded them — rules which remained in force until the hectic end of the What Cheer's career, in 1905. The What Cheer had other rules. One of them was: "Guests are requested to avoid the filthy practice of spitting on the carpets, smoking, lying upon beds with their boots on, or defacing the walls by lighting matches, driving nails or moving furniture." The management also took special pains to protect the house from cooties. If a prospective guest was suspected of being afflicted with graybacks, he was sent to a sort of delousing department, where he undressed and lounged around in his birthday suit while his clothes underwent treatment. This was, in fact, a service sought and greatly appreciated by the guests.

The average prospector never thought of going to any other hotel if he could get accommodations at the What Cheer. There he could get a room for fifty cents a night. He might have to share it with several others, but that did not matter. Miners usually bought a supply of lodging tickets when they arrived in San Francisco, each ticket good for one night. If the miner decided to leave town before his supply was used up, the management redeemed the tickets. Perhaps the What Cheer's rates were higher in earlier years, but the fifty-cent rate and the ticket plan prevailed in 1868 when Samuel Bowles visited San Francisco.[30] A few years later, according to the *Overland Monthly,* the rate was two dollars a week and up. For his two dollars the honest miner could get a clean bed, " in a room which is so clean for a hotel that its shortcomings are wholly unobservable by its average occupant, clean water, a towel, and a piece of soap." " What more can the honest miner want? " inquired the *Overland*. But the management gave the honest miner something more for his money. It had a library of five thousand volumes, and one of the largest and best-stocked newspaper rooms in the city. If the honest miner did not care to read, he could examine the large cabinets of assorted minerals and the " beautiful collection of stuffed birds."

If the What Cheer lost money on its rooms — many a hotel has had that experience — it made up the loss in its enormous bar-room and in the restaurant, in which were served some four thousand meals a day, at prices in keeping with the style of the house. They averaged about twenty cents apiece.[31] One could live as expensively or as cheaply in San Francisco as anywhere in the world, after the "feverish fifties" had calmed down a bit. As new hotels went up, the rates of old ones came down, and ten years made all the difference in the world.

Twenty-five years after the first forty-niners began pouring into the sleepy little Mexican village, the old Palace Hotel, the marvel of its day, was being built. It was conceived and started by William C. Ralston, head of the Bank of California ("the Rothschild of America," some called him), and it was completed in 1875 by Senator William Sharon, Ralston's friend and partner. Together they lavished almost five million dollars of Comstock Lode wealth on the building and its equipment in an effort to make it the largest and most magnificent caravansary in the world. They were conspicuously successful with respect to magnificence, but fell short of making it the largest, for in that same year the United States Hotel was opened (on June 20) at Saratoga Springs, with 768 single rooms and sixty-five suites, giving it just a little short of a thousand rooms.[32] But the United States was merely a summer hotel; the Palace was the largest in any city.

The Palace had everything that the best hotels anywhere had, and a few other things besides. Its tremendous cost was the first thing people thought of in connection with it. New York's finest hostelries had cost but a paltry million or two to build. Its size also was talked about, for it covered an entire block of ground. One of its early guests said the Palace was so huge that when one went upstairs and could not find one's room, the best plan was to " pretend you are full, let yourself loose and cuss. Someone will come and guide you to your room." Each of the 755 rooms of the Palace were twenty feet square, except a few of sixteen feet. Besides these bedrooms there were many splendid public rooms, including a lobby grander and more spacious than had ever been seen before, a sumptuous bar-room, a main dining-room 155 feet long and 55 feet wide (the world's largest at the time, so it was claimed); a breakfast room, music- and ballrooms, several private dining-rooms, a children's dining-hall, ladies' parlor, ladies drawing-room, reading-room, barber-shop and public baths, billiard-room with dozens of tables, and several " committee rooms," where one could draw to a pair of aces. In all these rooms, upstairs and down, the millionaire owners had put massive, plush-upholstered furniture, most of it made in San Francisco of native hardwoods. In all respects the Palace was impressively luxurious.

One of the most notable service innovations at the Palace was the introduction of the floor-clerk idea — an idea that was adopted a few years later by the Palmer House and the Grand Pacific in Chicago and by one or two hotels in New York. The Palace installed a desk with an attendant on each floor, near the elevators, and each floor had an annunciator, slots in which to drop letters to the main office, and pneumatic tubes for packages. Each floor clerk could communicate with the main office by means of oral annunciators, or " speaking-tubes."

The " Grand Central Court," or *patio,* of the Palace, with its crystal roofed garden, was one of the sights of San Francisco. It was a modern version of the old-time inn courtyard. The hotel was a hollow quadrangle, with an interior court 144 feet long and 48 feet wide. The promenade was tiled with marble; in the center of it was a tropical garden, filled with rare and exotic plants, statuary, and fountains.

Band concerts were given in it every afternoon and evening, and the city took great pride in the fact that at night the court was lit by 155 stands of gas, with 503 lights, the globes in all colors.[33] Into and out of this dazzling palm court rolled an endless line of carriages and livery rigs. In no city was more money squandered for buggy rides than in San Francisco, and no city had finer turnouts or more livery stables. Riding in fine carriages was a passion with almost every San Franciscan during the gold-rush decades. Tallyho parties and buses with passengers from the railway stations and ferries whirled into the court, and occasionally a stagecoach from some boom camp in the hills entered it. Day or night it teemed with life and color.

The staunch construction of the Palace was a feature that interested builders and architects. It was thought to be quakeproof and fireproof. Its seven stories rested on foundation walls twelve feet thick, and in the foundation and superstructure thirty-one million bricks were used, besides stone, marble, and iron.[34] Iron stairways throughout were enclosed in solid brick and stone, from basement to roof, and this massive masonry was enclosed in a wrought-iron skeleton that weighed three thousand tons. For added protection there were four artesian wells with a capacity of 28,000 gallons per hour, supplying water for a 630,000-gallon reservoir under the grand court, and seven roof tanks which held 130,000 gallons more. Three large steam fire-pumps forced water through forty-five four-inch mains, reaching above the roof and distributing it through 327 two-and-a-half-inch hose bibs. The floors were equipped with 15,000 feet of carbolized fire-hose, self-acting fire-alarms were in all parts of the building, and a thirty-minute fire-patrol was maintained.

Such was the old Palace, the pride of San Francisco, which lasted until the great fire which followed the earthquake of April 18, 1906. It was in advance of its time and for the first ten or fifteen years did not pay. It had cost too much to build and was too expensive to operate. None but a man with more money than he knew what to do with, coupled with an intense civic pride, would have thought of spending so much money on a hotel in the 1870's. But W. C. Ralston was just that sort of man. With him San Francisco's welfare was a passion and he was willing to go to almost any length to enable the city to outdo the world. " From the early days until he died he was more to San Francisco than any other man," wrote Judge C. C. Goodwin, who, during the bonanza days, published and edited the Virginia City, Nevada, *Enterprise,* on which Mark Twain was a reporter.[35]

The Comstock Lode, which made the whole coast dizzy with its wealth, gave Ralston his opportunity. But in the exciting days of 1874, when the hotel was less than half finished, a turn in the tide of Ralston's fortunes brought his bank and his private fortune into a financial snarl. Ill and discouraged, Ralston went one day to Harbor View, a resort north of the city, and swam far out into the ocean, until a current caught him and carried him to his death.

Construction of the hotel, which had begun in March 1874, was carried on by Ralston's friend and business associate William Sharon, trustee of the estate and one of the " Big Four " of the Comstock Lode bonanza. When the hotel was completed, Lewis Leland, one of the famous Leland family of hotel-keepers, came on from St. Louis with a complete hotel staff to manage the house. Things started off with a flourish, but in 1877, when Sharon saw that he had a white elephant on his hands, he tried to sell the hotel to the government to use as a post-office or customhouse. The government would not buy, and the hotel continued on. In course of time it became a big money-maker.

Two years after the opening of the Palace, Elias J. Baldwin, known to the world as " Lucky " Baldwin, one of

BALDWIN HOTEL

PALACE HOTEL. *Views of the old Palace and Baldwin Hotels, San Francisco*

the boldest and shrewdest speculators and gamblers San Francisco has ever produced, opened his famous Baldwin Hotel, in February 1877. It had long been Baldwin's ambition to build and own a fine hotel. He was a practical hotel man and had laid the groundwork of his fortune in the hotel and livery-stable business in San Francisco. But like Sharon and Ralston he had made his millions out of the Comstock Lode, though he was an "outsider" and had to fight the San Francisco "bank crowd," to which Sharon and Ralston belonged, for control of one of the richest of the Comstock mines.

Heedless of expense, Baldwin built and equipped his hotel in the grand manner, and although it was smaller than the Palace, having only 495 roms, it was an elegant house. And it became the headquarters of a faster crowd. Its barroom, perhaps the largest in San Francisco, was adorned with the finest collection of bar-room art in the country, outside the Hoffman House in New York, and the free lunch was a Lucullan feast. The Baldwin also was noted for the excellence of the meals it served in its dining-rooms. One of the hotel's novelties was a billiard-room exclusively for women. Or, if the ladies preferred to sew, there was a special sewing-room for them, "where the fair sex can pursue their tatting free from the interruptions of man." [36]

John A. Rice, who had been proprietor of the Grand Pacific Hotel in Chicago, was lessee and manager of the Baldwin for a time, but couldn't make a go of it. Baldwin himself took charge, and in years to come he made it one of the most popular hotels in the country. One of the things for which the Baldwin Hotel is remembered was the stylish four-in-hand coaches that rolled between the hotel and the ferries and trains. Drawn by high-spirited, high-stepping horses, groomed and harnessed to perfection, tossing their heads and champing their bits as they cantered along the streets, the Baldwin turnout always attracted much attention. Always a lover of horses — he was internationally known as a turfman in his later years — "Lucky" Baldwin kept up this show of style throughout the career of the hotel, which came to an end on the night of November 24, 1898, when it was destroyed by fire, with a loss of several lives. It was never rebuilt.

"Lucky" Baldwin was one of early San Francisco's most popular characters. He arrived in California by way of the Overland Trail in 1856 and fitted into the rough, devil-may-care life of the city like a glove. High society would have nothing to do with him in the years of his affluence; he scandalized the country too often to be in the good graces of the *bon ton,* but as a popular figure he was a success. Around his life many decorative legends have grown up. Unregenerate and game to the end, he died in 1909 at the age of eighty-one, the last of the bonanza kings to go, and by order of his last will and testament there was no religious service at the funeral. Instead a few old cronies delivered eulogies, and a band played selections from *La Bohême,* the grand march from *Aida,* and other operatic pieces.[37]

Like Chicago, San Francisco got a complete fresh start when all its splendid hotels, together with hundreds of other buildings, were wiped out by the big fire. Immediately the work of reconstruction began, and within little more than a year some of the city's largest and finest hostelries had been rebuilt. Half a dozen improvised hotels — quickly remodeled apartment houses that had escaped the fire — were opened within a few months. The Majestic, still standing at Gough and Sutter streets, was the first of these, opened on June 1, 1906.[38] The Fairmont Hotel was being built at the time of the fire. It was away from the main business district and escaped with minor damage. Rushed to completion, it was opened on the first anniversary of the fire, and once more the city had first-class hotel accommodations.

Meanwhile a number of smaller hotels had been completed, including the Grand Central, which opened on March 2, 1907; and a few months later, on November 30, 1907, a brilliant reception and dinner marked the opening of the rebuilt St. Francis, under the management of James Woods, who had managed the old St. Francis. It was announced as the third largest city hotel in the world, with 650 rooms, exceeded only by the Waldorf-Astoria, with about a thousand rooms, and the Belmont, with 750 rooms, in New York. The Grand, Manx, Argonaut, Golden West, Richelieu, Stanford, Union Square, and others opened in rapid succession, and finally the new Palace was opened on December 15, 1909, an event which may be accepted as signalizing the return of the city to something approaching normal, and the close of the first period of San Francisco's reconstruction. Since then San Francisco has kept on building hotels. A score of fine ones have been opened within the past half-dozen years. The city now claims third rank as a hotel center, and the claim is not seriously disputed.

Few Southern cities had any really pretentious hotels until about fifty or sixty years ago. There were exceptions, of course — notably New Orleans. Growing at top speed in the 1830's, when it almost tripled its population and passed the hundred-thousand mark, New Orleans got its first grand hotels partly as a result of a rivalry between the inhabitants of the old Vieux Carré and the newer American element above Canal Street. American capitalists, backed by the Exchange Bank, built the original St. Charles Hotel at a cost of $800,000 and opened it on February 22, 1837. It had a great gilded dome, in imitation of the national Capitol, and it was proclaimed the finest hotel in the world, which it probably was. All the ornate hotels were " the finest in the world."

Stung by the insufferable boastings of the Yankee capitalists, the Creoles, backed by the Improvements Bank, began plans to build a hotel that would be finer and larger than the St. Charles, at a cost of $1,500,000. But fate was against them. The crisis of 1837 made them trim sail, and Pierre Soule, head of the enterprise, was financially ruined. The architects' plans had to be revised downward, and finally a hotel that had cost a little less than $500,000 was opened in the summer of 1838. This was the historic old Hotel St. Louis, and although it failed to silence the Yankee boasts, it nevertheless was a splendid hotel. In 1841 it burned down and was immediately rebuilt, on a somewhat more elaborate scale, at a cost of $600,000.[39]

It used to be said of the St. Charles that "half the history of Louisiana" was written in it. The other half, then, must have been written in the old St. Louis, which flourished at high tide until the outbreak of the Civil War. The hotel's vestibule, forty feet wide and 127 feet long, its rotunda, open from noon to three o'clock for business only; its grand ballroom and its parlors were the centers of the city's Creole social and business life. It was also one of the greatest slave-auction centers in the South. For twenty-five years many slave auctions were held either at the St. Louis or in the bar-room of the St. Charles. Both hotels are perpetuated in the pages of *Uncle Tom's Cabin*. In 1845 the Louisiana legislature held its sessions in the ballroom of the St. Louis, adjourning from Jackson because Jackson was "too inconvenient." The hotel was later destined to become the state capitol. In 1874, during the carpet-bagger régime, the state bought the building and used it as a state-house for the next eight years, during which period it was the scene of many stirring political events. In 1884 it again became a hotel, known as the Hotel Royal, under the management of Colonel R. J. Rivers, who had once guided the destinies of the St. Charles. But times had changed and the olden glory of the St. Louis could not be recaptured. And so it closed, after a while, and stood vacant for many years before it was finally torn down, in 1914. It lives in literature in a sketch, "That Old Time Place," a charming picture of its decrepit days, by the novelist Galsworthy.[40]

The St. Charles found fairer sailing. Although its first proprietors, Floyd and McDonald, failed, their successors, E. R. Mudge and Watrous, were successful, and from their time on, the hotel enjoyed prosperity. Like many another fine hotel, the St. Charles was a bit ahead of its time and had to let the city catch up with it. This did not take long, but for seventy years its supremacy was unchallenged. In time the Creole element became as proud of it as they had once been scornful. It became a general social center and its sixteen-thousand-dollar gold table-service clanked and glistened at many a historic banquet. Politically it was always a storm-center, and its Parlor C was the scene of many big political deals.

There have been three St. Charles hotels. The first, designed by Dakin and Gallier, was the one that had the resplendent gold-leaf dome. The fire of 1850 wiped it out, and although the second structure, designed by Isaiah Rogers, was more up-to-date, it lacked some of its predecessor's architectural grandeur. The great gilt dome was missing, because construction costs had to be economized. In 1878 this house was remodeled and enlarged from three hundred to four hundred rooms. It was destroyed by fire on April 28, 1894, with a loss of four lives, and the present St. Charles was built immediately thereafter.

Only a few old hotels had gilt domes like that of the St. Charles. One was Stanwix Hall, opened in Albany in 1833, though the dome did not appear until 1844, when a large addition was built. Another was the American Hotel in Buffalo, opened in 1836. It burned down on March 10, 1850, the year the St. Charles burned. At the time these two hotels were being reduced to ashes, the old Burnet House in Cincinnati, in which Grant and Sherman planned the "March to the Sea," was nearing completion. It was opened on May 3, 1850. The London *Illustrated News* called it "the best hotel in the world," an opinion in which many concurred. The Burnet did, indeed, out-gadget the hotels of New York and was as sumptuously furnished and had as great a layout of public rooms as any hotel of its day. It was, besides, the most distinguished hotel architecturally. It remained one of the most famous and popular hotels in the country until it was closed, in 1926.

At the time the Burnet was opened, Cincinnati, then the largest city west of the Alleghenies, was booming at a great rate and had grown from a population of 46,328 in 1840 to 115,435 in 1850.[41] Sixth in size among the cities of the country, it lacked but a handful of being third in size. River trade was at its flushest and travel was growing heavier every day. Cincinnati supported two grand hotels, besides many smaller, less pretentious places. The Burnet's chief rival was the Spencer House, built at a cost of four hundred thousand dollars and opened in December 1853. During the Civil War days the Burnet was the Union headquarters while the Spencer was known as a "Copperhead hotel." It had a large soundproof room for professional gamblers between their trips up and down the Ohio and Mississippi rivers. During the war this room is said to have been used for many secret meetings of Southern agents and leaders.[42]

Before the Civil War St. Louis was Cincinnati's chief rival for the honor of being the largest city in the West. The Mound City caught up with the Athens of America in 1860, when each had 161,000 population. Thirty years prior to that time St. Louis had been a little fur-post with fewer than five thousand people, just beginning to grow as a result of Mississippi River traffic and settlement of the surrounding country. The budding young city then took pride in its National Hotel, a four-story frame building erected by

Thornton Grimsley, whose brother, William G. Grimsley, ran the house for several years. J. S. Buckingham, an English traveler, who visited St. Louis in 1840, wrote that " there are nine hotels in St. Louis, but they are among the worst we have seen in the West; even the best of them, the National Hotel, being greatly inferior to the second and third-rate hotels of the Eastern cities. But this evil will be speedily remedied by the completion of the large new hotel now erecting near the center of the city, which will soon be completed." [43] This was the second Planters Hotel, the first Planters having been a tavern opened in 1817 by Evarist Maury.

The second Planters was built by a community stock-company, chartered in 1837 and capitalized at a hundred thousand dollars. It had 215 rooms and was opened on April 1, 1841, with Stickney and McKnight, of Boston, as its proprietors. St. Louis, then a city of twenty thousand, could boast, and did, that it had a hotel comparable in size and elegance with the best hotels in the East. All the world was made aware of the fact that the Planters had " the largest ballroom west of the Alleghenies, 8,911 feet larger than that of the celebrated Tremont House in Boston." This famous hotel flourished until it was torn down to make way for the third and last Planters, which was opened on September 16, 1894, under the management of Henry Weaver. It closed thirty years later.[44]

Another famous hotel of early days in St. Louis was the Lindell, named after Peter Lindell, a pioneer merchant, and opened on November 25, 1863, with a grand ball and banquet attended by the city's high society. The Lindell was the hotel of St. Louis's aristocracy. It was a massive stone structure, but with the customary fire-trap interior, which sealed its doom on the evening of March 30, 1867. The Lindell that the present generation knew was the second of that name, opened on September 28, 1874.

Less exclusive than the Lindell, but more full of romance and color, was the old Southern Hotel, built by a stock-company that was organized in 1857. Because of war demoralization, however, it was not possible to complete and open the hotel until December 6, 1865. Flames destroyed it, with heavy loss of life, on the morning of April 11, 1877. It was rebuilt and reopened on May 11, 1881, and continued in business until 1913.

Like Buffalo in the 1830's and 1840's, Omaha was the country's foremost travel gateway in the 1860's and 1870's, through which, as Owen Wister said, "all America was draining prismatically." Omaha's cheap hotels prospered during this period, while its swagger hotels languished. It had several. The first hotel worthy of the name was the Douglas House, built in 1855, when "Omaha City" was still a village. Three years later the ornate Herndon House was built not far from the banks of the Big Muddy. It was run in magnificent style, but didn't pay and finally, about 1870, became the general offices of the Union Pacific Railroad. The eccentric George Francis Train, builder of the U. P., was its guest in 1867, by which time its proprietors had despaired of making it pay as a first-class house and were letting it go to pot. Train was eating dinner one day when a vicious wind came whistling through a broken window-pane. He complained about it to the manager, but nothing was done, so he paid a Negro ten cents a minute to stand in front of the broken pane until he had finished dinner. He vowed he would build a rival hotel, and that afternoon bought ten lots and put a crew to work digging a foundation. Within three months Omaha had another ornate hotel, the Cozzens House, managed by the Cozzens brothers, sons of William B. Cozzens, first proprietor of the Tammany Hall Hotel in New York. Like the Herndon it was badly located and was too elegant for its day. The building was put to other uses in 1871.[45] But Omaha was growing fast and other hotel builders took a chance on it. In 1873, when the town had a population of about eighteen thousand, a company spent two hundred thousand dollars on the five-story Grand Central Hotel, as good as any hotel in the country until it burned down, five years later.

The last of the famous old hotels of Omaha's callow days, the Paxton, built in 1882, made way for a modern successor some three or four years ago. Kansas City, the Big Muddy's other great jumping-off place, still has one of its pioneer hotels, the old Coates House (originally the Broadway Hotel), built by Colonel Kersey Coates, who also built the Coates Opera House, run in conjunction with the hotel. Construction began in 1860, but stopped for the duration of the Civil War. The hotel opened in 1868 under the management of Major Thomas B. Eldridge, whose historic Eldridge House at Lawrence, Kansas, figured prominently in the Kansas border warfare. The original part of the Coates House was torn down in 1889, when a new section, built about 1885, was enlarged.

The sudden rise of new cities in the West, with skyscraper hotels dominating their sky-lines, is by no means ended. Within the past ten years quite a number of boom towns have sprung up overnight and have tall fireproof hotels, with all modern conveniences and copying the style and service of New York. There are several such places in the Texas oil-belt. There are several others in Florida; Miami is the outstanding instance. Before the World War, Miami was a quiet little winter resort with a population of barely five thousand. Its great palace hotels have all been built within the past ten years. But Miami is a recreation center, and hotels are its life-blood, its substitute for factories. As a parallel to what Chicago and San Francisco were in the nineteenth century, Tulsa, Oklahoma, is more representative. Thirty years ago Tulsa had a population of less than a thousand. Then, in 1901, oil was found at Red Fork, across the river. For a time Tulsa was a wild and woolly camp. In 1907, when Oklahoma was admitted to statehood, Tulsa was still a crude boom town, with a population of 7,300. Today it is a magic city of 200,000, the indisputable oil-capital of the world. They will tell you down there that Tulsa is the largest twenty-year-old city on earth, and one of the most beautiful. Among its numerous skyscrapers are many fine hotels. There are thirty with more than three thousand guest-rooms. The tallest is eighteen stories high and has six hundred rooms, each with bath. Another is fourteen stories high, one of fifteen stories, and two of twelve stories. The others are of lesser height. Still another, taller than the rest, is being built.[46] Tulsa has its equivalents of the What Cheer House, but aside from these there are a dozen or more hotels that are plastered with pretension and that are as good as the traveler can find anywhere. In them Tulsa society cuts its finest capers.

CHAPTER IV

WELCOME, STRANGER!

LONG, long ago the landlords of American hotels discontinued the somewhat severe practice of locking their obstreperous guests in the stocks. Times are not what they used to be. Nowadays " the guest is always right " and has things pretty much his own way (within reason), except, perhaps, when it comes to settling his bill. But back in the days of ye olde innes of New England, and all points south and west, the guest was frequently, if not always, wrong and had to take the consequences if he demanded too much service or refused to knuckle down to puritanical rules. Decidedly, in the old inn days the common attitude of Mine Host toward his guest was quite different from the pose of the first-class hotel-keeper today. The hotel-keeper's policy has been, generally, to do his utmost to please his guests, while the policy of the innkeeper was, in the main, " Take it or leave it." The old-time landlord did not believe in catering to the whims of travelers. They were not entitled to have any whims, and must put up with whatever Mine Host volunteered to provide for them — which was usually an irreducible minimum of comfort and service.

This was especially true in America, but even in England it was the tavern-keeper, rather than the innkeeper, who became a jovial figure of literature — the tavern-keeper, whose principal business it was to sell roast beef and ale to steady customers (such as Shenstone, Dr. Johnson, and the Mermaid round table), rather than the innkeeper, whose chief business it was to sell a lodging for the night to unknown wayfarers, here today and gone tomorrow. The tap-room was the part of the inn that caused the poets to twang their lyres. And in both countries the innkeeper was quite a different individual from the roly-poly hail fellow well met that the latter-day romancers made him out to be. There were some of that sort, to be sure, but they were outnumbered ten to one. It is, of course, true that the English innkeeper was of somewhat different temperament from the innkeeper of America. He had to be, whenever His Highness or My Lord came along. Toward the ordinary run of travelers he was as arrogant and indifferent as he could afford to be. Mine Host of America could take a more contemptuous view of all his guests, for he was living under different conditions and had a different social status. He was, on the whole, a blunt and independent fellow, with nothing meek and humble about him, and with nothing cringing or subservient in his make-up. He was a man among men and was well aware of that fact long before Thomas Jefferson wrote the doctrine of natural equality into the Declaration of Independence. He was often, indeed, a man of eminence. The world was his oyster and he paid no deference to rank, wealth, or social position. His motto was: "Treat 'em rough — especially Englishmen."

The Englishmen were about the only fussy travelers with whom Mine Host had to deal. Those of the upper classes who came to America on various meddlesome missions and to see for themselves how the new experiment in democracy was working out were chagrined when they discovered that Mine Host would not jump through the hoop whenever they cracked the whip. Mine Host was perhaps the new nation's most ardent evangelist of democracy and he gave his English guests plenty of enlightenment on that subject. Then, too, in common with most Americans after the Revolution, he did not like Britishers any too well. They were still looked upon as enemies, and it was still a form of patriotism to make them squirm. They knew nothing about liberty and equality and made the mistake of scorning those principles.

Some few sympathetic British visitors seem to have got along very well with Mine Host and the accommodations he provided under his miserable roof-tree, but most of them, judging from the cries of anguish that sprinkle their books, paid dearly for their unwillingness to adapt themselves to conditions as they found them. To them Mine Host was an insolent fellow who absurdly considered himself their equal, as did also his servants — and woe be to anyone who called them servants. They were "the help," and as good as anyone, if not a little bit better — even the maids of all work, who wouldn't hire out unless they were granted bundling privileges. Mine Host was always extremely curious about his guests' personal affairs and used to put them through a sort of personal third degree. He had the impudence to sit at table with his guests and take the best cuts of meat for himself. If guests carried liquor with them, he drank it as though he had a right to it. He took offense whenever guests did not call him by his title of colonel, major, or captain — sometimes general — for he was frequently a militia officer or had served in the Army during the Revolution or the War of 1812. Worst count of all in the indictment, the visitors could not get him or his servants to do anything for them. He turned his back and walked away without a word, leaving them to their own devices. And, sometimes, if they got too nasty about it, he put them in the stocks.

This latter practice, however, is not believed to have been very widespread or of long duration. There is one record of it — perhaps the only one — by the American-born

Rev. Samuel Peters, graduate of Yale and pastor of Hartford, who, after he had been run out of the country, in 1774, by patriots because of his pronounced British leanings, wrote during his exile in London a *General History of Connecticut* — one of those now-it-can-be-told books, in which he let whole flocks of skeletons out of the New England closet, including the forty-five famous "blue laws." The *History of Connecticut* increased the Reverend Mr. Peters's unpopularity, and the short and ugly word was applied to him. But today he stands vindicated, for his blue laws and his accounts of bundling and other matters have been found to be gospel truth. Even his volume of history was accepted as such by the Connecticut Yankees, and a new edition of it was published in his old home town. Said the Reverend Mr. Peters in his enlightening volume:

> Europeans whose manners were haughty to inferiors and fawning to superiors were neither loved nor esteemed. An English traveler through Connecticut meets with supercilious treatment at taverns, as being too much addicted to the superlative mood, when speaking to the landlord. The answer is, "Command your own servants, not mine." The traveler is not obeyed, which provokes him to some expressions which are not legal in the colony, about the impertinence of the landlord, who, being commonly a Justice of the Peace, the delinquent is immediately ordered into custody, fined and put in the stocks. However, after paying the costs and promising to behave well in the future, he passes on, with more attention to his "unruly member" than to his pleasures. Nevertheless, if a traveler softens his tone, and avoids the imperative mood, he will find every civility from these very people, whose natural tempers are full of antipathy against all who affect superiority over them.[1]

One may infer from this that, as a cure for the imperative mood, a few hours in the stocks was what old-timers generally called "a sovereign remedy." Mine Host manifested his equality in various other emphatic ways. There is, for example, the cherished legend, long current in and around Coshocton, Ohio, of how the future king of France, Louis Philippe, was bounced out of a tavern there.

About the year 1800 Colonel Charles Williams, who had been a trader, trapper, hunter, and Indian scout in that section for several years, built a little log tavern at the forks of the Muskingum River, the future site of Coshocton. Louis Philippe, then Duke of Orléans, came to the tavern and presently voiced his dissatisfaction with the accommodations and service. It seems that he, too, was addicted to the imperative mood, which found no more favor in Ohio than in Connecticut. Colonel Williams's reply to the future king's commands was emphatic. Very likely it was quite profane, for the historian of Coshocton tells us the colonel "made a virtue of profanity."

The words that passed between the two are not on record, but it is related that the duke emphasized the fact that he was heir to the throne of France and would not condescend to bandy words with a mere "backwoods plebeian." The colonel retorted hotly — and probably in choice unparliamentary language — that he was an American citizen, and that every American citizen was a king. The national Constitution, and every state constitution, assured him of it.[2] And, by way of proving that he was as good a man as any scion of royalty, the colonel took the future king by the scruff of the neck and threw him out of the place. The tavern loafers — they were a ubiquitous breed — gave three cheers, and from then on until his death, on August 2, 1840, Colonel Williams was popularly known as "King Charlie." The old home town honored him with election to practically every municipal and county office at one time or another during his long career.[3]

There are skeptics who doubt the authenticity of this story, saying that although Louis Philippe and his brothers visited the Muskingum Valley during their three years' exile in America, they set sail for England in January 1800, in which year "King Charlie" is said to have built his tavern. Perhaps he built it a year earlier. At any rate, the tale ought to be true by this time, for it has been told and retold often enough. The colonel repeatedly related it and Coshocton pioneers used to swear that it was Simon Pure fact. It is even on record that a Coshocton lawyer who visited France got a verification of it from Louis Philippe himself.

And then, to illustrate further the distressing experiences that European travelers encountered in American hotels prior to universal spread of the doctrine that the guest is always right, there is the story that went the rounds in the early 1840's about Charles Dickens and Major Throckmorton, Mine Host of the old Galt House in Louisville. It was Dickens's first visit, the one that furnished the material for *Martin Chuzzlewit* and *American Notes*. By that time Americans — a great many of them, at any rate — had begun to soften toward their British cousins, and Dickens was lionized from one end of the country to the other. Major Throckmorton assigned to him the best room in the Galt House, and when the novelist was comfortabley ensconced therein, the major called to pay his respects.

"Mr. Dickens, we are mighty glad to see you," he said, effusively. "We know you and admire you, and will reckon it a privilege to be allowed to extend to you the hospitality of the metropolis of Kentucky. As your special host, I beg that you will command me for any service in my power to render."

The lion of the hour listened to this well-meant speech with a frigid stare. Then: "When I need you, landlord, I'll ring for you," Dickens said, pointing to the door.[4]

To say that Major Throckmorton, the friend of Clay and Calhoun, was flabbergasted is perhaps to put it mildly, and there was an instantaneous effort on his part to do exactly what King Charlie had done to the future king of France. But there were several people in the room, and the major was, not without difficulty, frustrated in the attempt. You can read *American Notes* from stem to stern and find no mention of the incident. All that Dickens says about Louisville is that he saw a pig rooting in the street. Few American cities were quite complete at that time without a few pigs rooting about.

Mrs. Frances M. Trollope, mother of the famous Anthony, who came to America in 1827 to establish a bazaar in Cincinnati, published such a stinging criticism of the country a few years later (when the bazaar had failed) that it almost brought on another war with Great Britain. She, too, had her troubles with Mine Host. Not caring to mix with the rabble in the dining-room of the Washington Tavern in Cincinnati, Mrs. Trollope ordered a waitress to serve tea in her chambers. Within a few minutes Mine Host appeared. " Any person ill? " he inquired, gruffly. He was assured that everyone was well. " Then, madam, I must tell you that I cannot accommodate you on these terms; we have no family tea-drinking here, and you must either eat with my wife, or me, or not at all in my house." Mrs. Trollope replied, perhaps acidly, that she had not known the manners of the country, hence her mistake. " Our manners are very good manners and we don't wish any changes from England," retorted the landlord. And that was that.[5] Joseph Bonaparte, ex-king of Spain, had a somewhat similar experience at the United States Hotel in Saratoga in 1825, when he and his two daughters and his sister, Caroline Murat, were guests there.

But Mine Host did not concentrate all his fire on guests from foreign lands. He was a czar to any Tom, Dick, or Harry who did not come up to his expectations. He laid down the law to one and all, and his general ultimatum was: " If you don't like it, get out." In the way of service he gave them just what he felt like giving them, and no more. Along in the 1820's he began posting stern and uncompromising house rules, but these merely embodied precepts that had been in force in New England and other sections since colonial times, except that one brand-new rule was added — the strict enforcement of prohibition of liquor on the hotel premises. Strange to say, quite a number of innkeepers were prominently identified with the temperance movement which began early in the nineteenth century and which had spread all over the country by 1830. It was a complete reversal of attitude from that of earlier days when inns were built next door to churches so that parishioners could take a few drinks before and after sermons. The law varied, of course, in various places and at various times, and no doubt the tithing men were more lenient toward home-towners than toward strangers. They kept their eagle eyes on guests at the inns and regulated the amount of liquor they might drink. Thus travelers, besides having to guard against the touchiness of the innkeepers, also had to be careful not to run afoul of constables. Those were, of course, days of much hard drinking, and the guest rarely had any trouble getting all the liquor he wanted, provided he carried it fairly well. The innkeeper himself was subject to fine in Massachusetts if he refused to sell the quantity of booze allowed to be drunk on the premises. Samuel Adams Drake, historian of the old Boston taverns, says, however, that he found no record of a prosecution under this singular statutory provision.[6]

Tobacco got the traveler into trouble oftener than liquor did. Smoking was a grave offense, forbidden by colonial New England and severely restricted in early republican days. One of the first Massachusetts laws against smoking in taverns read: " Nor shall any take tobacco in any wine or common victual house, except in a private room there, so as the master of said house nor any guest there shall take offence thereat; which, if any do, then such person shall forbear upon pain of two shilling sixpence for every such offence." Long after the Revolution, New England continued its war on tobacco, and it is said that less than a hundred years ago men were haled into police court for smoking on the streets of Boston.[7]

It was in the New England inns that the guest encountered the severest house rules. In some the guests were fined for swearing and in others they were required to accompany the landlord and his family to church services. In colonial days in practically all the colonies guests were prohibited by law from arriving at or departing from inns on Sunday. Perhaps the first temperance hotel in America was the old Marlboro, which opened in Boston in 1820.[8] When Nathaniel Rogers became proprietor of it a few years later, he posted the following notice:

> Family worship to be attended morning and evening.
> No intoxicating liquors to be sold or used about the house.
> Smoking of cigars not allowed on any part of the premises.
> No money to be received at the office on the Sabbath, nor will any company be received on that day, except in case of necessity.
> Cold and warm baths are provided here for boarders, and vegetarian diet for those who prefer it.
> The best efforts are promised by the landlord to furnish the table with the products of free labor.[9]

Much New England social history is reflected in those rules. They were imposed by one of the last upholders of the old Puritanism, for by this time strict enforcement of Sunday observance and other blue laws were becoming dead letters. De Tocqueville, author of the great treatise *Democracy in America*, mentions that although constables had the right, as late as 1830, to arrest those who traveled on Sunday, unless they could give good reason for it, the law was seldom enforced. Sunday stages were by now running unmolested in practically all parts of the country, and tithing men were no longer yanking Sunday saddle-travelers off their mounts, as they had been in the habit of doing up to about 1810, not only in New England, but in many other sections.[10]

There were few hotels as late as the 1820's that refused to admit guests on Sunday, and that required guests to attend daily worship, except some summer hotels run by or in the interest of some religious organization. (There still exist several of these.) The Marlboro was an outstanding exception. It was a small, popular-priced house (the first caravansary in Boston to be called a hotel from the beginning of its career), and it clung to its antiquated rules for many years. Unable to get accommodations at the leading Boston hotels when he arrived there in 1847, Sir Charles Lyall went to the Marlboro. " Ours is a temperance house, prayers orthodox, but if you and your lady should not attend prayers, it will not be noticed," said the landlord.[11]

In some places the guest seems to have had a much easier time of it, especially in New York, where there seem to have been no very severe rules imposed on him, and no very harsh laws after the Revolution. There a spirit of liberalism prevailed, as it prevailed everywhere a few years later. There is no record of hard and fast rules modeled according to Mine Host's individual predilections.

But the guest did not win his full place in the sun until the coming of the modern hotel, for not until then was he waited on hand and foot and provided with numerous luxuries undreamt of before. Mine Host of the modern hotel did his utmost to cater to the whims of his guests and rarely imposed his own whims on others. Nor was he puritanical and severe, beyond the necessities of protecting the reputation of his house. The hotel was changing, as were conditions in all branches of life. Long before the middle of the nineteenth century hotels were on much the same footing in their dealings with guests as they are today. By that time even most British visitors had learned to like American hotels and hotel-keepers and had ceased to jot down in their note-books observations on Mine Host's idiosyncrasies and the insolence of the servants. General condemnation of hotels turned to praise. Dickens on his first trip to America made many criticisms, but when he came a second time, he frankly said our hotels were superior in accommodations, service, and management to those of his own country. George Augustus Sala, London journalist, who wrote perhaps more about our hotels of the 1850's and 1860's than any other visitor, always wrote in a friendly spirit and found many things to praise.

Mine Host in America has always, for the past century, classified his guests in two main divisions: transients, who came from outside points, remained for a while, and then went on their way; and permanents, consisting of hometown people who, for one or another reason, preferred to live in hotels. The impression prevails today that the family hotel is a comparatively recent development. As a matter of fact, all the pretentious hotels of the nineteenth century, and many that were not pretentious, catered to the business of permanents. Even before the Revolution there were permanent guests at inns, but it was not until after 1800 that their number began to attain proportions. All the first-class houses from the Tremont House onward had parlor-and-bedroom suites, occupied chiefly by bachelors and married couples. These suites were the choicest rooms in the house, and Mine Host counted on them to afford sure revenue. With them and his bar he was fairly safe against any period of business depression that might curtail the transient business. The suites were generally filled, and Sala lamented the inability of transients to get them.

In the old days the bachelor permanents were known as "hotel hermits," and many of them acquired a great sentimental attachment to the hotels in which they lived. They clung to their suites as long as possible and grieved if they were turned out because the hotel was to be torn down. Every hotel, even today, that closes its doors after a career of thirty or forty years or more turns out a few regretful old-timers. One of the old Fifth Avenue Hotel's guests in New York had lived there forty years when it closed, on April 4, 1908. He boasted that during that time his meals, rooms, bar bill, and other expenditures in the hotel had cost him more than eight hundred thousand dollars.

Perhaps this early popularity of hotel life was due, as Sala said, to the fact that the American " is emphatically a gregarious animal," with " restless vanity and ambition," loving crowds and to be in a crowd.[12] Undoubtedly the color and sociability of hotel life had a strong attraction, but the habit of living in hotels was, more likely, an economic manifestation, partly due to housing shortage. This is indicated by occasional references to the matter in the press, as, for example, the following item that appeared in Greeley's *New Yorker* shortly before the opening of the old Astor House: " We hear that half the rooms are already engaged by families who give up housekeeping on account of the present enormous rents in the city." [13] Frederick Marryat, the British novelist, who toured America two or three years later, noted that many young couples lived in hotels because it was cheaper than to establish homes, at least for a while after marriage. But *Harper's Weekly* ascribed the popularity of hotel life to " stilted ideas " and a conception of economy founded upon a false standard of the necessities of life.

> If the tastes of our people were better regulated, and mere show was not preferred to substance [said *Harper's*], there would be less resort to the hotel or boarding-house on the plea of money-saving.

If gingerbread furniture, damask curtains, tapestry carpets, and a French cook are essential to happiness, there is no doubt they can be secured in greater perfection and at a less price by the gregarious hotel system than by individual effort. Such luxuries, however, as we all know, are not essential to happiness, and however permissible as superfluous enjoyments, they are certainly too dearly paid for when at the expense of domestic virtue and happiness.[14]

Again, hotel life solved the vexatious servant problem, which was as acute then as it is now. Hotel men throughout the nineteenth century stressed this point in their bids for business. Then, too, the very tempo of life in America helped to popularize living in hotels. Most people, eagerly on the make, were seldom rooted to any particular spot and were always willing to move on to some more advantageous place. They got the hotel habit easily. American cities were all booming, and because many of the newcomers could not get suitable housing, or did not know how long they might remain, they went to hotels for a few weeks or months. Some, taking a liking to hotel life, remained over a period of years. Thus the Tremont, the old Astor, and hundreds of other hotels, large and small, were built partly to meet this need. In New York, naturally, more people lived in hotels than elsewhere, and it was family hotels that led the van in the northward business growth of the city. Commuting already had begun in the 1840's, when the city got its first rapid transit, the old Harlem and New York Railroad. This road was opened to White Plains on October 26, 1844, and at that time began running eight trains a day to the Harlem station at One Hundred and Twenty-fifth Street, and one every fifteen minutes to the Twenty-seventh Street station, which was then far uptown. Soon thereafter a number of strictly family hotels sprang up, on Union and Madison squares and thereabouts. Even Forty-second Street had its hotels before the Civil War, the first being Robinson's Hotel, opposite the "upper depot" of the New York

Central. This was enlarged and renamed the Reunion Hotel in 1866, and a few years later the name was changed to Grand Union, a name that became known from one end of the country to the other in the succeeding forty years. The first hotel at Times Square was called the Broadway Hotel, opened in 1861 and run by Benjamin Rathbun, builder of the old American Hotel at Buffalo. Seven years later the old St. Cloud Hotel was built at the southeast corner of Broadway and Forty-second Street. It was opened as an elegant European-plan house on May 7, 1868, and was the last word in family hotel accommodations at the time.

Apartment-hotel life and its effect on America and Americans has always been a sort of puzzle to Europeans and is still debated with great seriousness by overseas writers, who invariably see evil consequences in it. As early as 1822 John M. Duncan of Glasgow was writing from New York to the folks back home, telling them that "the inn is, with us, proverbially the traveler's home, but here it is the home of a great many besides travelers. This feature in the American system I cannot admire; nor can I imagine what comfort there can be amidst the bustle and noise of a public tavern." Marryat was convinced that hotel life was demoralizing to women, and Harriet Martineau and others took a similar view. They were horrified at the shocking exhibition of a woman playing a piano in a hotel parlor. Miss Martineau mentions that young ladies were actually *taken* to the piano to play and sing before a promiscuous company. Marryat, however, had seen the bold hussies go to the piano without any urging, and play and sing " with all the energy of peacocks before total strangers and very often without accompaniment." [15] He was forced to conclude that for women hotel life was "a life of idleness and vacuity of outward pretence, but of no real good feeling," for scandal raged among them and there was much gossiping.

American journalists gravely discussed the subject up to about 1890, and then began taking it as a matter of course. Here is what one of them said in 1885:

> Human nature is human nature the world over, and there is no greater error than the prevailing one among us that domesticity is not the leading virtue of American married couples. That there is too much hotel life in American families I concede, and I am fully conscious of the faults and evils of the system, but that it entails any impairment of the higher domestic virtues I have failed to discover. It is not easy to see how a woman is deteriorated as the companion and friend of man — as the participator in his aspirations, his study, his higher life — because her conditions release her from the duty of devising the details of a dinner, from the irritation of demoniacal domestics, from the drudgery of checking the grocer's passbook and the sad realization that all bakers are liars and mostly robbers as well.

After all, of course, it was but a very small percentage of people who lived in hotels, just as it is a small percentage today, though the number has grown greatly in New York and other large cities since the World War. There was so much discussion of the matter, however, that Europe got the idea that nearly everyone in America lived in hotels during the period between 1830 and 1870. E. L. Godkin has been already quoted on this point.

Transient guests grew rapidly in numbers during the first three decades of the nineteenth century — the golden age of the stage-coach, and the beginning of the era of steamships and railroads. European visitors were astonished at the great number of well-filled stages on all highways, the multitude of coastwise ships plowing back and forth between Boston, New York, and other cities, and the swarms of packet-boats racing one another up and down the Great

Lakes and every navigable stream. The advent of the railroad (the centenaries of the first modern hotel and the iron horse in America both fall in the same year) gave another great impetus to travel. The little jerkwater lines of early days did a rushing business, and crowds piled in and out of the flimsy wooden coaches at every station. Habitual mobility had seeped into the American blood like a germ. Everybody was going somewhere, or coming back. That extraordinary restlessness which is looked upon today as a fixed American characteristic had begun in colonial days, and by 1800 Americans were recognized as the world's greatest nation of gadabouts. Even the passion for politics was secondary to the mania for traveling, for only the men talked politics, whereas traveling affected the very women and children.[16] This, of course, was an outgrowth of general conditions — the settlement and development of the country, the westward sweep of the frontier, the steady pursuit of opportunities, which opened up everywhere, and the lack of ancestral ties to bind anyone to a particular spot. The cheapness of travel and hotel rates were other contributing causes. John Robert Godby, a British visitor in 1842, found he could travel from New York to Albany, a hundred and sixty miles, for $1.50, and from Boston to New York, two hundred miles, for less than $2.50. The highest hotel rate was two dollars a day (American plan), " and at many excellent hotels it is only $1.50 a day." [17] The volume of travel at Buffalo in the early 1840's, when Buffalo, then little more than twenty years old, had a population of about thirty thousand, may be taken as an example.

> The inns are as large and as numerous as in any city in the world [wrote a visiting Englishman], the influx of travelers brought to this city by the canals, railway, stages, and private waggons every day being enormous; indeed, it is calculated that for seven months of the year at least five thousand persons pass through on their way to the west every day. These, with the few returning, and the merchants

from Canada and from the interior of the country, always give the city a business-like appearance, something resembling New York and Philadelphia.[18]

Only a small percentage of all this travel throughout the country was by train. It took the railroad nearly two decades to reach a point of development where it could be of much help to the hotel business. Prejudices had to be broken down. Up to 1840 and later stolid citizens viewed the railway with alarm, and almost everyone except promoters opposed it. People generally believed innumerable evils would follow in its wake. There were only 2,775 miles of track in 1840, scattered about the country in short lines, manned by amateurs. Only a few people had ever seen a train. The puny little wood-burning locomotives puffed along at a top speed of ten or fifteen miles an hour. Roadbeds were almost as bumpy and treacherous as turnpikes; the tracks were wooden rails with strips of iron nailed to them, and accidents were numerous. All in all, a trip on the railway was as much to be dreaded as a stage-coach journey. But during the decade from 1840 to 1850 the trackage increased to 8,571 miles, and by then the railway was asserting itself as a great revolutionizer of travel. Cities and towns that had rail connections were filled with strangers as they had never been filled before, and new hotels were being built at a great rate to take care of the new rush of business. From then on, the growth of railroads and hotels went hand in hand. There was more than a casual kinship between them. Hotel men built, or helped to build, many railroads; and many railroad companies built hotels. A great many innkeepers had operated stage lines. Now many of them were enthusiastic promoters of railway lines, organizing and helping to finance new companies. Mine Host often became a railway president. In turn, nearly all railroads had extensive hotel buildings, either directly or by means of subsidiary companies. This was true of England as well as of America. American railroads have generally (but by no means entirely) gone out of the hotel business; in Canada the three great railroad systems still build and operate many great hotels.

Travelers who came by stage were carried direct to the inn door. The railroad and steamship companies reversed this process. Mohammed had to come to the mountain. Near steamboat landings the "Steamboat House" appeared, and near railway stations stood the "Depot Hotel" and the "Railroad House." The hotel-location problem was not, however, solved by such a simple process. The best houses were generally a considerable distance away from the terminals; and so arose the bus and runner system. Runners met every incoming ship and train and fought over the spoils. No puller-in in front of a second-hand-clothing store was more zealous in pursuit of business. Buses raced to plant themselves in vantage positions at stations and landings, especially the latter, for ships came in at uncertain hours. Hotels in cities on main-traveled waterways depended to a large extent on steamer business. In Cleveland the two leading hotels were the American and the Franklin houses in the latter 1830's and early 1840's. Each had a little tower on its roof, with a sentinel stationed day and night to watch for steamers. The sentinels signaled whenever they saw a steamer coming, and carriages and runners hastened at breakneck speed to the piers, to pre-empt the best positions.[19]

Great as the increase of travel had been before the Civil War, it was insignificant compared to the increase after the war. Long journeys became commonplace events. One could go almost anywhere and everywhere by rail, and almost everyone did. This perpetual restlessness of Americans worried some folks. "The humblest village school child expects two or three excursions a year," said one writer.

WELCOME, STRANGER!

" Every servant and shop hand stipulates for holidays long enough to pay distant visits; in short, our lives are becoming much like those festive gnats at play of a warm evening. Sometimes we pause to suck a flower or to bite somebody, but we soon return to the perpetual locomotion which seems to possess unfailing charm." [20]

Several distinct groups of hotel guests grew up when railroad travel began to become general. The most important group of all was the commercial traveler, successor of the old-time Yankee peddler. Back in the days when Ulysses S. Grant traveled for a Galena leather and hide house, commercial travelers were known as bagmen, because they carried carpet-bags. They were a picturesque crowd, and before many years they swarmed all over the country.

The commercial traveler originated in England, about 1780. During the first two or three decades he did most of his traveling on horseback, and after that (until a network of railways came into existence) he either traveled by stage or drove his own gig,[21] as did Tom Smart in *The Pickwick Papers* — jolly Tom, with his clay-colored gig with red wheels, and his vixenish bay mare, on their way through the stormy night to the inn, where Tom used to sit at ease in the snug parlor, drinking punch and speculating on what he would do when he married the widow. The bagman appeared on the scene in America about 1830. Manufacturing and wholesaling firms started in a small way and at first depended largely on peddlers to merchandise their products. Gradually, as the firms expanded and conditions changed, business partners made occasional trips to pick up orders, or sent a trusted clerk. Within a few years the traveling salesman had become a recognized feature of American life, seen in every city and village. Presently he discarded his carpet-bag and began using sample-grips and trunks. He then became known as a drummer, drumming up business for his firm. He became one of the chief mainstays of the hotel business, providing about seventy-five per cent of the transient business in those houses classed as commercial hotels and nearly a hundred per cent of it in a great majority of little hostelries of the smaller towns. When the boom burst in a little town in a God-forsaken region out west, the Boniface there voiced his despair and his friendship for the drummers in some verses he tacked on the door of the hotel he was deserting:

> A thousand feet to water!
> A thousand miles to wood!
> I've quit this blasted country;
> Quit her! Yes, for good.
> The hoppers came a buzzin'
> But I shooed them all away,
> Next blew the hot winds furious;
> Still, I had the grit to stay.
> There's always something hap'ning;
> So, while I've got the pluck,
> Think I'll strike another country
> And see how runs my luck.
> God bless you, boys, I love you.
> The drummer is my friend.
> When I open up my doors again,
> Bet your life for you I'll send.

By 1860 there were about sixty thousand commercial travelers in the country, according to one authority, and the number grew steadily. The *Hotel Gazette* of 1883 estimated there were then more than two hundred thousand of them in the United States.[22] The ranks have been greatly thinned in recent years by the growth of the chain-store system. It is said there aren't half as many on the road today as there were twenty years ago.

The bagman of old was a picturesque individual. Many

of the first generation were Englishmen, who brought over with them a taste (shared by Dickens) for flashy clothes, gay waistcoats, vivid neckties, diamonds, real or otherwise, heavy gold watch-chains and rings. One could spot a bagman anywhere by his attire, which set the fashion among a bumper crop of dudes.[23] Naturally, he was a gay dog personally, a heart-breaker among the ladies, with a lass in every port, and an industrious conveyor of smutty stories throughout the length and breadth of the land. Washington Irving dubbed him a knight-errant, and a newspaper poet of the 1870's sang:

> Who puts oup at der besht hotel,
> Und dakes his oysters on der shell,
> Und mit der frauleins cuts a schwell?
>   Der drummer.

 In the course of time the traveling man lost much of his native wildness and picturesqueness. Today he is no different in dress and deportment from the rest of the traveling citizenry. A considerable percentage of today's traveling men are members of the Gideon Society, sponsor of the well-known Gideon Bible, without which no first-class hotel is quite complete. This society was organized by a group of commercial travelers on June 1, 1899, at Janesville, Wisconsin, with Samuel E. Hill of Beloit as president.

 Another class of guests whose ranks have been shot to pieces in recent years is that of the actors. The system of traveling theater-companies was introduced in 1869.[24] Prior to that time only the stars had traveled, appearing in various cities with local stock-companies. In the palmy days of what theater people call " the road," a considerable part of the business of many hotels was supplied by traveling dramatic companies. Before the movies, the automobile, and other influences cut into the business, it was estimated there were more than eight thousand barn-stormers trouping through the country. Now there is scarcely a corporal's guard of them.

The hotel man found the Thespians, as a rule, a hard lot to handle and to please. In every one-night stand the troupers gave Mine Host much trouble, fussing and fuming because his humble hotel was not a Ritz-Carlton. They were the only class of travelers who carried cats, dogs, birds, and other pets about the country with them. They slept most of the day, so that chambermaids had to work late cleaning their rooms; and they held parties in their rooms after the show until break of day, keeping other guests awake and burning up the hotel's costly gas and electricity. Worst of all, they were chronic abusers of the hotel's property, doing much washing and cooking in their rooms and not caring a rap what happened to the furniture and bedding. Then, too, there was the matter of payment of bills. Theater troupes were not always sure pay. Country hotel-keepers suffered heavily from the collapse of barn-stormers in the mauve and other decades. Often the hapless Thespian had to leave his trunk behind and "walk the ties" back to New York, or wherever he desired to go. The stranded actor was a common enough spectacle, celebrated in song and story. "He belonged to a troupe that was stranded in Peoria" was one of the big song hits of the gay nineties.

This indictment does not, of course, apply to all traveling actors; they were not all black sheep, by any means. Besides, actors had many a just grievance against Mine Host, especially those who played the one-night stands, the last resort of the self-respecting Thespian. About the only redeeming feature of many of the little hotels of the smaller towns was that they were cheap and the wandering sons and daughters of Thespis could generally get board and room for a dollar a day.

A third group of hotel guests was that composed of the

women. Prior to the Civil War and for some time thereafter the lone woman traveler was a rarity and was looked upon with suspicion by hotel-keepers. But an increasing number of women accompanied their husbands on journeys and there were, of course, the permanent women guests, wives of local citizens occupying parlor and bedroom suites. These latter were the vanguard of the "new women." British visitors looked upon them with astonishment. Along with the little parlor stoves in guest-rooms, the battle-scarred spittoons in the lobbies, the cocktails and juleps in the barrooms, and the succotash and flapjacks in the dining-halls, the women who lived in hotels, and the poise with which they participated in hotel life, were a perpetual source of interest to observers from overseas. There was always a large "ladies' parlor" with a piano on which the ladies played and sang "with the same self-possession amidst crowds of visitors as if they were in their own sanctuaries at home," but the ladies by no means limited themselves to their special parlor. They even had the temerity to enter the lobby. "Custom renders this mode of life agreeable to many of them," wrote George Combe. "They prefer the busy throng." [25]

Travel had been robbed of its discomforts and terrors and the New Woman had progressed to such an extent that by 1870 she began to travel alone. But not yet in any great numbers. The New York *Tribune* in 1885 sent out an Inquiring Reporter to ascertain how many women guests were registered at the city's four largest hotels. Out of the first one hundred guests at each hotel he found a total of only forty-four women. The *Tribune* added that no woman traveling alone could find accommodations in any hotel unless she had an introduction or credentials and other evidence of her respectability.[26] Toward the end of the century this discrimination against the lone woman, and fear of her, had almost died out. A guide-book of 1898 said:

A lady, unescorted, may sometimes be refused admission to a hotel by a plea of lack of rooms or some evasion of that kind. It is well, therefore, for the "lone woman," especially if young, to write or telegraph in advance; or, better yet, to take a note of introduction. In case a lady finds herself unexpectedly alone and unacquainted in the city, and compelled to go to a hotel for the night, let her do so without hesitation, however, since the great probability is that she will meet with no more obstacle than if her father or her husband were with her.[27]

Separate dining-rooms were provided for men and women for several decades; every first-class hotel had its "gentlemen's ordinary" and its "ladies' ordinary." But by 1870 the idea had entirely died out. Although Mine Host no longer herded the women into a separate dining-room, he still kept the bars up against their unaccompanied invasion of certain dining-rooms in which he thought it improper for lone women to appear. The militant suffragists, determined to establish their equality in every possible way, disputed Mine Host's right to bar them and carried the matter to court. In July 1907 the Hoffman House in New York refused to serve dinner to Mrs. Harriot S. Blatch, a noted suffragette, who entered the roof-garden unescorted after six o'clock in the evening. Mrs. Blatch filed suit against the hotel, but at the trial the jury quickly decided that a hotel had the right to bar unescorted women diners provided it offered to serve them in another room.

Undoubtedly the influence of women guests kept American hotels more spruced up than they might otherwise have been. Mine Host was quick to perceive that women were more fastidious in the matter of general cleanliness, more conscious of any deference paid to their tastes and convenience, and more responsive to the little things he might do to please them. And he acted accordingly. Commenting on this, the Cincinnati *Enquirer* in 1884 said:

WELCOME, STRANGER!

It is amusing to note the different dodges employed by the managers of the great city caravansaries to please their women guests. At the most exclusive hotels in Boston it takes the shape of beautiful flowers in vases and jars scattered about the rooms, and the latest numbers of the latest magazines ready to the hand. At a New York hotel, facing Madison Square, at lunch, when the dossier is brought on, a plate of choice confections is placed before you, and while making use of a finger bowl, the deft-handed waiter whips out a sheet of fresh white paper, twists it with a turn of his hand into a cornucopia, empties the bon-bons into it, and presents it with Oriental obeisance for upstairs consumption.

There is really cleverness in this, for it has put a stop without vulgar remonstrance to the practice of women carting off to their rooms plates loaded with fruit, cakes and candy to nibble between meals. Another hotel on Madison Square, when a lady is seated in the dining room, the waiter has ready for her feet a dainty tapestry-covered hassock. No one but a short woman, who has spent a portion of her life sitting on the edges of chairs dangling her feet in the air, can fully appreciate this comfort.[28]

Astute hotel men today are making more of a bid for the favor of women than ever before, for the percentage of women guests is steadily growing. It is said they average about thirty per cent of hotel business throughout the country, all the year round, and in the dining-rooms about fifty per cent. During the motor-touring season the number of women guests is around fifty per cent. How to make hotels more attractive to women and how to give them more and more special service is a stock subject at hotel conventions and is frequently discussed in hotel trade journals. All the larger cities have hotels "for women only," catering to women who travel alone and to the growing army of single business women. The Martha Washington Hotel, opened in 1903 in New York, was the first hotel exclusively for women. As a rule, however, women do not like hotels exclusively for their own sex any more than men like "stag" hotels. Nor do hotel-keepers look upon the one-sex policy with a kindly eye, for it cuts down their potential business in half.

It is fairly safe to say that no other nation makes more general use of its hotels than does America. The habit began in colonial times, when the inn and the church, standing side by side, were the only places of public resort. The conditions that made for a heavier volume of travel in this country than elsewhere, including the greater economic ability of the average American to indulge his taste for travel and hotel life, together with the habit of home-towners in habitually frequenting hotels for every sort of reason, made the hotel an institution dear to the hearts of the people. An American writer of sixty years ago summed up this love of hotel life somewhat picturesquely:

> Wherever an American is to be for the next twenty-four hours, there is his home. He is a kind of civilized Bedouin, who carries his home in his trunk, the law and the constitution in his revolver, and his religion in his disposition to do as he pleases.[29]

But whether he traveled or not, the American took his ease at his inn as nonchalantly and as regularly as though he were born to the life. In his home town he mingled in large numbers with travelers in the lobbies and parlors, in dining-halls, bars, and reading-rooms. If he loved crowds, as Sala said, in hotels he found them thickest and most colorful. American hotels were built for crowds, and Mine Host's wish was "the more, the merrier." He, too, liked crowds. That is why he provided such a large lobby and so many other rooms producing no revenue. It paid him in the long run. Our hotels were planned to meet the needs of a surging democracy, and despite competition continued to be the great social centers of the general public, as the inn had been before them. Therein the American hotels and American public differed from the hotels and public of the mother country. " We are an odd sort of people at hotels, our insular habits not adapting us so completely as our continental and American friends to the social usages of hotels," said a London journalist seventy years ago.[30]

Changing conditions have not lessened the average American's relationship with his country's hotels, but the form of the relationship has changed somewhat. In other words, we make just as free use of our hotels as ever before, but not quite in the same way. One of the changes is the almost total disappearance of the loosely organized form of club life, out of which our present club system evolved. In olden days every prominent hotel was the headquarters of some distinctive group, who came at definite hours to gossip, dine, and drink together. Each group centered, generally, in some special patron, and its members were in similar professions or businesses. The system flourished at its best during the early decades of the nineteenth century. Regularly organized clubs, with strictly private membership and club-rooms of their own, gradually displaced the system. The first of such clubs in New York, for example, was the Union Club, founded in 1836. It is said to have grown out of an informal group known as The Club, which used to gather at the old City Hotel and was headed by Colonel Nick Saltus, a wealthy bachelor and retired merchant. Colonel Saltus, short, thickset, and pompous, sat each noon at the head of a special table surrounded by his cronies. In the evening they came again, drinking and gossiping until ten o'clock or so, then toddling off to bed. The chief survival of this sort of informal clubdom is the famous Round Table of the Algonquin Hotel in New York.

The City Hotel also was headquarters of James Fenimore Cooper's " Bread and Cheese Lunch," which met once a week after he moved to New York in 1822. The group comprised the city's best-known men in literature, law, science, and art, including such men as Halleck and Bryant,

Chancellor Kent, Morse, inventor of the telegraph; Verplanck, editor of Shakspere; Jarvis, the painter; and Durand, the engraver. The group gave a dinner in honor of Cooper on May 29, 1826, just before he departed for Europe. The speakers included General Winfield Scott, Governor De Witt Clinton, and Charles King, editor of the *American* and later president of Columbia University. After Cooper's departure the club soon fell to pieces, for he was the life and soul of it.[31]

Perhaps the most famous of the informal dining-clubs of the old days was the Saturday Club which used to meet at the old Parker House in Boston. It flourished during New England's golden age of literature, and its membership included Ralph Waldo Emerson, James Russell Lowell, Oliver Wendell Holmes, Henry Wadsworth Longfellow, John G. Whittier, Nathaniel Hawthorne, Francis Parkman, Edwin P. Whipple, Louis Agassiz, Thomas Bailey Aldrich, and several others. Once a week they forgathered to dine and chat — and what wonderful chat it must have been!

The Clover Club of Philadelphia — perhaps you remember the justly famous Clover Club cocktail — was another famous dining-club of the middle of the nineteenth century, organized in 1883 and for a long time headed by Moses P. Handy. The club met once a month for dinner at the little old Bellevue Hotel, where the late George C. Boldt of the Waldorf-Astoria got his start as a hotel-keeper. The last dinner was held in 1895.

Groups still meet regularly at hotels for luncheons and dinners, but they are such thoroughly organized groups as the Rotarians, Kiwanians, Lions, and others, or local trade associations, and sales and executive staffs.

The hand of time has also changed the hotel's prominence as a hotbed of political activity. Political history — lots of it — is still made in hotels, as when a group of Republican leaders at the 1920 convention in Chicago gathered in a hotel room and made the decision that resulted in the nomination of Senator Warren G. Harding for the Presidency. But there is no counterpart today of the Amen Corner over which Boss Platt presided for many years at the old Fifth Avenue Hotel in New York, nor is there any Room Eleven like that of the old Astor House, in which Thurlow Weed, Warwick of Republicanism, made his headquarters. The paths of political glory led to that room for twenty-five years. As Weed's grandson later wrote:

> Could that room speak, what a story it might tell! It was an audience chamber and council closet, where all sorts of persons went month after month, year after year. In it caucuses were held, campaigns arranged, Senators, members of the Cabinet, governors, ministers, and even Presidents were made and unmade. For nearly a quarter of a century more political power and influence probably emanated from that little apartment than from any other source in the entire republic.[32]

Likewise the hotel has gone out of politics in the sense that made it a partisan institution. There is no longer any such thing as a " Republican hotel " or a " Democratic hotel." Strict political neutrality in the conduct of the hotel's business is Mine Host's policy today, but at one time he took great pride in having his hotel identified with one or another of the great parties. The end of that sort of thing came in the early 1880's, by which time Americans had begun to take their partisan politics a little less seriously. The New York *World*, noting the change in January 1890, said:

> In the old days each political party had its own hotel, and it was considered little less than treason for a man to patronize any public place outside his own hotel. The politician who violated this unwritten law was compelled to go to all sorts of explanations. Gradually a change has been going on. The Fifth Avenue Hotel and the Hoffman House are nominally the headquarters of the Republicans

and Democrats, but in name only. There is now no distinctively Republican or Democratic hotel left. The result has been to improve all hotels. Each now stands on its own merits. The day has gone by when a man will put up with poor service, bad food and a cold room for the sake of political sentiment. The inference is that the stomach is built on a non-partisan basis.

Despite all the surface changes that have come over his guests, Mine Host finds them essentially the same today as they were a hundred years ago. He puts his O. K. on most of them, but admits that a small percentage of them are very bad eggs. They cause him heavy losses in various unpleasant ways.

There is the guest who carries away " souvenir " spoons and other trifles, such as towels, sheets, rugs, lamp-shades, electric bulbs — anything and everything that is portable and can be pried loose. One New York hotel loses nearly two thousand napkins a month, worth $1.25 apiece. Another New York hotel reports a loss of $78,000 a year by thefts. A third figures about eighty cents average loss per guest, and still another has found that about one out of every six hundred steal. During a national convention of women in Cleveland a few years ago one hotel is said to have lost six hundred *demi-tasse* spoons. The losses from theft at this hotel two years ago amounted to $33,000. The secretary of the Ohio Hotels Association gathered figures showing that the hotels in its membership lost approximately twenty thousand towels a year. One could go on endlessly citing similar figures. All large hotels have heavy losses. It is part of the overhead. These losses are not caused by any particular type of guest, but by all classes. Three or four years ago the Milwaukee Railroad opened a resort hotel in Montana. Many invited guests were present, all people of prominence. The losses by theft on that occasion amounted to $1,800.

The light-fingered guest is a cousin of the one who is

extremely careless and wanton in his treatment of the hotel's property, especially the furniture and fixtures of the room he occupies. He drops cigarette stubs on costly carpets and bedspreads and burns arms of chairs and edges of tables and otherwise defaces the furniture. He tears blankets and sheets, he cracks mirrors and makes memoranda and weird smears and drawings on the walls. He spills ink on carpets, table scarfs, and furniture, and sometimes he holds a " party " in his room, leaving the room a wreck, with everything breakable smashed and even the plumbing fixtures wrenched from their moorings. Only a small percentage of guests go this far, but the losses they cause in a year mount into dizzy figures. One guest can, through pure wanton vandalism, cause a hotel a loss of several hundred dollars, as did the late Enrico Caruso in 1907 when, in a burst of artistic temperament, he smashed the clock in his apartment because the ticking annoyed him. This upset two hundred and twenty-five clocks run by a master system. The entire system was out of order for several hours, and expensive repairs were necessary.

It is hard to understand why so many people abuse hotel property. A very few do it for spite because of some fancied grievance against the management. More often it is owing to thoughtlessness or moronic wantonness. One well-known hotel man explains it this way: " A large proportion of our guests are not regular hotel patrons. They are away for ' a good time.' When they enter a hotel, they relax — that is, they let down the bars. They change their standards, their habits; and forget their dignity and self-respect. Everyone goes off standard when he gets into a hotel. A few seem to go the limit. Maybe the relaxation is a good thing for them, but it is expensive for us. The depreciation of our equipment is twice as rapid as it should be."

Added to these losses are those caused by outright crooks. There are two main groups of these — skippers and check-passers. The skipper jumps his hotel bill, leaving behind a cheap suitcase or trunk, probably filled with telephone books or bricks. There have been skippers at least as far back as the beginning of the nineteenth century, as is indicated by an entry made by Mine Host in an old register: "Couldn't pay his bill; stripped him almost naked and made an exhibition of him in the rotunda." This was reminiscent of the Connecticut innkeepers who put their guests in the stocks. In 1877 Potter Palmer of the old Palmer House in Chicago similarly took the law into his own hands, thus bringing down a storm of criticism and public indignation on his head and getting himself into several damage suits. Porters and house officers stripped several guests of their coats and waistcoats, cut off their trousers at the knee, and forced them to stand in the lobby, placarded "Hotel Deadbeat." One was forced to stand in front of the hotel thus attired and labeled, after having been kept in his room all day without food.[33]

The hotel man's biggest loss-problem, however, is the check-passer. All hotels cash checks, and large metropolitan hotels do a banking business of this sort in excess of that done by many banks. Joseph Reddington, credit manager of the Hotel St. Francis, San Francisco, said in a recent address that the St. Francis in 1927 and 1928 cashed checks and other paper averaging more than ten thousand dollars a day, or about four million dollars in each year. Most of the checks were presented by guests, but the San Francisco public came in for its share.[34] These large hotels have to be as careful in handling this business as any bank. The losses, therefore, are comparatively light. It is the smaller hostelries, where less care is exercised, that suffer most.

In spite of skippers, check-passers, souvenir hounds, and all the rest, Mine Host clings, generally, to his faith in human nature. But he will admit, privately, that the guest is not always right.

CHAPTER V

RAGS TO RICHES

WHEN the North American Hotel was built, in 1826, at the corner of Bayard Street and the Bowery, in the heart of what in later years became New York's Chinatown, one of the last survivors of those tall trees which gave " the Bouwerie " its name stood at the Bayard Street side of the hotel, its branches spreading down to the very windows of the tap-room. The North American was one of those missing links between the old-time inn and the new-style hotel, and its landlord was of the old school. His guests came by stage-coach and on horseback, and he did a thriving business, for the neighborhood already was taking on those characteristics which were to make it both famous and infamous as a center of early New York night life and rowdyism. The day of Chuck Connors was fifty years in the future, but the chin-whiskered Bowery boy who preceded Connors was plentifully in evidence. With his plug hat slightly askew and his trousers tucked into his boots, he loafed at street-corners, chewing tobacco and whittling shingles, always ready for a rough-and-tumble fight.

The landlord of the North American was polishing ale-glasses in his new hostelry one day when he observed a boy leaning against the Bayard Street tree. It was mid-afternoon of a cold winter day, but the boy had no overcoat. He stood dejectedly, his hands stuffed into his pockets to keep them warm. Moved, perhaps, by an impulse of pity, the landlord went to the door.

"Here, my lad, come in a minute and warm yourself by the fire," he invited, benignantly, and the boy accepted the invitation eagerly.

"You'll catch your death of cold, standing there like that, my lad," said the landlord. "Haven't you got nothing better to do?"

"No, sir," said the boy; "I've been trying to find work, sir, but can't find any."

"Well, now," said the landlord, warmly, "if it's work you want, maybe I can help you out a bit. How'd you like to take a job here, helping me? I could use a likely lad like you, and you'll get your bed and board, and a bit of spending money, besides. Think you'd like it?"

The boy said he thought he would, and thanked the landlord, and thus in true Horatio Alger fashion began the familiar journey from rags to riches.

The boy's name was David Reynolds, a name that later became familiar to all of the two hundred thousand New Yorkers of that day. He had come to the city from Liverpool a few days before, according to one version of the story; and when he stood under the tall Bayard Street tree, he was without friends or funds. The meal he ate that afternoon in the kitchen of the North American was the first he had eaten that day, and the bed he slept in that night was the first he had been in since his arrival at Castle Garden. It was a stroke of luck, David thought, to fall into a good job like that, and the proprietor discovered, too, that it had been fortunate for him to pick up such a valuable assistant, for David Reynolds developed into the best kind of a right-hand man, and his personality was such that he made friends everywhere. Within a few years he became one of the minor institutions of the town, and when the landlord died, a few years later, David succeeded him as proprietor of the hotel.

One of the first things he did when he became proprietor was to commission a wood-carver, skilled in the making of tobacco-shop Indians and figure-heads for sailing-ships, to chisel a life-size effigy of a ragged boy leaning against a tree — reproducing Reynolds himself and the Bayard Street tree — and this effigy was placed on the cornice of the North American, as an expression of appreciation of the country and city that had done so well by him, materially and spiritually. When Reynolds died, in 1855, the hotel passed into the hands of Patrick Fay, but the wooden statue of the urchin leaning against the tree remained on its pedestal, a landmark and a constant inspiration to writers of the Optic and Alger school, until the hotel was torn down, in 1891. It was one of the curiosities of New York for sightseeing strangers to see and to talk about when they returned to their homes.[1]

In its later years the North American Hotel was known as the New England House, and during its sixty-five years it was enlarged twice by the annexation of adjoining buildings. It was never a first-class hostelry, but during David Reynold's régime it attained great popularity among a certain Bohemian, easy-going crowd that clung to it until the center of the city moved too far away, after which it deteriorated into little better than a flop-house. In its palmiest days theater and circus celebrities were steady patrons of its bar and its basement restaurant. In the 1850's and 1860's every actor and actress of prominence — the Hamlins, the Booths, James W. Wallack, John B. Scott, Colonel Mann, and many others — ate there. Star performers of the Sands and Nathan Circus, out of which P. T. Barnum's first show was recruited, also dined at the North American, and prominent sporting men used to divide their time between it and the notorious Branch Hotel, which was run by the celebrated Tom Hyer, who in 1849 fought "Yankee Sullivan," escaped convict from Australia, who was America's first ring champion. The two hotels were the scene of many exciting skirmishes of various sorts. All the political disorder with which the city was persistently afflicted was quickly reflected in the neighborhood. On the corner of Bayard and Mott streets, adjoining the North American in Reynold's day, stood the Butts and Shaw livery-stable, where the belligerent "Stable Gang" originated and made its headquarters. Reynolds saw Boss Tweed begin fighting his way to power in Tammany politics as the leader of this gang.

Measured in dollars and cents, Reynold's success was not remarkable; he left no huge fortune. He was, we may suppose, one of that numerous class of nineteenth-century hotel-keepers who were good hotel men, but not particularly good business men. They knew how to run a hotel in first-class style, but couldn't make much money at it. This was perhaps the result of too direct contact with the general public in its taking-it-easy mood. Then, too, there was the tradition of "old-time hospitality," which was all very well, perhaps, when Mine Host, assisted by his wife and family, was running a little inn, but was not so well adapted to the operation of a large modern hotel, for it produced too much cirrhosis and too many lean bank accounts. Mine Host too often died young and died poor. Generally speaking, of course, Mine Host was not greatly different from other business men; there were all sorts and conditions of hotel men. But their successes and their failures were more conspicuous than those of other business men, for Mine Host was always a figure of romantic interest, and never more so than during the nineteenth century, when his business changed so astonishingly. In a century remarkable for the greatest changes that had ever happened in human life, Mine Host took on a new picturesqueness and was more in the public eye than ever. If his material successes were small, on the whole, his success otherwise was considerable. He made many friends and the spectacular nature of his business brought him into the limelight as a very smart fellow. The public knew him only as a good Boniface and cared nothing about whether he had a comfortable bank account. The men running the big showy hotels were doing their jobs so well from the standpoint of commercialized hospitality that their cleverness became proverbial. "American enterprise is perhaps in nothing more strikingly exhibited than in the establishing of hotels and the competition which exists among Mine Hosts," said George M. Towle in the 1860's. "The very slang of the streets hints this. It is said of a man whose cleverness is doubted, 'he can't keep a hotel.'"[2]

When the Boydens withdrew from the management of the old Astor House, and John Jacob Astor was casting about for someone to take charge of the hotel, Charles A. Stetson, who had been clerking for the Boydens at the Tremont House, was an applicant for the job. Stetson boasted that he was a hotel-keeper, not a tavern-keeper, and would run the Astor House in first-class hotel style. When Astor asked him to define a hotel-keeper, he said: "A hotel-keeper is a gentleman who stands on a level with his guests." That was a view of Mine Host that prevailed through most of the nineteenth century. It was expressed by numerous travelers, especially those from England, who could not help noticing the contrast between the social status of Mine Host in America and his contemporary in the mother country. One English traveler went so far as to say that hotel-keepers and steamer captains formed the only aristocracy he had encountered in America, while another observes that "the keepers of American hotels, who consider themselves on an equal with Senators, and who not unfrequently become Senators . . . have the manners not of a headwaiter, but of a gentleman of fortune dispensing the hospitality of his mansion." Mine Host was sitting on top of the world in a ringside seat and enjoying life with great gusto, even though he might be on the brink of financial failure. His reputation in those days was somewhat like that of a theatrical star or a noted politician, and if he was known from one end of the country to the other as a good host, he had nothing much to worry about. His services were always in demand. Which is all quite different from nowadays, when nobody seems to know or care much who is running a hotel, except the owners, who prefer a manager with business ability as well as other qualities.

There was, however, one fly in the ointment. As the temperance movement grew in strength, Mine Host began to be classified with " the sinful race of publicans." In the tolerant cities this had little effect on his standing, but in the smaller places it was a distinct handicap. In the old innkeeping days pillars of the church and everyone else drank Mine Host's liquor. Toward the close of the eighteenth century sentiment against John Barleycorn began to crystallize, and in 1808 it reached the organization stage, when a society was founded at Saratoga. In 1826 a national organization, the American Temperance Society, came into existence, and the *American Almanac* noted that in 1830 this organization had 1,605 branches. There were numerous smaller organizations.[3] In succeeding decades the movement gained ground rapidly, enrolling millions of " signers of the pledge," sincere and otherwise. Reformers of oratorical ability — among them John B. Gough, Neal Dow, and James Appleton, " Father of Prohibition " — were dealing mighty blows against the Demon Rum. These orators and their followers looked upon the hotel-keeper as a vicious agent of the Powers of Darkness, tarred with the same brush as the saloon-keeper. The Cary sisters — Alice and Phœbe — and other poetasters began to write narrative verses about the wicked innkeeper and he was assailed in many of the tracts with which the country was flooded.

And so, toward the end of the century, Mine Host, like

Lucifer, fell. He was no longer a part of the small-town aristocracy, but a shady fellow at whom society looked askance — notwithstanding that, judged by the standards of humanity in general, he was not any worse than the rest of his fellow citizens. He remained more or less of an outcast — though in many places he continued to be one of the foremost village politicians — until the time of the Eighteenth Amendment, since which time the cloud has lifted and he has regained the position and influence that were formerly his. The cloud cast by the Demon Rum had, of course, its silver lining. Without his bar-room the old-time landlord — whether in city or village — would have been utterly lost. The first question he asked when he opened negotiations for acquiring a hotel lease was: "What are the bar receipts?" That was the all-important thing to know. He depended upon his bar to pay his bills for rent, heat, light, and a few other items of overhead. Without the bar the four big American-plan meals of the old days would never have been possible — at least, at the rates Mine Host charged in those days. Little as he knew about cost-finding and all the other fine points of modern book-keeping and accounting, Mine Host knew well enough that he was losing money heavily on his dining-room. But the bar was his big ace, and it more than made up for his dining-room losses.

The temperance movement gained even a few recruits from the ranks of hotel-keepers, and as a result there were quite a number of temperance hotels, here and there, during the early days and, in fact, all through the nineteenth century. E. T. Coke, a British army officer, mentions that he saw many hotels in 1832 with "Temperance Hotel" inscribed in large gilded letters over the door or on the sign.[4] One of the first temperance hotels of any prominence, as was said before, was the old Marlboro in Boston, bone-dry from its beginning, in 1820. Nathaniel Rogers, Mine Host of the Marlboro, later became proprietor of the famous old Delaven House in Albany, which was built in 1845 by Edward C. Delaven, one of the wealthiest total-abstinence zealots of his day. Rogers managed it for four years and kept it as dry as its owner could wish, but when he was succeeded by Theophilus Roessle, the house went soaking wet, and from then on until it burned down, on December 30, 1894, there were few hotels, if any, in which more champagne corks went popping toward the ceiling, especially during sessions of the legislature. The old Delaven House is remembered as the scene of some of the fiercest political fights known to New York State, including the Tweed charter uproar of 1869 and 1870 and the memorable Conkling-Platt contest in 1881.

Even New York City had its temperance hotels. The first was the Croton Hotel, at 142 Broadway, which George D. Ives and John L. Moore opened on April 1, 1843. Horace Greeley commended the idea and expressed the belief that it was possible to run a hotel successfully without relying on the sale of rum. The *Tribune* was a strong supporter of the temperance movement from the beginning. The Croton, appropriately named after New York's new waterworks system, ran for many years, apparently thriving on the business of white-ribboners. In 1847 there were four temperance hotels in the city, the fourth being Taylor's Hotel, at 28 Cortlandt Street, opened in that year. The *Tribune* regarded this as ample proof that a hotel could be run without the assistance of John Barleycorn.[5] But all of these were small hotels, run on the European plan. The American-plan Astor House, whose wine-cellar was "mentioned with reverence, even in foreign capitals," continued unregenerate.

Mine Host did not always limit his activities to running a hotel, nor did he always remain an innkeeper. Often he had other irons in the fire and figured conspicuously in the fields of politics, education, law, and even in arts and letters. Many men who rose to prominence in other walks of life were at one time or another in the business of commercialized hospitality. In colonial days Mine Host often was a justice of the peace or incumbent of some other village or county office. When the Revolution began, many of his number became officers in Washington's army, and at least one, Israel Putnam, rose to the rank of general. Patrick Henry, silver-tongued orator of the Revolution, married an innkeeper's daughter and tended bar in his father-in-law's tavern in Virginia, even after he had been admitted to the bar, when he found it hard to get enough law practice to keep him busy. It was seldom that a state legislature did not have its sprinkling of Bonifaces, and almost every city has elected Mine Host at one time or another to the mayoralty. Occasionally one was elected governor or sent to Congress, and at least one, Jeremiah Lane Rusk, sat in a president's cabinet. Rusk was the first Secretary of Agriculture, appointed by President Benjamin Harrison. For many years he ran a hotel and a stage line at Viroqua, Wisconsin, during pioneer days. Potter Palmer of Chicago declined appointment, in 1870, as Secretary of the Interior in President Grant's Cabinet.

Few men in recent years have wielded more political power than did Thomas Taggart, veteran Democratic boss of Indiana, who died a multimillionaire on March 6, 1929, at the age of seventy-two. During his long career in politics he made governors, senators, at least two vice-presidents, and some presidential nominees. He was mayor of Indianapolis, national chairman of his party, and senator — a very fair record for a boy who had to go to work at fifteen and walked a hundred miles two years later to get a job as a waiter at a railway lunch-counter at Indianapolis. A few years later he began running a small hotel near the railway station and in course of time became proprietor of the Grand Hotel in Indianapolis and builder and general manager of the elegant French Lick Hotel at French Lick Springs, Indiana, of which he was president until 1921.

Mine Host can even claim, with at least some warrant, that one of his number scaled the heights to the presidential chair. During at least one of the six years that he spent at New Salem, Illinois, Abraham Lincoln was a licensed tavern-keeper, as the records of Sangamon County show. On March 6, 1833 a tavern license was issued to him, William F. Berry, and John B. Green. It was for one year and they paid seven dollars for it, as the county treasurer's receipt shows. The license granted them the right to charge 12½ cents per night for lodging, 25 cents per night for keeping a horse, 12½ cents for a single feed, 25 cents each for breakfast, dinner, or supper, with a rate of 37½ cents per meal for stage passengers. The license also listed the prices for half-pints of brandy, gin, rum, whisky, and other liquors. The bond, required by law, read as follows:

> Know all men by these presents that we, William F. Berry, Abraham Lincoln and John Bowling Green, are held and firmly bound to the County Commissioners of Sangamon County in the full sum of $300, to which payment well and truly to be made, we bind ourselves, our heirs, our executors, and administrators firmly by these presents, sealed with our seals and dated this sixth day of March A.D. 1833. Now the condition of this obligation is such that, whereas Berry & Lincoln have obtained a license from the County Commissioner's court to keep a tavern in the town of New Salem to continue one year; now if the said Berry & Lincon shall be of good behavior and observe all the laws of this State relative to tavern keepers, then this obligation to be void, or otherwise to remain in force.
>
> Abraham Lincoln (Seal)
> William F. Berry (Seal)
> John Bowling Green (Seal)

But destiny had greater things in store for Lincoln than mere tavern-keeping; and before his tavern license had expired, he was taking the first definite step toward those higher reaches of life and affairs in which he attained such high distinction. As a business man of the rough little frontier town the witty and sociable Lincoln, ever ready to pitch horseshoes with fellow-townsmen during idle hours, or to act as judge of horse-races, cock-fights, wrestling-matches, and foot-races, had become the idol of the village, and in the following year (1834) he was elected to the legislature from New Salem, the beginning of his office-holding career. The life of Lincoln had still another link with tavern-keeping, for his first and greatest love was Ann Rutledge, the daughter of James Rutledge, who combined the pursuits of tavern-keeper and miller at New Salem.

During the first quarter-century of the railroad in America, the days when a two-hundred-mile line was an extraordinarily long one, many hotel men were builders of railways. Some innkeepers, of course, were among those who set every possible obstacle in the way of railroad construction, as Caroline E. MacGill points out in *The History of Transportation*;[6] but it must be remembered that at the beginning of the railroad era a great majority of people opposed railroads. It was natural for some hotel men to fight against a new mode of transportation if it threatened to isolate their properties and ruin their business. Hotel-keepers on the Conestoga wagon-trails through Pennsylvania, the popular gateway to the West, were especially successful in their opposition, but only for a short time. On the other hand, many progressive hotel-keepers were owners of stage lines and, understanding the inadequacies of the stage-coach, were quick to appreciate the advantages of steam travel and to foresee its revolutionizing character. They took a leading part in promoting and organizing railroad companies, and many of them were the presidents of those companies.[7]

Cornelius Vanderbilt, the old "Commodore," was

perhaps the most conspicuous example of a hotel-keeper who engaged in the transportation business — first as a steamship man and later as a railroad man. Like many others he had no enthusiasm for railroads at first, but changed his views quickly when he saw their possibilities demonstrated. The Commodore was for many years landlord of the old Bellona Hotel, on the waterfront at New Brunswick, New Jersey, before and after he became a captain, in 1817 (at a thousand dollars a year), of the first steamship to run between New York and New Brunswick. The Commodore's wife, who had been a tavern maid, helped him run the hotel, and it was at the Bellona that the Commodore's eldest son, William H., who inherited most of the Vanderbilt fortune, was born.[8]

"Uncle Dan'l" Drew, a picturesque figure of early nineteenth-century New York, built no railroads, but he had a lot to do with the affairs of the Erie when that railroad was in the clutches of Drew, Jay Gould, and Jim Fisk. Drew was the landlord for many years of the Bull's Head Tavern on the Boston Post Road (Third Avenue), near the present Twenty-sixth Street — a tavern which, with its cattle market and surrounding village, was for nearly fifty years the main outpost of the city in its northward march. Before becoming landlord Drew was a drover who brought cattle down from up-state to Bull's Head village. On one trip he fed his drove a quart of salt apiece at a Harlem farm and kept them absolutely away from water until the next day, then went on with them to the tavern. While he dickered for the sale of the cows at three and a half cents a pound in the bar-room, his herd-boys pumped water for dear life in the tavern stockade. The cows scaled fifty pounds apiece heavier. The first butcher thus stung kept it a secret, but never bought from Drew again. Others were similarly victimized, and thus arose the expression "watered stock," which followed Drew to Wall Street when he began his operations there.⁹ We are told that " Uncle Dan'l " was not a hearty, genial host, but that he kept a "comfortable, economical house." He took with him to Wall Street the blue swallow-tail coat with brass buttons in which he used to pace solemnly back and forth, " his hands folded beneath the tails, his head bent down and his introspective eyes partly shaded by the rim of a tall bell-crowned hat." It was understood that at such times " Uncle Dan'l " was planning business, and it behooved all and sundry with whom he dealt to be strictly on their guard.

One of the most romantic figures in hoteldom's early days was Benjamin Rathbun of Buffalo, America's first " Get Rich Quick Wallingford." Rathbun began as an innkeeper at Sherburne, New York, but went to Buffalo and built the Eagle Tavern, which opened in 1825. It was Buffalo's first caravansary of any importance and Rathbun's first step toward transforming Buffalo into a great city. Buffalo had a population of less than five thousand, but the great westward tide of travel via the Great Lakes was setting in. Rathbun began building steamships and wharves and established nearly forty stage lines to bring land-hungry travelers to his ships. Later on he built a railroad. He employed steadily from one to two thousand workmen in various forms of construction. They erected warehouses, factories, wharves, many fine business blocks, churches, schools, theaters, bank buildings, and hotels. The finest building in the town, and one of the finest in America, was the five-story American Hotel, surmounted by a belvedere and a large gilded dome. It rivaled the Astor House in splendor, was almost as large, and was superbly managed. On August 3, 1836, a few weeks before it opened, Rathbun was arrested.¹⁰ He and his colleagues had been fraudulently financing their operations by means of forged bank-notes. Discovery of this was the sensation of the day, and Rathbun's alleged rascality was a tale to be told all over the world, for here was "the Girard of the West," a superman of business, come to grief. They sent him to prison for five years. Just before the term expired Governor Seward granted him a pardon, in response to petitions signed by nearly everyone in northwestern New York, including fifty members of the legislature. The day Rathbun returned home was a gala day in Buffalo. There was a general suspension of work in the city, and all stores were closed during a big welcome-home parade. With banners flying and brass bands blaring, hundreds of prominent citizens in carriages and thousands of others on foot escorted Rathbun from the railway station and through the principal streets, after which there was a banquet at the American Hotel. At this banquet a purse was presented to Rathbun, to start him in business again, for he was penniless. His fortune had at one time been estimated at more than two million dollars. Thousands of clerks and workmen had given one day's wages to the fund and store-keepers, professional men, and employers in general had contributed a day's profits.[11] It was a generous gesture of Buffalo's appreciation of what Rathbun had done for Buffalo. He had come to it when it was but a village, second in importance to the near-by rival village of Black Rock as the starting-point of westward travel at the head of the lakes, and he had built it up overnight into one of the most prosperous and best-built cities in the country, its victory over Black Rock complete and overwhelming. Moreover, he had not misused a penny of the money he had obtained fraudulently. It had all gone into construction work that, with Buffalo growing like a weed, netted handsome returns. No one had lost a cent on his financial manipulations. And so, if Buffalo people no longer thought Rathbun "the greatest and wisest man in the United States," he was still their martyred hero. But Rathbun was unwilling to remain in Buffalo. Instead he came to New York, where he opened Rathbun's Hotel, on lower Broadway. He ran it until 1861, when he opened the Broadway Hotel in the quiet pastoral neighborhood of Broadway and Forty-second Street. He retired in 1870, worth seventy-five thousand dollars, and died three years later.

New England supplied the entire country with hotel-keepers for several decades. It seemed as though no new palace hotel was quite complete without a New England

CAPT. ROBERT COLEMAN, *early proprietor of the Astor House, New York City*

landlord. The New Englanders had a great reputation for hotel-keeping before the Civil War and indeed throughout the first half of the century. The hotel men of the period from 1830 to 1900 are already known as hotel-keepers of "the old school," though many of them doubtless would be shining lights in the profession today. The Boydens of the Tremont House; Captain Robert Coleman of the old Astor House, and later of the Eutaw in Baltimore, the

National in Washington, and the Burnet in Cincinnati; Charles A. Stetson of the Astor House; Paran Stevens of the Revere House in Boston and the old Fifth Avenue Hotel in New York, and his partners, Alfred B. Darling and Hiram Hitchcock; the famous Leland family of the old Metropolitan in New York and later of many other hotels

EUTAW HOUSE, Baltimore, Md.

in cities far and wide; Harvey D. Parker, founder of the Parker House in Boston; Uriah Welch of the St. Nicholas in New York; Hiram Cranston of the Eutaw House in Baltimore and later of the New York Hotel; Richard French of French's Hotel in New York; Lewis Rice, first proprietor of the American House in Boston; David Barnum of Barnum's Hotel in Baltimore, and his sons and grandsons, identified with many of the old hotels in various cities; the

POTTER PALMER, *founder of the old Palmer House, Chicago*
PARAN STEVENS, *pioneer chain hotel man*
DWIGHT BOYDEN, *first proprietor of Tremont House, Boston, and Astor House, New York—From a painting by Chester Harding. (Courtesy of Charles Boyden, Boston)*

LUCIUS BOOMER, *president of the Hotel Waldorf-Astoria Corporation. Mr. Boomer became president of the old Waldorf in 1917, after the death of George C. Boldt in 1916*
ELLSWORTH M. STATLER
JOHN McENTEE BOWMAN, *President Bowman Biltmore Hotels Corporation and Bowman Management Inc., another operating company*

Willard brothers — Joseph, Caleb, and Henry A. — who ran the old Willard House in Washington; Colonel R. J. Rivers of the old St. Charles in New Orleans; J. McDonald Crossan of the old Monongahela House in Pittsburgh; William B. Cozzens of the Tammany Hall Hotel; J. Reed Whipple of Boston; John B. Drake of the Grand Pacific Hotel in Chicago; and Potter Palmer of the Palmer House; Captain Daniel Howard of the old Howard House in New York, first proprietor of the old Hoffman House; Colonel Selden Crockett and his son, S. Frank Crockett, of the old Bromfield House in Boston; Colonel George E. Presbury and John H. Billings, partners in the operation of the old Girard House in Philadelphia; Colonel James H. Breslin of the Gilsey House in New York and the Auditorium Hotel in Chicago; Henry Milford Smith of the old Grand Hotel in New York; Charles B. Waite of the Brevoort Hotel in New York; the Huggins brothers of the old Cosmopolitan Hotel in New York; W. D. Garrison of the old Grand Union Hotel in New York; Tilly Haynes, E. L. Merrifield, Horace H. Brockway — these were some of the outstanding hotel men of their time, many of whom are well remembered by oldsters of the present generation.

In the middle decades of the nineteenth century Paran Stevens was generally regarded as the greatest Boniface of them all. This "Napoleon of hotel-keepers," as he was often called, bestrode the hotel world like a colossus and was the great exemplar of his generation, as Ellsworth M. Statler was of a later generation. Stevens was the first to demonstrate, in an impressive way, that it was possible to be a good hotel man and a good business man as well. When he died, in New York on April 27, 1872, he left an estate of about three million dollars. Strictly speaking, he was the first chain-hotel operator — and, incidentally, there were hotel chains in this country before there were chains of any other sort of business enterprises. While other hotel-keepers were generally of the opinion that a hotel of six hundred rooms was "too unwieldy to handle, requiring almost as much vigilance as the affairs of a nation," Stevens demonstrated that he could conduct not only one hotel, but several. His was a centralized-control chain, and not a mere family affair, with one brother running one hotel, another brother running another hotel, and so on.

Stevens was a native of Claremont, New Hampshire — born September 11, 1802 — and came of old New England stock.[12] His grandfather Elihu Stevens was a justice of the peace in Claremont in the eighteenth century, puritanically stern in his punishment of offenders, especially Tories. His son, Josiah, the father of Paran, was a store-keeper who introduced luxuries into the town — a hogshead of molasses and a chest of tea, "which some of the citizens declared was a piece of foolish extravagance that would certainly lead to no good." He was the first postmaster of Claremont, from 1802 to 1813, when it cost six cents to send a single-sheet letter thirty miles, and twenty-five cents to send it four hundred miles. In 1800 Captain Josiah built the Tremont House at Claremont, and when he died, in 1827, his four sons took charge. In a few years Paran became sole proprietor and ran it so well that in 1843 he was called to Boston to run the New England Coffee House. There, too, he made a reputation and three years later was chosen as the most desirable man for the proprietorship of the Revere House, which had been built by a company of men connected with the Charitable Mechanics Association, of which Paul Revere, the midnight rider, was the first president. The Revere House was opened on May 19, 1847 and within a few years had enshrined itself firmly in the hearts of the public as few other hotels have since done.

Harvey D. Parker, a short little man of slight build, but with an exceptionally keen mind and an indomitable energy, was another Boston Boniface whose fame was nation-wide. Parker was born on May 10, 1805, in the little town of Temple, in what was then the District of Maine. When he was twenty years old, he walked to the nearest sea-coast town, carrying a bundle of clothes, and ten dollars tied in a handkerchief. He took passage to Boston on a coastwise packet and there got a job at eight dollars a month. After a while he got a job that paid a little more, as coachman for a family living at Watertown, near Boston. During his two years at that job he frequently had to drive members of the family to town. These trips took the better part of a day, and on such occasions Parker ate luncheon at a little restaurant kept by John E. Hunt in the Tudor Building on Court Square, which was later remodeled into Young's Hotel, known in its palmiest days as " the Delmonico's of Boston." Within seven years after he had left home, Parker became owner of this restaurant, paying almost every penny he had saved, $342, for it. A few years later he opened a large, elegant restaurant and in 1854 began building the original Parker House, which opened on October 8, 1855. He, too, knew how to run a hotel well and make it pay. When he died, on May 31, 1884, at the age of seventy-nine, his estate was appraised at $1,272,546.[13]

Perhaps the most widely known family of hotel-keepers of the Parker and Stevens generation was that of the Leland brothers, whose name cast a very potent spell over the traveling public for more than half a century. The family consisted of Simeon Leland and his five sons — Aaron, Simeon Jr., William, Charles, and Warren. They and their numerous progeny spread out all over the United States and were known almost everywhere. Every city, at one time or another, either had a Leland Hotel or a hotel of some other name managed by a Leland. Simeon Leland, gray-haired chieftain of the tribe, was Mine Host of the Green Mountain Coffee House at Landsgrove, Vermont, during the early decades of the century. There his sons were born and got their early training. As each son grew up, he migrated to Boston or New York. Charles was perhaps the first to come to New York. He was a clerk at the old Carleton House at Broadway and Leonard Street in 1843. In later years he clerked at other hotels, and in 1850 he and Warren became proprietors of the Clinton Hotel, in Beekman Street.[14] The Clinton was one of the few top-rate (two dollar) hostelries of New York at the time, the others being the Astor House, the American Hotel, the Carlton House, the old City Hotel, the Franklin House, at Broadway and Dey Street; the Irving House; Howard's Hotel; Rathbun's Hotel, at 165 Broadway (between Liberty and Cortlandt streets); and the New York Hotel, at Broadway and Waverly Place.[15] Two years later Charles and Warren sold the Clinton and, with their brothers Simeon and Aaron, opened the famous old Metropolitan Hotel, which they continued to operate until about 1870. Meanwhile they had become proprietors, in 1864, of the Grand Union Hotel at Saratoga, and after the Civil War ran various other hotels.

The last stand of the brothers in New York was at the Sturtevant Hotel, from which the family retired in 1886. By that time there was only one of the five brothers left, Warren, who died at Port Chester, New York, on June 8, 1893. Their sons carried on the name and prestige of the family for many more years. Of these Lewis Leland was perhaps the most widely known. " Portly, good-natured, with a thunderous voice," as one eulogist said, " there was no jollier, heartier host in America." Lew had a host of friends in theatrical circles, and none more staunch than E. L. Davenport and John B. McCullough, the Shaksperian star. " If Lew Leland kept a shanty on one side of the street and there was a palace on the other side," said McCullough, " you can bet your life I'd stop with Lew." Lewis Leland was the first manager of the old Palace Hotel in San Francisco and in the middle 1880's managed the Occidental Hotel there. At the time of the World's Fair in Chicago he was managing the Renfost Hotel in that city, while two cousins, Warren F. and Charles E., were running other Chicago hotels. Warren was running Leland's Hotel and also managed a temporary hotel of nine hundred rooms, called the Ingram, in the fair-grounds, facing the Midway Plaisance. Charles managed the principal fair-grounds hotel, a temporary structure of eight hundred rooms, immediately opposite the main entrance.

John B. Drake and Potter Palmer were the two outstanding figures of Chicago hoteldom in the old days. Drake, whose two sons, Tracy A. and John B., carry on the business established by their father, is remembered by older Chicagoans as the *bon vivant* whose annual game dinners were red-letter events in the social life of the city, and as one of the men whose business enterprise and acumen contributed much to the growth of Chicago. To the traveling public he and his now-vanished Grand Pacific Hotel were institutions of more than mere national fame. Drake was a native of Lebanon, Ohio — born on January 17, 1826 — in which town another famous old-time Boniface, Harvey Bates, of the old Bates House in Indianapolis, also was born. Drake was eleven years old when his father died and he had to go to work in a store to help his mother support a family of five other children. A few years later he got a job in the Williamson House, a stage inn on the main turnpike between Cincinnati and Columbus. The Williamson House was left high and dry when a railroad was built, a few miles away, in 1845, and young Drake went to Cincinnati with fifteen dollars and a letter from Governor Tom Corwin in his pocket. He clerked for ten years in the Pearl Street House and the Burnet House and in 1855 went to Chicago, where he bought an interest in the old Tremont House, of which he was proprietor at the time of the big fire.[16]

While the fire was still raging, Drake, fleeing from the embers of his own burning hotel, passed the Michigan Avenue Hotel (on the site of the present Congress Hotel), which was still unharmed. Near-by buildings were bursting into flame and it seemed but a question of minutes when the hotel would catch fire. There was a chance, Drake thought, that it might be spared — one chance in a thousand, perhaps, but still a chance on which he was willing to gamble. "How much will you take, in cash, for your lease and furniture?" he asked the worried proprietor, who did not believe, at first, that Drake meant business. "You must be crazy," he said; "within an hour there'll be nothing left of this place but cinders." "Maybe so," said Drake, "but if you want to sell, I'll buy, and here's a thousand dollars down. You'll get the rest in two weeks." A contract was drawn up on hotel stationary, and the binder was paid over. Though an extremely long chance, it turned out to be a lucky chance, for the Michigan Avenue Hotel escaped destruction. Drake rechristened it the Tremont House, annexed some adjoining buildings, and did a rushing business, for there was practically no competition and sightseers immediately began flocking into the stricken city by the thousands.[17]

Drake's contemporary, Potter Palmer, had become a national figure before he undertook, when past middle age, to run a hotel. Born near Albany, New York, on May 20, 1826, he began his career as a clerk in a bank and store at Durham, New York, and later ran stores at Oneida and Lockport, New York. In 1852 he went to Chicago on a visit and was so captivated by the opportunities there that he induced his father to finance him in establishing a dry-goods store in that city. In that store he inaugurated many new ideas that revolutionized retail trade. It is said he was the first to make big window displays, the first to use big advertising space for a department store, and the first to send goods on approval to homes and to hold bargain sales and special sales.[18] He was as brilliant a hotel man as he had been a merchant, though some hotel men thought him " erratic, inconsistent, and peculiar " because he applied a lot of department-store methods to the operation of his hotel and could see no reason why clerks, chefs, and head waiters should not be subject to the same discipline as floorwalkers and counter-jumpers. Nevertheless he was one of the most successful hotel men of his day and introduced administrative policies and systems that prevail in all well-conducted hotels today. He could be seen at all hours in the lobby and corridors of the Palmer House, watching and directing, always speaking in short, jerky sentences, and tugging nervously, perpetually, at his whiskers. He never went behind the desk. " He is tall, lean and spare, with a clean look and the good color of a good man who has regular and simple habits," said the *Hotel Gazette*. " He has a kindly, regularly featured face ornamented with a slightly grey moustache and a short chin beard. His eyes are blue and express great reserve. Mr. Palmer, like most successful men, is more inclined to reserve than expansiveness." This was not the sort of Boniface the average guest was accustomed to seeing.

There has probably never been a better Horatio Alger story in the annals of American business than that of Ellsworth M. Statler, admittedly the greatest hotel man of his time. Statler began life as a glory-hole boy. A glory hole is a furnace in a glass-factory, similar to the kilns in pottery works — the finest kind of place to destroy the spirit of a spindle-legged youth of nine years, such as Statler was when he began work in the glory hole of the La Belle Glass Works at Wheeling, West Virginia, in 1872. He worked twelve hours a day in alternate day and night shifts, and got twenty-five cents a " turn," six hours to a turn. When he left the glory hole, at the age of twelve, he was getting forty-five cents a turn, or ninety cents a day. The family lived at

Bridgeport, Ohio, across the river from Wheeling, to which place Statler's parents had moved from Somerset County, Pennsylvania, where he was born in 1863. His three years of glory-hole experience ended when his brother, employed in the old McLure House in Wheeling, got him a job as bell-hop in the hotel. The McLure House, five stories high, was the show-place of Wheeling, with stores on the main floor front, and an elevator that carried guests to the upper floors. But not bell-hops. They had to trudge wearily up the back stairs whenever a guest rang for ice-water or whatever else was wanted. Statler got six dollars a month at this job, but he also got nickles and dimes, and occasionally quarters, from appreciative guests, and on the whole it was much better than the job in the glory hole had been.

There were dull hours when bell-hops were expected to perform other duties than answering bells, and it was in the performance of these duties that young Statler became acquainted with Tom Duffy, bar-tender. Duffy took an interest in the bright little lad who always seemed to be eager to learn, and taught him many things. The story of how Duffy gave Statler a lesson in the use of good English is related by one of his biographers:

> Young Statler came to the hotel rich in knowledge of economic strife but poor in the rudiments of speech and manner as practiced outside of a glory hole. He comprehended his lack of polish but covered it up by keeping his mouth shut and getting his lessons how and where he could. He and the bartender, Duffy, became great friends, and one day Statler told Duffy an incident of his career. "I seen it wasn't right," he said. Tom Duffy stopped him in the middle of his tale. "Never say, 'I seen,'" he corrected the boy; "say, 'I saw.' That's English." Statler swallowed his lesson and never forgot it.
>
> Tom Duffy was not the only one from whom the boy learned the essentials of speech and conduct. He used to watch the manners of guests and take lessons. General Nathan Goff once stayed at the

hotel, an imposing figure. He rang for a boy and Statler was sent up to his room. He made it in double quick time. "Bring me a cuspidor, boy," said the general. "Yes, sir," answered Statler, and waited, half expecting to get the money with which to go out and buy it. The general looked at him closely, then grinned. "I reckon you don't get me, son," he said. "I want a spittoon." He got it and Statler added a new word to his vocabulary.[19]

And thus the former glory-hole boy began his upward climb to the presidency and general management of one of the largest and best-known chains of hotels in the country. He learned as he went along. At the McLure House he was successively bellboy, check-room boy, night clerk, and day room-clerk at fifty dollars a month. From the brother of the proprietor he picked up the rudiments of book-keeping and accounting, " and thus got an inkling of the profits made by hotel-keepers." Finally, when he was in his early twenties, he became lessee of the McLure's billiard parlor, his first business venture, and also took over the railroad-ticket concession. A few years later he leased the old Wheeling Musee and installed billiard-tables and a lunch counter in two-thirds of it, leasing the remaining space to a barber. Within fifteen years after he had left the glory hole, he was making between four and five thousand dollars a year and had become a moderately prosperous man of the world.

The thing he had missed most as a child was play. He began making visits to Canada, to fish, and stopped at Buffalo on the way. In that city he subsequently began his career as a hotel proprietor. In 1898 he leased restaurant space in the Ellicott Square office building, the largest in the country at that time. It was a move that led directly to the beginning of his hotel chain, which was founded when he opened the first Hotel Statler in Buffalo on January 18, 1908. In this hotel he incorporated ideas he had been picking up for years. Very few hotels then had private baths with every room. It is said, in fact, that no strictly transient hotel was thus equipped. But every one of the four hundred and fifty rooms in Statler's new hotel had either tub or shower. He remembered, too, the iced water in the halls on each floor of the Ellicott Square Building and installed running ice-water in every room of the hotel. He remembered that Charles Vendig, of the old Vendig Hotel in Philadelphia, had put pincushions in every room, with needles, thread, and a few buttons, and he adopted this idea. Mine Host of Craig Hall in Atlantic City had put the keyholes of guest-room doors above the door-knob, instead of under it, so that guests might have less difficulty in unlocking their doors. And there was another idea he made good use of. It had long been a custom in many first-class hotels, dating back to the days of the old St. Nicholas and Metropolitan hotels in New York, to deliver a newspaper each morning to guests at their rooms if they notified the clerk or head waiter that they desired such service. Mr. Statler improved on this idea. Each guest-room door had a thin slot at the bottom, just big enough for a newspaper to be slipped through it into the room, and when each guest awoke in the morning, there was a paper for him. These and many other service ideas which he had worked out himself or picked up in earlier life and stored away for future use were put into practice at the first Statler Hotel, and at each of the others as fast as they opened. He seemed to have an inexhaustible fund of ideas, many of which were at first looked upon as fantastic and unnecessary, but which were, nevertheless, copied more and more as time went on and have become standard features of hotel practice and administration. At the old McLure House while plodding up and down the stairs with pitchers of ice-water, and later in other capacities, he had learned that it is service that makes a hotel and he was determined to do for the guests of his own hotels a little more than had even been done for them before. On this cardinal principle his great success was built.[20]

RAGS TO RICHES

John McEntee Bowman, head of the Bowman-Biltmore chain of hotels, is another hotel man of today who had no easy time of it in his boyhood days, though he never had to work in a glory hole. When he first came to New York from his native Toronto, in 1892 — he was then seventeen — he arrived with the traditional lack of funds and a willingness to take the first job that came along. In his pocket he carried a letter of introduction to the manager of the old Manhattan Hotel at Madison Avenue and Forty-second Street. He called at the hotel to present the letter, but was kept waiting hours for an interview and left without seeing the man. Then he mailed the letter, asking permission to call. There was no response, so he wrote again, asking for the return of the letter. Even then he got no reply, and he formed a strong opinion of the character of the man who had exhibited what seemed to him such gross and needless discourtesy. He knocked about New York in various jobs, including a few months as a riding-master at the old Durland riding-academy, work that was close to his heart, for he had always had a great fondness for horses and had spent one or two summers in Canada in connection with a stable of racehorses on the county-fair circuit. But although the work was agreeable, he was convinced there was little future for him in a riding-academy, and he was equally convinced that his future lay in the hotel business. He got his first taste of hotel life when an employment agent sent him as clerk to a summer hotel in the Adirondacks, and the following winter he went south in a similar capacity. This sort of thing went on for two or three years, and finally he got a job as clerk in the old Holland House, on Fifth Avenue, then operated by Gustave Baumann, who took a liking to the brilliant, debonair young fellow from Canada and appointed him as his private secretary. He became Baumann's right-hand man, and when the Biltmore Hotel was opened, on New Year's Eve 1913, with Baumann as president, Bowman was announced as vice-president and managing director. In the summer of 1914 Baumann, in a fit of despondency, leaped from an upper-story window of the Biltmore, and Bowman succeeded to the presidency of the company. The outbreak of the World War ushered in an era of extraordinary travel to New York and other financial and industrial centers, and the Biltmore rode on a high tide of prosperity. The company began to acquire other hotels, and the Bowman-Biltmore chain, now one of the largest in the country, sprang into existence.[21]

Lucius M. Boomer, who guided the destinies of the old Waldorf-Astoria during the last dozen years of its life, and who is president of a chain of swagger hotels in New York and elsewhere, also had his struggles against adolescent adversity. He was born in Poughkeepsie, New York, in 1878, and was brought up in Chicago. Legend has it that he wanted to become a violin virtuoso and took lessons from an old German teacher, but had to give up this ambition when his father died. Instead he went to work as a stenographer in a railroad office at fifty-five dollars a month. This left him no time to practice the fiddle. He was then aged eighteen. Presently he got a letter from a friend who was clerk in a hotel at St. Augustine, Florida. "I am getting out of here and you can have my job if you hurry down," wrote the friend. Winter was coming on and — again the legend speaks — Boomer had no overcoat. In Florida he would not need an overcoat. So he went south, ran afoul of an epidemic of typhoid fever, and spent the winter in a hospital. Joseph Greaves, owner of the old Oriental Hotel at Manhattan Beach, Coney Island, was one of his fellow patients in the hospital, and in the spring Greaves brought Boomer north to a job in the store-room of the Oriental. Evenings, as he rolled barrels, opened crates, and did other sweaty work in a pair of overalls in the basement, Boomer could hear the music of Sousa's band on the esplanade, hear the cheers of the crowds watching the bicycle races, and, peering through the window, see the glare shed by Paine's fireworks. But the work agreed with him; he regained his strength, and next fall he again went to Florida. For three years he alternated between the Oriental and St. Augustine and after that held various hotel jobs in New York and Boston and at Canadian resorts. At this period he was studying to become a lawyer, but his eyes failed and he decided to stick to hotel work. He finally got a job as secretary to Fred Sterry, manager of the Plaza Hotel, and from him learned many secrets of hotel efficiency. Finally, in partnership with Henry L. Merry, he became proprietor of the Nassau Hotel at Long Beach, Long Island — the hotel in which, back in Spanish War days, an impulsive Miss Arnold of St. Louis started a craze that spread throughout the country when she ran up to the dashing young Lieutenant Richmond Pearson Hobson and cried: " May I kiss you ? " [22] When the McAlpin Hotel was opened in New York, in 1912, Boomer became its managing director, and thus at the age of thirty-four had become director general of a house of seventeen hundred rooms, the world's largest at the time. He succeeded to the management of the old Waldorf-Astoria when George C. Boldt died, in 1916, and within the next few years, as president of the Boomer-duPont Properties Corporation, was the head of a chain of hotels of Waldorf rank. It is this company that is building the forty-million-dollar Waldorf-Astoria that is to carry on the name and traditions of the old house.[23]

George C. Boldt, Boomer's predecessor at the Waldorf-Astoria, was another New York hotel man who had climbed up from a lowly beginning. Born in 1853 on a Baltic island, he landed in New York when he was sixteen, without a friend and with not much money. His first job was as dishwasher in the Merchants' Exchange Hotel at Broadway and Chambers Street. Subsequently he had various other kitchen jobs. While he was working as cashier in Parker's Restaurant in New York, a patron who owned a small hotel at Cornwall-on-Hudson took a liking to him and offered him the proprietorship of the hotel. It was Boldt's first important stepping-stone. Later he managed the Philadelphia Club and became proprietor of the Bellevue Hotel, a small house, with a fairly large restaurant, which became very popular. Subsequently he also operated a restaurant in the Bullitt Building in Philadelphia and two summer hotels in New Jersey.[24] In 1888 he became lessee of another Philadelphia hotel, the St. George, which had been closed for remodeling. He reopened it on November 17, 1888, as the Stafford Hotel, and was still running this and the Bellevue when he got his long-desired chance to enter the New York hotel field. William Waldorf Astor had bought the southwest corner of Fifth Avenue and Thirty-fourth Street, on which the Waldorf-Astoria was to rise. The Waldorf section of it opened on March 13, 1893, with the erstwhile humble dish-washer as proprietor. He became a world-famous Boniface and so prominent and popular in his own city and state that the Democrats tried to draft him as candidate for governor in 1908. He died on December 5, 1916. Even more widely known than Boldt himself was his *maître d'hôtel,* Oscar Tschirky, generally known as "Oscar of the Waldorf." He was with the hotel from its opening to its closing. He came to America from his native Neuchâtel, Switzerland, in 1883, when he was fifteen years old, and had been with Delmonico's and the Hoffman House prior to joining Boldt's staff to help prepare for the opening of the Waldorf.

One of the shining lights of hoteldom in his day, not long past, was Edward M. Tierney of the Arlington Hotel at Binghamton, New York, known among hotel men throughout the country as the "Silver-tongued Orator of Hoteldom." He was born November 11, 1860, at Susquehanna, Pennsylvania, and in association with George W.

Sweeney, now managing director of the Hotel Commodore, he was proprietor for many years of the old Marlborough and Victoria hotels in New York City and later was managing director of the Ansonia. Meanwhile he was co-proprietor, and later sole proprietor, of the Arlington from the time of its opening, on April 24, 1888, until his death, on August 9, 1927. He was very active in association work, serving six terms as president of the New York State Hotel Association, two as president of the American Hotel Association, and one year as president of the Hotel Men's Mutual Benefit Association.

Past generations of hotel proprietors have, generally speaking, come up from the ranks. They learned the business " from the ground up," beginning as bellboys, waiters, bar-tenders, or clerks or in other menial jobs. The great majority were poor boys who got most of their education as they went along. They were taught readin', 'ritin' and 'rithmetic in the little red schoolhouses and picked up the rest of their knowledge in the school of experience. The present generation is somewhat less of that type, but not greatly so. Future generations, perhaps, will be chiefly college-trained men, for there are now scientific courses in hotel administration. These courses — chief of which is that of Cornell University, sponsored by the New York State Hotel Association some eight years ago — are designed to make the academic road of progress toward success in hotel-keeping easier and quicker traveling than the older road of experience. As one writer wittily put it, the object is " the educational transformation of Mine Host into a successful hotel executive, so that he may tend to be as well-rounded intellectually as he used to be physically in those days when he was the traditional fat and jolly fellow of imaginative literature. Mine Host, standing so round and smiling (as one likes to imagine him) in the doorway of the Pig and

Chickens needed little by way of education in comparison with the hotel manager in the private office of a palatial skyscraper named, after the fashion of democracy, to suggest the residence of at least a duke."

Naturally, opinions within the ranks differ. While none are opposed to education as such, there are those who believe that whether hotel men come from the class-room or the glory hole, experience is still a prime essential to the greatest successs. The fact is recognized by those schools that have courses in hotel administration. They give the students practical training during the school year and get them minor jobs for vacation periods. Many of the students are the sons of hotel-keepers.

CHAPTER VI

DIAMONDS TRUMPS

TIME and changing conditions have stripped the hotel clerk and his job of all their old-time glamour. Today the clerk is an unnoticed nobody among the horde of prosaic white-collar workers, a standardized cog in the wheel, devoid of any special distinction. He fits into his place and performs a routine duty — in an all too routine manner oftentimes. Fifty years and more ago it was different. Then he was one of America's magnificoes, a conspicuous and romantic type in the life of the nation, basking pleasantly — and more or less constantly — in the limelight. Old-timers will tell you (drawing the long-bow a trifle taut, no doubt) that once upon a time it was next to impossible to pick up a newspaper that did not contain either an article, a joke, an editorial, or a bit of doggerel about the clerk. He was a favorite source of reportorial copy, talking glibly on the peculiarities and difficulties of his work, and he figured as the hero of many amusing encounters with greenhorn travelers, for it was at the beginning of the clerk's palmy days that city life began to take on many new characteristics, with which the artless rustic was unfamiliar. Up to about a hundred years ago there were not many differences between city and rural life to make a countryman stand out as a figure shy and uncouth. But after 1830 those differences multiplied rapidly and he began to feel more and more like a fish out of water whenever he went to the city, and whenever he put up at a first-class hotel. And so he became the anecdotal victim of the supercilious urbanite, of which class the hotel clerk was an unreserved representative.

Old-timers also will not forget to mention the hotel clerk's diamonds, swearing by the beard of the prophet that every clerk lived in an incessant blinding glare of these precious stones. As a matter of fact, only a minority owned diamonds. Those who did own them, however, seem to have been firm believers in the policy once enunciated by Diamond Jim Brady: "Them that has 'em wears 'em." And so the impression became widespread that hotel clerks, as a class, could out-trump any other class on diamonds.

The flamboyant decades of America's development from about 1840 to 1890 were the Augustan age of the hotel clerk, when he was universally accounted a man of position and parts. During half of this period he was a novelty, a new phenomenon in the expanding life of the country, and it took four or five decades for the interest in him to wear away — about the same length of time that it took the American public to get fed up on the Wild Man from Borneo. While his fame lasted, the clerk made the most of it. He played his role with skill and aplomb, taking himself quite seriously, if no one else did. He regarded himself as a professional man, a personage gifted of the gods, and he dressed the part. Like all the rest of mankind in that day, he wore a beard, but no one kept it more neatly trimmed or more trigly combed and waxed than he. Generally it was not a full beard, but one or another of the numerous variations of French beard. The beard was characteristic of all the rest of him. He was one of the "Broadway dandies" of the 1840's and 1850's and in post-bellum days was a fervent disciple of Kyrle Bellew and E. Berry Wall, striving to be a glass of fashion, in which role he succeeded admirably with his black Prince Albert coat, his stove-pipe hat, his high gates-ajar collar and lurid necktie, his pointed mustache, his

Chesterfieldian manners, his daily polished shoes, and his white, round, detachable cuffs. He gave the diamonds, or whatever other stones he could afford to buy, the best possible background. One of his severest critics said of him: " The clerk is generally an appalling example of the extent to which dress may be carried. His shirt is always openworked at the bosom. His waistcoat is of radiant velvet with perhaps gold buttons, and he wears diamond shirt-studs, and diamond sleeve-links that, if he came by them honestly, must have cost him a couple of years' salary." [1]

When the clerk first began to wear diamonds, a few years prior to the Civil War, he was prompted by a mercenary motive, as well as by vanity. The same may be said of his clothes. It was profitable for him to dress in dandified fashion and to adorn himself with jewels during the period from about 1850 to 1880. In his position, meeting so many traveling parvenus and being reverenced by them as an authority on city life and an expert in numerous intricate matters in which the average person was supposed to be a witling, it was possible for him to direct much business to favored jewelry-stores and tailors, who paid him a commission. This gave him a great opportunity, for his pay was pitifully small, ranging from ten to fifteen dollars a week, sometimes less. Well-to-do guests, especially women, openly admired his sparklers and made inquiries about them. To many parvenus of the day, America's first big crop of millionaires and near-millionaires, the diamond was a mysterious bauble, wholly beyond their knowledge. Few had seen diamonds and still fewer owned them. During the first half of the nineteenth century the family jewels in America consisted principally of semi-precious stones. Cameos were a popular jewel, and it is probable there were many Cameo Kirbys behind the front office desks of hotels. It is said that the leading piece of jewelry shown at the Crystal Palace, America's first " World's Fair," in 1853, was a seed-pearl necklace, worth about a thousand dollars.² But when Americans did begin buying diamonds, they went in for them hot and heavy. A New York correspondent, writing in the Charleston *Mercury* in 1859, said:

> The common use of diamonds as an ornament in this country, (where these precious stones are more generally worn than anywhere else in the world), dates back only to the discovery of gold in California. The increasing disposition to extravagance which made its appearance at that epoch was early manifested in an active demand for diamonds. The price of diamonds has gone up 30 or 40 per cent within the last dozen years, and stones of large size and the first water are now held at fancy prices.³

It was during this period that the hotel clerk began to profit by America's newly born weakness for diamonds. The Pennsylvania oil bonanza, the crop of Civil War profiteers, and the dawn of the first great period of financial prosperity after the war, widened the market and furnished a rich field for the clerk's abilities as salesman. Diamonds began to adorn the necks and fingers of all and sundry. The importation of diamonds, amounting to less than two million dollars a year prior to 1860 (the South African field was then unknown), grew rapidly and has ever since continued to grow, until today more than half the wealth of the world in diamonds — sixty to a hundred million dollars a year — comes to the United States.⁴

The clerk's method of helping to popularize diamonds was to bedeck himself with them and be a sort of walking display window. He was always willing to talk freely about his diamonds and about diamonds in general. He posed as an expert, ever eager to demonstrate the genuineness of the gems he wore. He was always willing to sell what he had and he knew where other stones like them were to be purchased, and at what prices, and he was always willing to be a first aid in making a selection. On all such sales he received a commission from the jeweler and in this way added thousands of dollars a year to his income. By this means many of our early hotel proprietors got their start. But some clerks made so much money in this way that they preferred to cling to their jobs behind the desk. After a few years of money-making on a commission basis, some clerks went into the diamond business on their own account, buying and selling the stones independently of retail jewelers, who complained bitterly of this "unfair competition." One of the early Palmer House clerks in Chicago in the 1870's is said to have made more than sixty thousand dollars in this way in four or five years.[5]

But as the general public steadily became more prosperous and more familiar with diamonds and gained confidence in judging and buying for themselves, the hotel clerk's function as a diamond-salesman and dealer gradually petered out. This came to pass during the gay nineties. During the elegant eighties the newspapers had helped to spoil this profitable side-line. Paragraphers and columnists made merry over the clerk's diamonds and even the hotel trade papers, which flourished by the dozen, took frequent flings at the clerk and his diamonds. "We have often wondered," said the *Hotel Mail*, "at the depraved taste of certain hotel clerks, especially in some Western cities, which could induce them to wear large, blazing diamond scarf pins and shirt studs. The display of such gems at all hours during business, or when on pleasure bent, is vulgar and unseemly."

Times were changing; the clerk's star was setting and his job was losing its glamour — and its profit. Public interest had turned to other idols, and the clerk was becoming one of the common herd. Even his enemies, who accused him of haughty insolence and indifference toward guests, grew silent. Some of these had at times been rather severe, as was the one in 1857 who wrote:

I have discovered a sovereign remedy for hotelkeepers and their clerks. It is simply Billingsgate. The fellows are all cowardly at heart, and if you treat them civilly they, true to coward instinct, will ride over you roughshod. If, on the other hand, you treat them in the most severe and contemptuous manner, they will cringe at your feet.[6]

A traveling man who thirty years later wrote a book of reminiscences described the clerk as " the concentrated embodiment of dignity." Said he:

Christians who are always striving to humble and abase themselves — whose besetting sin is pride — should take a dose of hotel clerk. Whenever I feel that I need taking down a peg or two, and that I am getting too big for my clothes, I have a never-failing remedy. I merely step into a first-class hotel, and approach Mr. Diamond Pin, and ask: " Is Mr. Smith stopping here? " The great man, after four or five minutes, lifts his eyes, he speaks. I am crushed.[7]

In a similar chastening vein the *Hotel Gazette* said, in 1885:

The fraternity of hotel clerks in this city [New York] is a large one, and they comprise all sorts and conditions. There are some that assume more importance than their masters, particularly when he is out of the way. Their special delight is to make smart (?) answers and to " sit down " upon anyone that they may imagine is not up to all the peculiar city ways. There is too much of this, and the sooner more politeness and consideration is displayed, the better it will be for the reputation of our clerks.[8]

There were, of course, all varieties of hotel clerks, and among them were many models of modesty, courtesy, and efficiency. Simeon Ford, for many years Mine Host of the famous old Grand Union Hotel in New York, once rose to the defense of the hotel clerk, in a speech in which he said:

A very important feature of a hotel is the " man behind the desk," the hotel clerk. A good hotel clerk must be a walking encyclopedia, directory, railway and steamship guide, and, in short, a universal fountain of knowledge and information. No man is more maligned than the hotel clerk. In current fiction he is described as a haughty and unapproachable despot who, entrenched behind a large diamond shirt-stud, superciliously assigns trembling travelers to remote and cheerless chambers. As a matter of fact, he is usually the most good-natured and accommodating of mortals. Were he not of a serene and placid nature he would long since have decorated a cemetery. He is expected to remember everybody, and to give everyone the best room in the house; to laugh at every humorous anecdote related to him, no matter how antique; and to lend a sympathetic ear to every traveler who is in distress, or imagines that he is.[9]

The hotel clerk was distinctly an American creation. Hotels in Europe managed to get along without him until about the time his star had begun to set in America. As late as the early 1880's only one or two London hotels employed clerks, and these were young women. Clerks in American hotels have always been men, except that during the World War many hotels had to employ young women in that capacity. The first hotel clerks are said to have been those of the old Tremont House in Boston, that having been the first hotel to divorce the bar-room from the front office, or lobby. Back in the old inn days the innkeeper himself served as clerk. Generally he had plenty of time to "room" the few guests who came per day — on some days. That, indeed, was the smallest part of his job. In the cities, as business grew, Mine Host had to have an assistant. Chiefly this assistant's function was that of tending bar. He was Mine Host's right-hand man, serving as bar-tender, cashier, and clerk all in one. Sometimes, too, he was postmaster and justice of the peace.

The clerks of the Tremont House, and of other first-class hotels during the 1830's and 1840's — a period when the railroad was still a new thing and travel comparatively light — had other duties besides their work behind the desk, and one of them was that of helping Mine Host to carve meats during meal hours. During the old inn days the landlord sat at the head of the table and did his carving there, but when the overgrown inns of the pre-Tremont days sprang up, with their dining-rooms apart from the reception-room and bar, the carving was done at a side-table, sometimes screened from view of the diners. The bar-tender and landlord, and later the clerk and landlord, donned white aprons and began the task of cutting the fowls and roasts. At first the clerk took this duty as a matter of course, but when he began putting on airs — and it did not take long for this to happen — carving became a distasteful task. But it taught the clerk many things that would be of value to him if he became a proprietor or manager. Wielding a carving-knife taught him how to cut meats to the best advantage, from rigid rules that date back beyond the ancient *Boke of Kervynge*. He learned how to make direct, incisive cuts, the keystone of good carving, and he also learned where to cut, how to hold the knife, the thickness of various cuts, the proportion of fat and lean, how to disjoint a fowl, and other fine points. Henry S. Mower, who was a clerk in Boston and New York hotels in the days before the Civil War, relates his experience when he began as a clerk at the old Revere House in Boston, in 1855:

> At this date the carving was done in the gentlemen's ordinary at the upper end of the room behind a screen and here each and every day, robed in a long white apron, with a flashing knife in hand, stood the master of his business, Paran Stevens. Each clerk in those days was expected to do his share of carving, and though it became to some of them a come-down to put on an apron and spend the time until the rush was over, yet many of them lived to rejoice in after years that they through this means acquired a knowledge that was ever after useful to them. My own apprenticeship was served here and I shall never forget the first day of my novitiate into the mysteries of wing, leg, second-joint, side bone, pope's nose, etc.[10]

The clerk had begun to grow priggish several years before Mower's time. Perhaps he had priggishness thrust upon him, as is indicated by Alexander Mackay, a British visitor in the latter 1840's, speaking of a sojourn at the United States Hotel in Boston:

> We apply for rooms at the bar, which, in the usual sense of the term, is no bar, but the counting house of the establishment, in which a clerk, elaborately caparisoned, sits enthroned, at a considerable elevation, before a desk, which in point of cost and construction would be a piece of extravagance in the Bank parlour. The walls around him are literally covered with bells, each having beneath it the number of a room, to which it corresponds, and they count by the hundreds. My flesh creeps at the bare contemplation of their being rung all at once.[11]

"Bishop" White of the old Everett House in New York was a typical example of the old-time hotel clerk. The Bishop was known from one end of the city to the other. Tall and straight as an arrow, he carried himself like a lord and was the essence of politeness. He was born in Lancaster, New Hampshire, in 1814 and traced his ancestry straight back to the *Mayflower*. In 1836 he began clerking at the old Maverick House, which had just opened in Boston. This hotel was named after the father of that Colonel Maverick whose name is perpetuated in the common noun meaning unbranded cattle on the ranches of the West. The Bishop also clerked in the old Adams House, run by the son of "Oliver Optic" (William T. Adams), and at the old Marlboro Hotel in Boston, where guests had to attend prayers every morning before breakfast. For forty-seven years he was clerk at the old Ocean House at Newport, Rhode Island, during summer seasons. He came to New York in 1868, when the Everett House was opened on the north side of Union Square, and remained with that hostelry until his death, at the age of seventy-nine years, on January

31, 1893. The Bishop lived right through the golden age of hotel clerking, from the period of carving meats on through to the decline of the diamond shirt-stud, and it was said that he knew more people of high and low degree than any other man in America. On duty he always wore a black skull-cap, after his curly white hair had all disappeared. His neatly trimmed beard and snowy white mustache remained to the last. When he died, he was mourned as few men are mourned when they die.

OLD OCEAN HOUSE, Newport, R. I.

Perhaps the best-known of former hotel clerks was Richard A. Canfield, the most celebrated gambler America ever produced, who flourished in New York and at Saratoga Springs during the last two decades of the nineteenth century and the first few years of the twentieth. Canfield spent five or six years (in the 1870's) as night clerk at the old Union Square Hotel in New York, then operated by his cousin, Andrew J. Dam, target of a merry toast in the days when Allen and Dam were running the old Astor House. Mad wags at the bar must have bored him to death with their frequent repetition of "Here's to Allen and Dam his partner." Canfield also managed the original Monmouth Hotel at Spring Lake, New Jersey, for four years.[12]

About ten thousand of the country's hotel clerks are banded together in an organization known as the Hotel Greeters of America, which has branches in fifty or more cities and districts. The name Greeters was originated by Stanton U. Kohler, long connected with New York hotels, and one of the organizers of a New York association of clerks in 1908. This organization became a part of the national organization, which was founded at a convention held in Denver on June 2, 3, and 4, 1910, chiefly through the efforts of Leigh A. Fuller, known to Greeters as "Daddy," who was then president of an association of Denver hotel clerks. The national organization maintains headquarters at Denver and a few years ago established a home there for ill and indigent members.

Nothing better illustrates the growth of hotels than a comparison of the lobby staffs of the Tremont House of a hundred years ago and of a superdreadnought hotel of today. Mine Host with two clerks behind the desk and with three or four "rotunda men," who served in the dual capacity of porter and bellboy, could get along nicely. Today bellboys and elevator men — nearly a hundred of them in the largest hotels — form a distinct department under a "superintendent of service." The porters and drivers, a score or more, are in still another department, under a head porter, or "superintendent of transportation." Half a dozen assistant managers are on hand on the lobby floor, aiding all and sundry in a thousand different ways, and a corps of telephone-operators big enough for a town of fifty thousand is at work behind the scenes. Then there is the "front office" itself. Today you will find a dozen or more clerks of various ranks behind the desk of any large hotel, each with some definite duty. There are rack clerks, mail clerks, information clerks, reservation clerks, a battery of cashiers, a credit manager, room clerks and assistant room clerks and, last but not least, the captain of the crew, known as the office manager, who is also in charge, sometimes, of the floor clerks, those courteous and efficient women who have desks near the elevator on each floor. Also aiding the office manager, behind the scenes, is a force of stenographers and typists, keeping records, answering telegrams, taking room reservations over the telephone, and doing many other things connected with the orderly operation of a hotel's front office.

The first office manager, it is said, was Alexander Hamilton Palmer, a dapper little old man who was for many years chief room clerk at the old Fifth Avenue Hotel in New York, where the job of office manager was finally created for him. When George C. Boldt opened the Waldorf-Astoria he engaged Palmer as office manager, in which position he continued until he was eighty-three years old, when he was put on a pension by L. M. Boomer, who became proprietor of the Waldorf-Astoria after the death of Boldt. Palmer died on July 21, 1922, at the age of eighty-seven. Many of America's most notable hotel men of the present generation got their early training under old man Palmer.

Like the clerk, the register over which he presides has undergone a number of changes in the past hundred years. Its old-time romance has been sacrificed on the altar of modern hustle and efficiency. It has, in fact, begun to disappear, for, contrary to general belief, keeping a register is purely a matter of custom in the hotel business in this country and is not a legal requirement except in four or five states.[13] The old-style folio register that never closed — because clerks feared that if anyone shut the book, business would be bad for the rest of the day — is now giving way to a card-index system in some hotels, and in others it is being supplanted by loose-leaf sheets, fresh each day or hour. Wherever that has happened, it has dealt a hard blow to one of America's most popular indoor sports, reading the register. "Another of the common people's inalienable rights," Harrison Rhodes once said, "is to know who is staying in a hotel, hence the pitiless publicity of the register. This volume is indeed at times the center of hotel social life, its perusal the daily pleasure of hundreds."

The register was not an American invention, though it had some American peculiarities. Perhaps the register originated in China. At any rate, the first mention of it in literature is to be found in the writings of that observant Columbus of the Orient, Marco Polo, who, A.D. 1250, found a city in China — now supposed to be the smaller Hang-Chow-Foo — called Kin-Sai, which was, Marco said, a city of several million people. He devotes several chapters to a description of this city and mentions that "all the innkeepers and public houses inscribe in a book the names of those who take up their occasional abode with them, particularizing the day and hour of departure; a copy of which is transmitted daily to those magistrates who have been spoken of as stationed in the market square." Thus the register seems to be at least six hundred and seventy years old and possibly had been in use a few centuries before Marco Polo discovered it. Before the discovery of America inns of some countries in Europe were forced to keep registers, but the practice seems to have died out in more modern times. There were statutes providing for the keeping of registers in France and other countries during the closing years of the medieval age, and the object of these statutes was exactly the same as it had been in China. As W. C. Firebaugh points out, the inns of France were hotbeds of crime and the favorite rendezvous of radicals, propagators of heresy, free-thinkers, and the like.

There is no mention of a hotel register until the year 1407 [says Firebaugh], but on November 29 of that year a regulation was prescribed which compelled keepers of inns and hotels to provide a register in which they inscribed the name and quality of the guest lodging with them. This was a prudent measure, and it did more to remedy the defects of the situation than all preceding legislation. . . . It is probably true that this custom was in force at Rome before its adoption in the realm of France, and, if Marco Polo is to be relied upon, in Cathay."[14]

The most interesting characteristic of the register of the old inns of America was that the guests used it freely for expressing themselves, in poetry and prose, on various subjects, and that Mine Host used it as a sort of combination register and day-book record of transactions, spiced with blunt comments on the peculiarities of his guests. This habit of writing all sorts of things in the register perhaps dated back to colonial days. One of the earliest mentions of the habit is made by William Faux, an English farmer, who went west as far as the great Looking Glass Prairie of Illinois in the 1820's. He relates of an inn at which he stopped in Zanesville, Ohio: " Here is kept a folio register, in which travelers write their names, from whence they come, and whither they are bound, with any news which they bring with them."[15]

Yankee peddlers and their successors, the bagmen of the early railroad days, invariably put down the names of their firms or wrote a few lines recommending their wares. Often, too, they wrote little messages addressed to one another. Facetious ones sometimes recorded the fact that they were " sober " or " at large." Some graybeards among traveling men continued to write down the names of their firms up to a comparatively recent date, and advance agents of theatrical productions and circuses to this day have the same habit, because of its publicity value.

Much that was written on the old registers was too robust for family reading; Mine Host, his guests, and the tavern loafers sometimes displayed a too Rabelaisian grossness of expression. But some entries were gems of humor and wit. It must have been quite a pleasure in the old days to read such bits as this from the register of the hotel at Trenton Falls, New York, a once famous but now almost forgotten resort:

John Graham and Servant.
G. Squires, wife and two babies. No servant, owing to the hardness of the times.
G. W. Douglas and Servant. No wife and babies, owing to the hardness of the times.[16]

Or a contribution such as this from the register of Ball's Hotel, at Brownsville, near Pittsburgh:

> Old Connecticut, to frogs once fatal,
> Is the State I call my natal;
> Which most of other States surpasses
> In pumpkins — johnny cakes — molasses —
> Rogues — priests — attornies — quack physicians —
> Blue laws and black-coat politicians;
> Where many a father's son — yes, plenty —
> Is father of a son at twenty,
> And many a mother's maid has been
> A mother made at seventeen,
> And many more at twenty-seven;
> Pray for more husbands than for heaven.
>   — James Wilson [17]

The few old registers of the early days of the republic that have survived have yielded many similar scraps of entertainment and have shed some light on the social life of the times. They have even had some degree of historic interest, like the old register of Columbia Hall at Lebanon Springs, New York, in the 1820's. Ezra Cornell, founder of Cornell University, scanning the worn and faded pages of this old register in 1873, jotted down the following entry on the fly-leaf: "Aug. 4, 1873.—I have looked through this old register today with great interest and some profit."[18] One of the entries Cornell found was this, dated June 13, 1825:

> Marquis de La Fayette and son, Gen. Solomon Van Rensalaer, Col. Clinton, Col. Bloodgood, Major J. B. Van Schaick, Major R. V. De Witt, Capt. S. V. R. Bleeker, Lieut. Webster . . . the above, with Capt. Spencer (of Col. Cooper's Regt) dragoons, formed part of the escort to the Massachusetts Line. Gen. La Fayette did them the honor to express sensible regret at parting with them. The intention was for the escort to have gone on to Pittsfield, but " a little brief authority" deprived them of the anticipated pleasure.

The " brief authority " was exercised by the Massachusetts authorities, who were determined to have a monopoly of General Lafayette the moment he crossed the state line, which was but a few hundred feet east of the hotel. The New Yorkers had given a reception and banquet in honor of the general at Columbia Hall and kept him there as long as they could, much to the annoyance of the Massachusetts patriots, who got even by exercising their state's rights.

Columbia Hall stood on the old stage road between Albany and Boston, and there was a great rolling in and out of coaches, public and private, to and from its doors. Many of the landlord's guests were, naturally, " gentlemen with srvts. and horses," for Lebanon Springs was a fashionable place, and its guests traveled in the grand manner. These aristocrats signed themselves in this wise:

R. L. Livingston, 2 srvts. and 5 horses.
De Witt Clinton and Lady.
Mr. Longfellow and Lady, Portland.
Alfred Conkling [father of Roscoe].

One of the lady guests at Lebanon Springs wrote after her name: " Oh, Lebanon, thou dear, delightful spot," a sentiment which evidently is not widely prevalent today, for the resort has fallen into decay and is now seldom heard of. Under date of May 1, 1824, " Moses Rathbone, Village of Buffalo," checked in at Columbia Hall, and a facetious guest signed himself " a foreigner from Detroit."

An old register of the early days of the Cataract House at Niagara Falls, which was established in 1814, reveals many interesting inscriptions. One of the entries of 1828 was this: " Sally Wiggins arrived, of Boston, very much fatigued, took a little wine, felt better." The landlord could not resist the temptation to follow this with a few words pointing out that Sally's inscription was an excellent testimonial of the quality of the hotel's wine. Fred Urquhart, who inscribed himself " a bachelor," jotted down the statement that he had " come 1,200 miles to see Niagara," and another traveler, evidently of a pious turn of mind, wrote: " See the creator and adore the created." Still another lapsed into doggerel:

> I wish I had a bowl of punch,
>   Of ice a half a pound;
> Into the punch the ice I'd launch
>   And stir it round and round.
> And when I'd stirred it round and round,
>
> I'd take a cup and drink it up,
> Nor leave one drop behind.
> Temperature 96.

Under this the next arrival aired his views of hotel-register poets by writing:

> Let Newton rhyme no more,
> Let Watts lie in his tomb;
> Let Milton go behind the door,
> And give these poets room.

Many travelers were, it seems, addicted to scribbling poetry, so-called, on the register pages. Some of it was of the backhouse variety; some was of the thee, thou, and thy school. When Henry Weeks, Jr., arrived at the Cataract House on September 13, 1827, from Youngstown, Ohio, he wrote:

> Man's life's a vapor full of woes,
> He cuts a caper and down he goes.
> He's born in trouble, lives in sin,
> And then — into the grave falls in.

Just below this, in another fist, someone wrote: "A man no more can't make himself a poet than a sheep can make himself a goat."

One of the religious guests of the Cataract House in the 1820's wrote: "John McNair, a late graduate of Jefferson College, who has this day heard the roar and saw the dashing of the mighty waters. The spectacle was beautiful and sublime, but the emotions it produced were serious and awful, inasmuch as they reminded me of the mighty power of God, before whom we must shortly stand." An irreverent reader of these rhetorical lines added under McNair's words: "If John McNair is a graduate of Jefferson College, I advise him now to return to some common school and learn his native English, that his productions may no longer disgrace his Alma Mater. — No Graduate." [19]

Another of the poetical efforts found on the old Cataract House register was this, under the name of " John C. Lord, attorney-at-law, Buffalo, New York ":

>John C. Lord of his own accord,
>Went down to see his sister;
>Mary Lord of her own accord,
>Went down to see her sister;
>Jason Lee, as brisk as a flea,
>Jumped right up and kissed her.

A spiteful fellow who signed himself " One Who Knows " wrote: " Yes, John C. Lord, attorney-at-law, you are the fellow who ran away first from the United States to Canada for stealing, and from thence (for a similar reason) back again." Cutting remarks of this sort perhaps did their share toward curing the traveler of any desire to do more scribbling than was necessary in hotel registers, but, even so, it took time to discourage him. The practice went on for many years, especially at resort hotels and village inns.

Hotel registers of the early days of the republic bristled with declarations of political faith, especially during presidential years. The present-day quadrennial pastime of taking straw votes began on the pages of hotel registers. Presidential campaigns were of a hotter, more personal nature than those of today, and such a thing as an " independent voter " was unknown. Every man was a strict party man and a rabid rooter for his candidate at all times. Mine Host himself, although he tries nowadays to maintain strict political neutrality, was as violent a party man as anyone in the olden days, had very positive views on all political questions, and was very assertive about them. His guests argued with him and aired their views on the pages of the register. Thus on the register of the Cataract House of July 21, 1824, we find this: " N. L. Keyser from Philadelphia, bound for Detroit. In favor of J. Q. Adams for President and R. Rush for Vice-President." J. S. Buckingham, a British visitor to this country about 1840, who has been quoted before, mentions this custom in connection with Ball's Hotel at Brownsville, Pennsylvania. He says:

> In the hotel in which we staid, called " Ball's Hotel," a Register was kept, after the usual fashion in this country, in which all persons coming to the house, though they should remain only for a few hours, are expected to enter their names, their town of residence, and their places of destination; but in this was an additional column for remarks, in which each person entered the name of the Presidential candidate for whom he intended to vote. Thus the column contained the entries of — Harrison against the world — Van Buren for ever — Henry Clay, the Pride of Kentucky — Little Van, the Magician — Old Tippecanoe, and no Sub-Treasury — The Farmer of North Bend — Hurrah for Jackson — Van Buren again — Log Cabin and Hard Cider — and so on, page after page. In this way some attempt is made to ascertain the strength of the parties, but the best is most imperfect.[20]

Mine Host's notations in the register often were of a business nature, a sort of book-keeping, like the following by the landlord of Columbia Hall:

> Aug. 22 — Applied for mutton and was disappointed.
> Aug. 4 — Beef and veal. Could not get any.
> Aug. 8 — Applied for lamb and could not get any; had none for dinner that day of him.

The Cincinnati Historical Society preserves an old register of the Dennison House, which was built by Senator William Dennison and opened in the early 1820's. The landlord, with a sort of frontier wildness in his spelling, jotted down the following:

> Wednesday evening Dutch lady began to bord and her husben on Friday with mare and colt.
> Mr. Nelson and friend began Bord. Friend paid his bill.
> Young man with ague began bord.
> Mr. Homer put his mair in my stable.
> Sick man for licker, pt. whiskey.

3 dutchmen to supper.
At breakfast six Kentuckians.
Settled acct. with cook, paid her $1 week.
Two ladies began Bord at 4 dollars per week for the two.

One of the treasures of the White Sulphur Springs Hotel, the famous "Old White," in West Virginia, are the worn, leather-bound registers of the 1820's. Their yellowed pages contain many famous names. On July 20, 1818, "Henry Clay, servant and three horses," arrived at the hotel. Under his name are the following notations:

Three days board,	$4.50
Two grogs for servant	.12
Dinner for servant	.12
One dozen segars	.25
One gal. extra grain	$1.50
Two gal. grain	.33

Sometimes Mine Host jotted down after guests' names such trenchant remarks as these by an old-time tavern-keeper in Philadelphia: "Travels on his honor"; "This man was drunk and made a beast of himself in his room"; "Had dinner and owes me nothing"; and "Forgot to settle." Perhaps it was some tavern loafer who wrote: "Fair, fat, and forty" after the name of a woman, and "General shyster" after the name of a man.

At the bottom of the page, as in the old Philadelphia register, some landlords jotted down a report of the day's weather, such as: "This was a wet, gloomy day," or: "Snowing all morning; bright in the afternoon."

Nowadays one finds the hotel register simply a list of names and addresses. The naïve custom of writing other matter in the book died out long ago, and such signatures as "Mr. Longfellow and Lady" are no longer good form.

There are no hard and fast rules about registering in hotels. The last two generations of married males used to write their names and put down " and wife " if she were on hand. But that, too, is old-fashioned and for some years past doggy guests have been writing " Mr. and Mrs. So-and-so." Indeed, in some of the ultra-fashionable hostelries of New York Mr. So-and-so signs his name on one line and then lets Mrs. So-and-so sign hers on the next line. This is even required in one or two swagger places.

It is regrettable that more of the old registers of the days when guests scribbled various things in them were not preserved, for no doubt many of them would have yielded material of rich interest, if not of importance. Registers of more recent days are now being contributed to public libraries, for the edification of future generations. These registers are the greatest autograph albums in the world. There's not a man who travels whose signature is not scattered all over the country. And since all prominent men and women travel, their signatures appear often amidst solid pages of signatures by nomadic nonentities. There may be only two or three examples of the chirography of Button Gwinnet extant, selling at twenty-five thousand dollars and up per sample, but the preservation of old hotel registers alone will prevent any such scarcity of the signatures of the celebrities of the present generation.

If the present trend keeps on, however, even the old-style register will soon be a thing of the past. Lamenting this fact, an editorial writer in the San Francisco *Examiner* recently said:

> The guest feels that he is applying for a job to the personnel director of a big corporation or asking for admission to a clinic, so businesslike and bare does that lone card look in its ordained place on the huge desk. One of those newfangled pens in a socket stands officiously ready. With a dismal sense of being one more cog in a sandwich ma-

chine the guest enters his name on a card, which is then whisked away to the electric icebox where heartless efficiency experts keep their statistics.

The good old register, that gravid folio, was different. Just to look at it was to think of Mine Host and tankards of ale, or at the very least of a good five-cent cigar and stories told by drummers on rainy Sunday afternoons. Down at the left-hand corner it was always rumpled, where the inscribed leaves had been turned over as the years went oozing by. M. Bertillon, the well-known authority on Who Stole the Jam, could have spent a month in sheer ecstacy transcribing all those thumb prints. The pen was rusty, and as you entered your name, there was a squeak and spatter appropriate to the importance of the occasion. Unraveling the mysterious chirography of your predecessor, you learned that J. Blennerhasset Oofendorffer at French Lick, Indiana, had also sat in the red plush sofa beside the potted palm.

The good old days! They are gone forever. Some hotels won't even let the bellhop put his thumb in the ice-water pitcher.

CHAPTER VII

THE GROANING BOARD

THE GREAT test of a hotel in America throughout most of the nineteenth century was its table. The fame and fortune of a caravansary depended chiefly upon the quality, variety and abundance of its food. Architectural grandeur and interior ostentation were of no avail as a business lure if the house did not provide good grub, and plenty of if. The average American wanted style plus good food, and if he had to make a choice between the two — which was very seldom — he went where he could gratify his palate to the greatest extent. Almost all Americans were birds of a feather in their devotion to the hotel table, and Mine Host catered to this trencherman proclivity by setting Gargantuan meals of the best possible quality. The period was the golden age of the American plan of hotel operation. The American plan was the trencherman's seventh heaven, for it gave him a room and four whacking big meals — generaly served at two or more long tables down the length of the dining-hall — for a flat rate, which, in the days before the Civil War, was at most a dollar and a half or two dollars a day in the best hotels, and in post-bellum days ranged from about two to five dollars a day. Those were low prices, even for that period, and European visitors admitted that it was incomprehensible to them how Mine Host could give so much for the money. But the home-grown guests were inclined to grumble. They recalled the good old days when

Mine Host served free brandy and whisky with each meal — or a bottle of imported Madeira — and charged only a dollar a day or less.[1]

Every meal was a banquet, and it is hard to see how any special blowout could be any better. The difference seems to have been that for everyday meals Mine Host set down only fifty to sixty dishes and at a special feast provided a hundred or more. Perhaps that is why banqueting became so popular in America. Immediately after the Revolution Americans developed a fondness for banqueting that persists to this day, despite the fact that it was predicted prohibition would kill off this feature of national life. Most of the post-Revolutionary banquets were political. Americans sat for many hours, eating, drinking, and toasting. Each diner was expected to deliver at least one toast, either fulsomely praising his party and predicting great victories for it, or smiting the opposing parties hip and thigh. After each toast the diners would shout: "Hip, hip, hooray!" and otherwise voice their approval. Columns of these toasts were often printed in the newspapers. It was not until about 1840 that postprandial addresses began to take the place of toasts.[2]

The American plan of hotel operation dates back to early colonial days. The old-time inns served three meals a day, strictly pot luck for a century or so. The guest ate whatever the landlord and his family were having for breakfast, dinner, or supper, and the quality and size of the meals depended on how well Mine Host kept his larder stocked and on the ability of his wife to cook. It takes no great stretch of imagination to conjure up a picture of those heavy, coarse, plain-cooked fireplace meals, with Mine Host sitting in his shirt-sleeves at the head of the table, carving thick slices of meat, while his wife toiled in the kitchen and his buxom daughters brought the food to the table.

But when the towns and country became more populous,

and boarders more numerous, meals had to be specially prepared for guests. Pot luck gave way to a definite cuisine. It was an abundant and varied cuisine, and it seldom lacked a selection of such game as venison, wild turkey, and wood-pigeon. Nowhere in the world could the guest get so many good things to eat and help himself to so unlimited a supply. Landlords of the busy inns of Boston, New York, and Philadelphia, and those in town on main-traveled stage routes, began to pride themselves on the excellence of their meals. The superiority of the American *table d'hôte* soon became traditional.

In those days, and on up to about 1830, the food was put on the table all at one time — large tureens of soup, huge platters of meat, capacious dishes of vegetables, great bowls of pudding. The guest ate as though he were possessed, wolfing his food with such rapidity that he was able to stow away an incredible quantity in a short space of time. He wasted little time in conversation, and when he was through, he pushed his chair back and went away, with a quill toothpick sticking in the side of his mouth. Fate could not harm him; he had dined that day. Such, at any rate, is the picture of the American hotel boarder drawn by his severest critics, though it is not likely that all Americans of that period were of this voracious type, or that they were any different in this respect from the rank and file of the rest of the world. Gross feeding was a popular indoor sport the world over at the time, and nowhere more popular than within palace walls.[3]

At the *table d'hôte* American eating-habits and table-manners were on wholesale parade, providing a spectacle that was unique and therefore impressive — and, to supercilious travelers from abroad, grotesque. Europeans who came to take stock of the workings of the Great Experiment, and on various other meddlesome missions, put the strong-stomached Americans under observation as though they were animals in a zoo or pygmies from Africa. It was a novelty to them to see two hundred or more people of all types and stations of life sitting in an ornate dining-hall, eating, with varying degrees of gusto, the prodigious and incomparable American-plan meals. As the Rev. George Lewis (one of those who did not criticize) said, speaking of the Tremont House in 1845:

> Everything appears large — large ante-rooms for smoking and lounging, and reading the newspapers — spacious parlours, and a still more spacious hall where the common meals of breakfast, dinner and supper (our tea) are served. Travelers come in twenties and fifties to our dozens. You live in a crowd — eat in a crowd, sitting down with fifty, a hundred, sometimes two hundred at table, to which you are summoned by a sonorous Chinese gong. The only place of retirement is your room, to which you have the key.[4]

During the latter half of the eighteenth century the inns seem to have provided about half a dozen sorts of meat at each meal, together with vegetables and puddings or other desserts. The spur of competition increased the number as time went on, until finally, by the middle of the nineteenth century, the peak was reached. The *Magazine of American History* observed that in 1794 the Tontine House, " the best in New York," set from twelve to sixteen dishes each day. Mine Host Hyde charged three hundred and fifty to four hundred dollars a year for board and room, " without liquor."[5] Hyde's menu, typical of its time, included such morsels as venison, bear steaks, wild turkey, wild ducks, lobster, terrapin, oysters, wild pigeons, and other game, besides the general run of butcher-shop provisions. Henry Wansay, an Englishman who visited America in 1794, mentions that at the Boston inn where he stopped, the dinner included " veal, beef, mutton, ham, fowl, salmon, roots, puddings, &c., &c.," and a pint of Madeira was served to each guest at dinner.[6] Wansay added that the charge was five shillings a day for board and room, "for they made no separate charges, nor do they abate their charges, were you to dine out every day." Another traveler, of somewhat later date (1831), says of a dinner at Niblo's Tavern in New York: "The dinner was more excellent in its material than for its cookery and arrangement. We had oyster soup, shad, venison, partridge, grouse, various sorts of wild ducks, and a host of other dishes, all set at once upon the table."[7] Even on the edges of the frontier the meals were "universally plentiful" and "quite luxurious." As one traveler said: "The dinner ordinary has almost everything to recommend it except conversation, which according to American notions is unnecessary to the enjoyment of dinner; so completely sensual are they at that meal." It would appear that no one had grounds for complaint; nevertheless, there were kickers. In 1853, at a time when fifty or more dishes were set at a meal, and everyone could have as much of them as he liked, one querulous traveler said:

> Twenty years ago all the tavern and hotel tables in the States were twenty times more liberal, served in the good old English way. Brandy was even put on the table to help yourself, till the dessert came on; and the servants were not so evidently in a hurry to get rid of you. Delicacies were not rare nor stinted as now.[8]

This traveler, one of the chronic carpers, noted also that a change in the method of service had come into general use. Instead of "the good old English way" of putting all the food on the table at once, it was now being served in the good old French way. That is, the waiters were dividing their "squads of cattle off into sixes and eights" for service, giving each whatever he ordered. This system, introduced into the country by French restaurants, was first employed at the Tremont House in 1829, and within a few years was in general use in hotels. It was one of several table-refinements that, coupled with all its other avowedly aristocratic features, made the Tremont stand out as a hotel *par excellence*. It was in keeping with the Tremont's silver table-service, which included America's first four-tined forks — called, in derision, " split spoons " — which did more to abolish the ancient art of " sword-swallowing." The Tremont also introduced a sort of military drill for the waiters and thus further ceremonialized the *table d'hôte*. This, too, became general in all first-class hotels, and though it has long since disappeared as a dining-room formality, a trace of the custom may still be observed at banquets when the waiters march in simultaneously with each course. Colonel A. M. Maxwell of the British Army, who toured America in the late 1830's, said that the entire staff of the old Astor House in New York — the staggering number of a hundred and three male and sixty-five female employees — " are drilled as regularly as I drill my regiment." The colonel added that if there were a trained regiment of employees of that size in some of the little principalities with which Europe then abounded, it would scare the princes to death.[9] Perhaps the best description of the waiters and their drill was that given by a writer in 1859:

> There will be seen a magnificent set-out dinner-table for a hundred or more guests, with a line of table napkins, in upright fantastic form, stuck into every tumbler, which range along each side of the table, from end to end. The meals — all previously prepared and brought up — are placed on side tables, and there delivered to the white or colored waiters, each one of whom has four or six guests to wait upon. It is one of the most novel sights for a stranger to see in one of these immense dining halls, a whole regiment of Sambos, waiting for the signal to uncover such of the dishes as are placed on the table before the guests. After all the company are seated, say twenty to thirty of these waiters are ranged, one half on each side of the table, behind the guests, in military line. At a given signal, each one reaches over his arm and takes hold of the handle of a dish. That is the first motion. There they all hold for a second or two, when, at another

signal, they all at the same moment lift the cover, all as if flying off at one whoop, and with as great exactness as soldiers expected to " shoulder arms." This is the case in the $2 and $2.50 houses in the large cities. In the smaller or cheaper houses the same formality or order is not to be seen in that respect, nor are the dining halls, of course, so splendid. . . . The meals, one and all, may be said to be " royal " in the fullest sense of the word. Even in hotels where the charge is only $1 a day, or $3 or $4 per week, the set-out is not to be despised.[10]

One of the odd features of the *table d' hôte* in the early part of the nineteenth century was that separate dining-rooms (called " men's ordinary " and " ladies' ordinary ") were provided for men and women. This was a survival of the old Puritan custom of separating the sexes at worship and at social events. Edward A. Kendall, a British visitor during the first decade of the nineteenth century, describing a visit to Stafford Springs, Connecticut, observes:

All of the women sat together, beginning at the lower end of the table; and all of the men sat together, toward the upper; and the only communication between them resulted from the necessity under which the men appeared to labor to be helped by the women. . . . The separation of the sexes prevails, in New England, through all the intercourse of society, even where the condition of life is many removes from the rustic. On that awful occasion, a *tea-party*, all the ladies occupy one side of the room, and all the gentlemen the other; and one consequence is that the gentlemen talk politics, and the ladies listen in silence; for the ladies are rarely politicians. " In monarchies," says a French writer, "the women are everything; in republics, nothing." [11]

It was probably not until the opening of the Tremont that the menu card, or bill of fare, became a necessity at the *table d' hôte,* for guests had no need of consulting a card when all the food was put on the table. The diners marked on the cards the various dishes they desired. " But the *maître d'hôtel* was not satisfied with sending in those dishes alone which we marked," says a guest at the old City Hotel in New York in 1832, " but besides these, furnished everything which he himself thought best."[12] Mine Host adopted, about 1870, the plan of having diners write out their orders, thereby effecting a considerable reduction in the wastage of food.

At first the menu cards were written in pen and ink, but early in the 1830's they were being printed from type. The Astor House in New York had its own printing-plant for the production of its bills of fare and was probably the first hotel to have such a plant.[13] The bill of fare of the opening banquet at the Tremont House in Boston was the first facsimile of handwriting ever printed in this country.[14] The bill was written out and signed at the bottom by Mine Host Dwight Boyden. When a banker present at the opening was informed that the card was printed from a lithographic stone, he became alarmed and asked: " If Dwight Boyden's signature is printed, what are our checks worth?" Only two hundred of these bills of fare were issued and it is said that there are not more than two or three in existence now.

Menu cards of the middle and latter decades of the nineteenth century were generally very large and were gaudily ornamented with gastronomic emblems and symbols. At first a single sheet was used; later a double-fold sheet, almost the size of a tabloid newspaper. In the 1860's and 1870's the gastronomic symbols were still being used on the double-fold sheets, which also contained advertisements along each side and at the bottom.

There is not a great deal of romantic tradition in connection with menu cards, though Schubert is said to have written one of his loveliest songs on one. There is a legend that menu cards were a deciding factor in the choice of Montgomery as the state capital of Alabama, back in 1846. Originally the capital was at Wetumpka, at the head of navigation on the Coosa River, thirty miles from Montgomery, which was then known as Yankeetown, or New Philadelphia. Enterprising citizens of Montgomery started a campaign for removal of the capital and built a hotel called the Exchange, to help their cause along. But there seemed to be a clear majority of the legislature in favor of Wetumpka. On the day the vote was to be taken, however, handsomely printed bills of fare of the new hotel at Montgomery were given each legislator as he sat eating a miserable dinner in the hotel at Wetumpka. The Montgomery menu cards, listing all the luxuries of the season, were quite a contrast to those of Wetumpka, badly printed on coarse brown paper, and listing but a limited assortment of foods. And so, when the vote was taken in the afternoon, Montgomery won by a handsome majority.[15]

It was quite a common thing for proprietors of "resteraws" in booming cow-towns and mining-camps of the West's wild and woolly days to use menu cards copied direct from those of Delmonico's, though these establishments were prepared to serve only a limited selection of frying-pan and boiling-pot victuals. Owen Wister relates the legend of the traveler who saw "*vol-au-vent*" on a bill of fare in Texas and ordered some. The proprietor yanked out his six-shooter and said, grimly: "Stranger, you'll take hash."[16] Colonel Cyrus Jones, whose "eating palace" stood near the U. P. station in Omaha, handled the situation somewhat differently. The colonel's menu swarmed with French and listed all the good things served in swagger Eastern refectories. One day a customer ordered frogs' legs. "Wants frogs' legs, does he?" said the colonel, his eyes narrowing to a slit. Then: "Too many brain workers before you come in, professor. Missionary ate the last leg off me just now." So the customer probably took pork and beans, or ham and eggs. The colonel may have been an indifferent restaurateur, but he deserves his niche in the hall of literary fame, for he was the first story-book character to narrow his eyes to a slit. Thousands have done it since then.

According to legend, it was in the happy-go-lucky West that the jovial custom of calling poached eggs on toast "Adam and Eve on a raft," black coffee "a dipper of ink," and milk toast "graveyard stew" survived longest. The short-jacket waiters of the old horseshoe-counter restaurants were supposed to be geniuses at nicknaming items on the bill of fare, but in reality this was a pastime of waggish guests, dating back to the time when pigs' feet were known as "Cincinnati oysters," prairie chicken was "Northern Pfd.," and bean soup was "Old 365," because it was served every day of the year.

Both before and after the advent of the menu card Mine Host sometimes preferred to ballyhoo his *table d'hôte* in a sort of Coney Island barker manner. Perley Poore, old-time Boston and Washington journalist (one of the famous Civil War correspondents), relates in his reminiscences an interesting story of Jesse Brown, landlord of the Indian Queen Tavern in Washington at the time Congress held its first session there (in 1800). Brown set the customary bountiful table and as he sat at the head of it, industriously carving the meats, would shout in a full-throated voice: "Here's a rare slice for Mrs. A"; "Ah, a nice bone cut for Colonel B," "Pass your plate, Miss J, for this splendid cut"; "Mrs. Z, you *must* have another helping of the floating island "; "General, can't I help you to some more pigeon pie?" "Joe, pass the sweet potatoes to Major S"; and so on.[17] General McMackin, who used to run the McMackin Hotel in Vicksburg, Mississippi, in the 1850's, had a similar method. The general was reputed to be the politest man in the country, a Southern gentleman of the old school. He used to stand at the carving-table in a corner of the spacious dining-hall and cry out: "Nice turkey hash, fresh sausages, cold ham, the best beefsteak in the world," and would direct his waiters to hurry up with the hot cakes, to pass the rolls, and to see that everyone had plenty of food. Bishop Pierce, who was a guest at the general's hotel, wrote of him:

> All his various directions worked into a sort of song; and were it not that the tune is a nondescript, one might imagine that the old Roman fashion of combining music and feasting had been revived on the banks of the Mississippi. This plan is a substitute for printed bills of fare, now common in all the best city hotels. He says, I understand, that the reason he adopted this unique method was that some years ago he kept a public house in Jackson, and many of his boarders were members of the legislature, and could not read, so he had to *call out* for their information. Finding it cheap and easy, he had continued it.[18]

The era of the general and of Jesse Brown was also the era of the dinner-bell and its successor, the gong. The dinner-bell was rung, generally at two o'clock, at the doors of taverns and inns during the village days of Boston, New York, and Philadelphia, and as late as 1800 in Boston it was customary for Mine Host to ring the bell on the streets.[19] "The awful gong," as Dickens called it, " which shakes the very window frames as it reverberates through the house and horribly disturbs nervous foreigners," went out of use in cities before the Civil War, but was still in use at resort hotels and in smaller places until near the end of the century.

Until about the decade of the nineties American breakfasts, dinners, and suppers were practically identical. There were plenty of food fads, worthy and otherwise, during the nineteenth century, but none seemed to have much effect on the American-plan *table d'hôte,* which continued to be a meal of Gargantuan proportions right down to the threshold of the twentieth century; and those who preferred it continued to be prodigious eaters. Simeon Ford, Mine Host of the old

Grand Union Hotel in New York, once said: " I see by the papers that a scientist has discovered that the average man eats about one thousand times his own weight in food during a lifetime. Some of my boarders try to do that trick in two weeks." A great many guests were like the traveling man John Kendrick Bangs used to tell about. For his supper this fellow ordered fried eggs, bacon, " a little of that steak," baked beans, German fried potatoes, kippered herring, milk toast, cereal and cream, preserved peaches, hot biscuit, sponge cake, and a cup of coffee. After the commissariat had responded faithfully, an old friend came in and sat next' to the traveling man. " Well, Tommy, how's things? " he asked. "Business is all right," said Tommy, "but I ain't feelin' well myself. My stummick don't seem just right. I guess I been workin' too hard." " You'd ought to eat milk toast," said the new arrival. "Yes," said Tommy, " I've ordered some." At this point the waitress came up for the newcomer's order. Among other things he ordered buckwheat cakes. " Gee ! " cried Tommy; " I did't know there was buckwheats. Bring me a stack of 'em, too, Jennie." [20]

But in the 1870's the drift away from gormandizing began and made steady headway. Life was becoming softer and appetites more jaded. The army of vegetarians, dieters, and other " pickin' eaters " was growing more rapidly. Breakfast was the first meal to show the effects of this. Newfangled breakfast foods, advertised after the manner of pink pills, and a sudden passion for toast and eggs and oranges and grapefruit, finally routed the old-style matutinal meal, with its beefsteaks, chops, eggs, flapjacks, fried potatoes, hominy, and other selections.[21] Breakfast was the one American meal for which George Augustus Sala expressed sincere respect. It was, he said, " the foundation stone of the entire twenty-four hours, a ceremony almost religious." From the bill of fare, " a foot long," he ordered hominy, iced milk, whitefish, eggs, a cutlet, a prairie hen, corn-bread, and coffee.

Hominy was Sala's favorite American dish and he noted that Americans ate great quantities of it. The eggs were eaten raw, in a glass of milk, "after the custom of the country." After Sala had disposed of his eggs, prairie hen, cutlet, and other viands, the solicitous waiter, perhaps with a twinkle in his eye, asked: "Any hot cakes, mister?"[22] Sala was surrounded at the breakfast-table, he said, by "lean and sallow creatures" who made great inroads on the supply of spongy steaming bread and hot muffiny cakes. "That masculine yet bony authoress from New England," he said, "has actually built a monument to Mrs. Beecher Stowe of flapjacks; now she butters each layer, then pours libations of molasses on the whole, and lo! in less than ten minutes the monument is no more, and the strong-minded woman herself has stalked downstairs and gone shopping, in defiance of all dietetic laws, human and divine."

Proprietors of the old American-plan hotels did not, of course, hope to break even on their dining-rooms, for besides the prodigality of the meals there was a vast waste of food in the kitchens. Then, too, classic French cookery was in itself expensive, calling for high-priced ingredients and a great deal of labor in the preparation. Especially was this true of the chef's masterpieces, of which each chef had one or more. Mine Host was prepared to stand a loss and placed the burden of making up the loss on the bar-room, which generally came nobly to the rescue. The bar thus determined, to a considerable extent, the quality of the table. If Mine Host was making enough out of his bar, he could afford to spend more for food and cooks. The meals were advertisements for the hotel — none better — and Mine Host made them count in his favor as much as possible, unless he had so little competition that it did not matter. But practically all of the old-time hotel-keepers took great pride in their tables.

Of course, the price of food-stuffs had a great deal to

do with the hotel-keeper's ability to provide big meals. Throughout practically all of the long golden period of the American plan the raw materials for Mine Host's table, especially the meats (which were the most important thing of all), were dirt-cheap compared to today's prices. There was a great abundance of game in colonial and early republican days, and a surplus of barn-yard meats. Those were generations of great meat-eaters, and there was plenty for all. The market was more often glutted than not, for little could be shipped abroad. In the early 1800's Mine Host could buy venison for three and a half cents a pound. Bear meat was slightly higher. Wild pigeons were a drug on the market at a cent apiece. Men and boys with sticks could kill thousands of them as they roosted at night in the woods. Quail, prairie chickens, and wild ducks and geese were plentiful, and so were wild turkeys, full-grown ones weighing from twenty to thirty pounds. They were as numerous as were buffalo west of the Missouri. The *Magazine of American History* said in 1794 that wild turkeys were then selling for 62½ cents each (five shillings), and that for one shilling (12½ cents) one could buy enough " Albany beef " (sturgeon) to feed a large family. Oysters, the magazine said, were plentiful and large. Early American oysters, lobsters, and crabs were much larger than those of today. Thackeray, after trying his first American oyster, said that he " felt as if he had swallowed a baby." [23]

The hours of meals varied at different times and places, but the guest had to be punctual in those days, when Mine Host was somewhat like the landlady in one of Scott's novels who warned her hungry boarders to be on hand promptly, " for ye'll get nae mair meat till the naxt meal." The guests assembled near the dining-hall doors when the gong clanged, and went to their seats when the doors were thrown open. Some contemporary observers say there was a mad scramble to get to the table; others say there wasn't. The old Puritan meal hours, prevalent in Boston inns up to about 1800, were breakfast at six, dinner at twelve, and supper at six or seven. Tyrone Power, the Irish actor, a guest at the Tremont House in 1833, records that at half past seven the crash of the gong aroused all sleepers. Half an hour later breakfast was served. Dinner was at three, tea at six, and supper at nine. " It is yet a marvel to me," wrote Power, " first, how all these elaborate meals are so admirably got up, and next, how the plague these good people find appetite to come to time with a regularity no less surprising."[24] The City Hotel in New York had the same meal hours at that time.[25] Thomas Hamilton, popular novelist and member of *Blackwood's* staff, who visited America two or three years earlier, branded Mine Host as "the most rigorous and iron-hearted of despots" because of the *table d'hôte* and the fixed meal hours.

> And surely never was monarch blessed with more patient and obedient subjects [said he]. He feeds them in droves like cattle. He rings a bell, and they come like dogs at their master's whistle. He places before them what he thinks proper, and they swallow it without grumbling.[26]

Hamilton had no complaint, however, against the Tremont House. He thought it a splendidly managed and superb hotel in every way, except that its architectural beauty was much overrated. At the Tremont Captain Hamilton " enjoyed the blessing of rational liberty, had command of my own hours and motions; in short, could eat, drink or sleep at what time, in what manner, and on what substances I might prefer." Mine Host Boyden of the Tremont had quietly humored his English guests from the first by providing both *à la carte* orders and room service; and Hamilton, Power, and others availed themselves of these special favors. Toward the end of the decade Mine Host gave his boarders a wider range of meal hours. They need no longer be on the dot at the peal of the bell. In 1840 Coleman and Stetson of the old Astor House in New York posted a steel-engraved card in guest-rooms announcing meals at the following hours: Breakfast, half past seven in the ladies' ordinary, eight o'clock in the men's ordinary; dinner, three o'clock in the ladies' ordinary and half past three in the men's; tea, six to nine o'clock; and supper, nine to midnight.

These are the regular hours [said the announcement], but if it suits the interest or convenience of our patrons, we provide breakfast at any moment between daylight and dinner time. Dinners for one or more at any hour. In short, we take pleasure in providing for the wants of our patrons, regardless of the hour or our own convenience, without extra charge.

Ten years later the New York *Tribune,* remarking that " the gastronomic progress of the day is perpetual," quoted the following meal hours at hotels: Breakfast, five to noon; dinner (ordinary), half past one to half past three; " a princely banquet at 5 o'clock in the afternoon "; tea, six to eight; and supper, nine to midnight. An anecdote that went the rounds related that a farmer who checked in at a large hotel learned, upon inquiry, that the meal hours were breakfast from six to eleven, dinner from eleven to three, tea from three to eight, and supper from eight to midnight. "Wa — al, say," said the farmer, "that doesn't leave me any time to see the town."

The European plan of hotel operation, whereby the guest pays only for his room and takes his meals wherever he pleases, finally routed the American plan and is all but universal today. Chiefly the few remaining American-plan hotels are at resorts and in the smaller towns. The European plan (which originated in France) was introduced in this country about 1835, or possibly a little earlier. In that year two or three New York hotels were advertising adoption of the plan.[27] But only a very small percentage of hotels were operated on the European plan prior to about 1870, and those were chiefly in New York and other cities of the East. After 1870 the European plan began to spread. Hotels in all the larger cities that had been strictly American plan, and new hotels, such as the Palmer House in Chicago when it opened, in 1870, began offering guests a choice of either plan. When a guest registered, the clerk would ask: "American or European?" When Israel Zangwill paid his first visit to this country and was asked that question, he replied: "I'm European, but I don't see what business that is of yours."

Which hotel was the first to adopt the European plan is uncertain, but the honor was claimed for the historic old Tammany Hall Hotel by its proprietors in 1847 when they advertised the opening of a new addition. "At this extensive hotel," said advertisements in the *Tribune* and other newspapers, "the European Plan of lodging and table under distinct organizations was first introduced in this country." The plan was still so new and unusual in 1840 that John Cotter, when he took charge of the Washington Hall Hotel, at Broadway and Reade Street, found it necessary to give an extended explanation of it in the newspapers. Said he:

> The establishment will be conducted on the much admired European Plan, (namely) of letting the bedrooms, adequately furnished, at such terms as will square with the times — say from $3 to $5 per week.
> Gentlemen also may be accommodated with bedroom, breakfast and tea, the charges per week in proportion to the quality of the room.
> The restaurant will remain open from 7 o'clock in the morning till 11 o'clock at night, during which time the guest can always be accommodated from the daily bill of fare, and charged accordingly.
> This plan of hotelkeeping leaves the guests at liberty to dine when and where they please.[28]

The Washington Hall Hotel, by the way, stood on what was later the site of the Irving House. It was built in 1809, at a cost of about a hundred and forty thousand dollars by the Washington Union Benevolent Society and was perhaps the chief rival and competitor of the old City Hotel for the next twenty years. The corner-stone was laid on July 4, 1809, and exactly thirty-five years later (on July 4, 1844) the hotel burned down.[29]

The first hotel of any considerable prominence to adopt the European plan was the aristocratic old New York Hotel. S. Baptiste Monnot, who had full charge of the kitchen, dining-room, and cuisine in general, created somewhat of a sensation when he announced that the hotel would specialize in private dining (or room service), and that meals *à la carte*, with the food cooked to order, would supplant the *table d'hôte*. *Pro Bono Publico* and a number of New York editors viewed this announcement with alarm and expressed the fear that such a radical departure threatened the very foundations of the republic. Although room service and *à la carte* were not new to the country — for, as we have seen, both could be had at the Tremont, Astor, and other hotels, if the guest insisted — it was startling for such a house as the New York to go so completely contrary to established practice. Nat P. Willis, poet and journalist, led the attack on Monnot's highfalutin innovations. He objected particularly to the room service, on the ground that it was directly opposed to American ideals of democracy, and that it engendered the spread of dangerous blue-blood habits that might lead no one knows where.

> There are some republican advantages in our present system of hotels which the country is not yet ready to forgo [he said]. Tell a country lady in these times that when she comes to New York she must eat and pass the evening in a room by herself, and she would rather stay at home. The going to the Astor and dining with two

hundred well dressed people, and sitting in full dress in a splendid drawing room with plenty of company — is the charm of going to the city! The theaters are nothing to that! Broadway, the shopping and the sights, are all subordinate — poor accessories to the main object of the visit.

What good are hotels, Willis wanted to know, if folks " tolerably well dressed and well behaved " could not rub elbows and pick their teeth at a public table. Dining-room and drawing-room life in hotels, he declared, was " the tangible republic — the only thing palpable and agreeable that we have to show, in common life, as republican. . . . And when the hotel-garni draws its dividing line through this promiscuous community of habits," he added, " the cords will be cut which will let some people UP, out of reach, and drop some people DOWN, out of all satisfactory supportable contact with society."[30] As for Monnot's plan to cook food to order, it was simply ridiculous, and *à la carte* service was equally foolish, though it had its element of danger. No one but a nitwit would order a meal *à la carte,* Willis pointed out, when one could get for fifty cents a *table d'hôte* feast that would cost two to five dollars if each item were charged separately. These patrician whims, Willis predicted, would never win popular approval. But somehow or other they did; and the republic survived them nicely. As Willis had feared, however, the New York Hotel did become a rendezvous of what some commentators declare to have been the only true aristocracy America has ever known, the Southern planters, who, with their families, comprised a very large percentage of the visitors to New York at that time.

Many of the present generation remember the old New York Hotel, for it lasted until 1893. It is said to have figured in several Civil War romances and, like the old Spencer House in Cincinnati and a number of other hotels, it was constantly under suspicion during the war of being a hotbed of Confederate intrigue. Many of its guests were shadowed by secret-service men. Perhaps because of its popularity among Southerners, it was one of the few important hotels in New York that was not set afire on the night of November 25, 1864, by plotters who evidently hoped to burn down the city. During an interval of eight hours, extending into the morning of November 26, fires were started in the upper rooms of thirteen hotels, including the St. James at Broadway and Twenty-third Street, the St. Nicholas, the Metropolitan, Jonathan Lovejoy's Hotel on Park Row, the Tammany Hotel, the La Farge House, the Howard Hotel, the Hanford Hotel, the New England Hotel on the Bowery, the Fifth Avenue Hotel, the Astor House, the United States Hotel, and the original Belmont Hotel, at 133 Fulton Street, just east of Broadway. Barnum's Museum also was set afire.[31]

Men carrying black bags set the fires, and "Beware of the man with the black bag" became one of the slang phrases of the day. In each case the procedure was similar. The incendiary registered, was assigned to a room, and immediately piled bedclothes and furniture in the center of the room. Then he took from the bag a quantity of paper and cotton cloth, soaked with an inflammable compound, and set it afire. Locking the door and pocketing the key, the guest disappeared. Fortunately all the fires were discovered and put out before much damage had been done. But New York and the entire nation were greatly excited over the affair, and this excitement continued for months. Even the South was excited, for the Confederacy was blamed. Detectives discovered, however, that not more than ten people were involved in the plot, and that their acts, like that of Wilkes Booth, were self-imposed.

It was a presidential year. Lincoln had just been reelected; Sherman was marching through Georgia; Grant and Lee were at grips in Virginia; and the war was drawing toward its close. But the fire plot was as big a sensation as any news from the battlefront. The New York Hotel-keepers' Association, the first organization of hotel men in America, published an announcement in the newspapers of November 29, 1864, offering rewards totaling twenty thousand dollars for the capture and conviction of the perpetrators of the plot. The anouncement, signed by Richard French of French's Hotel, president of the association; Samuel Hawk of the St. Nicholas, vice-president; and H. L. Powers of Powers' Hotel, secretary, offered five thousand dollars for the first arrest and conviction, three thousand for the second, two thousand for the third, and a thousand dollars for each of ten others. But the association never had to pay more than the first of these awards, for although many suspects were arrested and investigated, only one paid the penalty.

In January of the following year Robert Cobb Kennedy, a Louisiana planter who had attended West Point, was arrested, brought to New York, tried, and hanged at Fort Lafayette in New York harbor on March 25, 1865. During the weeks after his arrest he alternately admitted and denied his guilt and finally wrote a confession. On the scaffold, however, he branded his execution as " a judicial and cowardly murder " and just as the black cap was about to be adjusted, he burst into song:

> Trust to luck, trust to luck,
> Stare Fate in the face;
> For your heart will be easy
> If it's in the right place.

One hundred and eighty-five bounty-jumpers, who had been forced to attend the execution as a warning, heard the song and saw the hanging. " A more villainous looking set of rascals were never before collected together, perhaps," remarked the *Herald*.[32]

THE GROANING BOARD

Like the European plan and *à la carte* service, the strictly French cuisine made rather slow progress in the teeth of much opposition. French cuisine had begun its conquest of America shortly after the French Revolution of 1789. The chefs — men of the type of Vatel, who killed himself because something went wrong with a dish he had prepared for Condé and Louis XIV — were the spoiled darlings of the aristocracy, with swords dangling at their sides. When the Reign of Terror broke loose, they began scampering out of range of the guillotine. Perhaps more of them came to America than to any other country. Many went to New Orleans, the only distinctively French city in the country, and, at that time, of course, in French territory. They quickly gave New Orleans a reputation for culinary excellence and made her hotels and restaurants nationally famous. In the North their conquest was not so swift. Some got jobs in kitchens of the larger inns, but not as head chefs. Others cooked in French boarding-houses and inns catering to their countrymen. Still others opened restaurants, patronized by native blue-bloods and visiting foreigners.

The first to establish a restaurant in the North was Jean Baptiste Julien, who opened Julien's Restarator in 1794 in a house at Congress and Milk streets in Boston. Francis Guerin, another refugee, opened perhaps the first French restaurant in New York, about 1800, at Broadway, Pine and Cedar streets, directly opposite the City Hotel.[33] According to Samuel Adams Drake, historian of the old Boston taverns, Julien's soups soon became famous among Boston gourmets, while the novelty of his cuisine attracted custom. He was familiarly nicknamed "the Prince of Soups." Besides its main dining-room, there were smaller rooms that were used by dining-clubs, one of which was known as "Our Club."[34]

The French chef introduced culinary frills to America. He scorned simplicity and could never see the value of it.

But the average American preferred simplicity. For many years the public attitude toward *la cuisine française* was somewhat like that of today toward Chinese cookery — it was all right to eat it once in a while, as a sort of lark, but as a steady diet it was out of the question. As Thurlow Weed tells us in his autobiography, there was a general prejudice against "fancy French cookin'." Americans in general looked upon it with suspicion, surmising, as did Owen Wister's Virginian, that "it would give an outraged stomach to a plain-raised man." Nevertheless, the irresistible delights of the classic French cuisine gained wider and wider prestige, and when the Tremont adopted it, other hotels soon followed. The Astor House and other hotels that catered to "the bloods" had French cooks and bottle-washers. Swagger resort hotels at Saratoga, Cape May, and Newport had French cooking, and by 1840 chefs began to come north from New Orleans to take charge of hotel kitchens, while others were attracted from France by the high wages paid — sometimes as much as a hundred and twenty-five dollars a month. According to a writer in *Putnam's Magazine,* French cuisine was dominant in all hotels by 1853, and all first-class hotels used French terms on their bills of fare, except the Astor House, which insisted on giving English names to all dishes "capable of translation." By now French cooks and kitchen workers in general were swarming into the country on every ship. The triumph of *la cuisine française* was complete.

It was also during this decade that wealthy families began to employ French chefs, a field of employment that widened greatly after the Civil War. People of wealth vied with one another in giving expensive dinners and suppers in their mansions, which had banquet halls and kitchens almost as large as those of hotels, and as well manned and equipped as those of many a small hotel. The Lorrilards, Astors, Goulds, Vanderbilts, and all the rest bid against one another for the services of chefs who had won reputations, and hotels could scarcely compete with the parvenus in engaging the top-notchers of the profession. Salaries of hotel chefs in the 1870's ranged from $175 to $250 a month, but the latter figure was rare. In 1877 the *Hotel Mail* ridiculed a report that the chef of the St. George Hotel in Philadelphia was getting three hundred dollars a month. Such an extravagant figure, said the *Mail,* was simply absurd. Three hundred dollars a month was still considered a fancy salary for a hotel chef in 1883 when the Hoffman House in New York paid that amount to Eugene Laperreque, who had formerly been Rothschild's head cook in London and had just come from Paris, where he had been head chef of the Café d'Anglais. Meanwhile, salaries of three to five thousand dollars for private family chefs were common. It was said that George W. Childs, who for many years had the reputation of giving the best dinners in the country, paid his chef eight thousand a year. This may have been just a talking-figure.

Society then used to attend the annual dinner dances of the Société Culinaire Philanthropique, the oldest organization of kitchen workers in the country. It started in 1865 with a membership of about three hundred, and Louis Ragot, of Delmonico's was its first president. These annual events are still held, but society does not attend them, for long ago the chef dropped out of the picture as one of society's pet retainers. It is even said that the reign of the French chef in hotels and restaurants is nearing its end, and that within a few years the old-style chef will have disappeared entirely. The influence of the classic French cuisine on American cookery will not disappear, but for many years now the tendency has been more and more toward plain foods. Like everything else, cookery is subject to readjustment to changing conditions. Heavy meals of complicated preparation are no longer in vogue. " A few years more and we shall be one with the horse-car and the leg-o'-mutton sleeve," said the president of a New York association of chefs a year or two ago. "And our art perishes with us, don't forget that," he added mournfully. "It is not a thing of cook books, but of loving study of technique."

Meanwhile American cookery is becoming more and more distinctive and is "on the way to being the most delicious and varied in the world — a piquant and fascinating

ANNUAL BALL AND BANQUET OF SOCIÉTÉ CULINAIRE PHILANTHROPIQUE

mixture of all the nations," as Edna Ferber points out in the preface to her sister's cook book. But in addition to its borrowings and adaptations from other countries the American cuisine has many gastronomical triumphs that are purely American in origin, even the ingredients being indigenous to American soil. Some distinctively American receipts are the contributions of skillful housewives, while others were first prepared from receipts concocted by early hotel and restaurant cooks of native origin. Then, too, America, like all other countries, has had her share of dilettante experimenters in the *art culinaire;* such fellows, for example, as the late Sam Ward, whom Lord Roseberry once called " the Uncle of the Human Race." Ward was an industrious inventor of new receipts, his *chef d'œuvre* being stewed terrapin *à la* Maryland. More recently many new dishes have been produced by dietitians, college women who have made a success of the cafeteria and tea-room business, and the heads of home-economics courses in various state schools.

A long list could be made of American culinary creations. It would include such concoctions as clam and fish chowder, pumpkin pie, hominy, Saratoga chips, chicken *à la* King, Philadelphia pepper-pot, succotash, porterhouse steaks, Virginia's sweet-potato pie, catchup, and an endless variety of tomato preparations, including tomato soup; Indian pudding, flapjacks, Graham bread, cinnamon buns, Parker House rolls, corn fritters and other corn dishes, including corn on the cob; chocolate pie, the candied yams of Dixie — these and a wide variety of others. Delmonico's, that celebrated cradle of American epicureanism, was the birthplace of several dishes that continue to tickle the palate of the world. Founded just one hundred years ago by an Italian-Swiss pastry-cook, Delmonico's unquestionably did more than any other institution to change and elevate the standards of American cookery. Its style and menu were imitated everywhere. Before the Civil War it was practically the only restaurant whose cuisine could outdo that of the first-class hotels.

Lobster *à la* Newberg was the Delmonico dish that attained perhaps the widest fame. There is an interesting story in connection with this immortal midnight dainty. According to tradition, Skipper Ben Wenberg, owner of a line of fruit and passenger boats plying between New York and Latin America, was one of Delmonico's regular patrons in the 1870's and 1880's. He was one of the town's gourmets and fastidious dressers. One afternoon on his return from Central America he entered Delmonico's with some friends and, calling for a blazer, two large lobsters, half a pound of unsalted butter, six fresh eggs, a glass of Jamaica rum, and a pint of heavy cream, he showed Charles Delmonico how to prepare a new dish. A species of hot pepper which

BANQUET TO GEN. DAN SICKLES, at Delmonico's, Feb. 22, 1872

Wenberg had brought with him from Latin America was added after the cooking was completed and red pepper was sprinkled over each portion when it was ready for serving. Wenberg's friends were delighted with it, and it went on the Delmonico menu as " lobster *à la* Wenberg." Charles Delmonico substituted sherry, however, for rum in the receipt.

A few years later Wenberg got on the famous Delmonico black list because of a violent quarrel in the restaurant with some other patrons over the merits of President

Cleveland's pardon of Edward S. Stokes, who had been sent to Sing Sing for the murder of Jim Fisk. Delmonico also ordered that " lobster *à la* Wenberg " be changed to " lobster *à la* Newberg. Wenberg was but one of many free-spending victims of the Delmonico black list, devised to rid the establishment of objectionable characters. It was a rule that anyone who raised a disturbance or otherwise annoyed other diners was put on the list, and employees were forbidden to serve him. Black-listed persons were permitted to enter the place, seat themselves at table, and order. But the orders were never filled. After politely taking the order the waiter disappeared. After a tiresome interval the patron would summon the head waiter, who would promise to " see about it." The head waiter, too, would disappear, and presently the patron would take the hint and leave.

There are a number of other traditions in connection with the origin of various American viands. Of all the many ways of preparing potatoes, the Saratoga chip is perhaps the most ingenious. This appetizing dainty gets its name from the fact that it was accidentally invented in the early 1850's at the old Montgomery Hall, kept by Carey E. Moon, at Saratoga.[35] Legend has it that in 1853 George Crum, the chef, got an order from a fastidious diner to cut his French fried potatoes thinner. In a spirit of sarcasm Crum sliced off a sheet of potato as thin as a wafer and dropped it into the hot fat of the frying-pan. A few minutes later he fished it out and ate it. So good did it taste that he fried a few more slices, sharing them with his assistants, and with Mrs. Carey Moon, who had a quantity of them fried and put into paper cornucopias for the guests. The chips won favor at once and within a few years became an established viand throughout the country.

New England's culinary glory — despite that inglorious mixture known as succotash — would be secure if that section had given us nothing more than pumpkin pie. But pumpkin pie is but one of many gastronomical ten-strikes that have come out of Yankee-land. The time-honored New England boiled dinner still numbers its partisans by the million, and although hominy is not consumed in such wholesale quantities as formerly, it still is one of America's breakfast staples. According to Henry Wadsworth Longfellow, the world has New England to thank for clam and fish chowder, invented by French settlers along the coast of Maine and named " chowder " by the Indians because it was prepared in *chaudières,* or kettles. Fish chowder, generally made of cod or haddock, was Daniel Webster's *pièce de résistance*. He had a special receipt of his own and delighted in imparting it to cooks and helping them prepare their first batch of it. No mention of New England gastronomy would be complete without reference to Boston baked beans. In recent years Boston antiquarians have been compelled to rise nobly to the defense of Boston's claim to authorship of this traditional dish, a base effort having been made to steal Boston's thunder by a speaker at a convention of restaurateurs who stated that baked pork and beans originated in a Russian monastery a hundred years before the Pilgrims landed at Plymouth Rock.[36]

New England may or may not have been the first blessed corner of the world to smack its lips in delight over porterhouse steaks. There are several legends of the origin of this toothsome cut of meat, one of which is that it was first served at the Porter House, an old-time hotel at North Cambridge, Massachusetts, run by a Mr. and Mrs. Porter. A more likely version is that the steak was first served at Martin Morrison's porter-house at 327 Pearl Street, New York, near the old Walton House, about 1815.[37] Other porter-houses began serving the steaks and they speedily became known as " porterhouse steaks."

Even in bread-stuff specialties America has no mean achievement to her credit, for one of these is corn pone, most thoroughly American of all food preparations, the one great contribution made by the Indian to American gastronomy. The noble red man taught the making of it to early settlers in various parts of the country, and under various names — journey-cake, Johnny-cake, hoe-cake, ash-cake, corn-bread — it is known and eaten everywhere, though it has been discarded to a large extent in its native country. The art of making it and serving it in several tasteful ways was perfected by the Aunt Dinahs of the South, who, under the guidance of their mistresses, produced several other famous combinations, including that well-known liquid delight from New Orleans, chicken gumbo soup, and that vegetable jujube common throughout the South, candied yams.

Even the bewhiskered sourdoughs of California's Argonaut days have a few first-rate receipts to their credit. The oyster cocktail originated in San Francisco in the 1860's and was, so tradition says, invented by a miner who came back from the diggings loaded with nuggets. He dropped into a restaurant and ordered a big meal. "How long will it take you to get it ready?" he asked. "About fifteen minutes," said the waiter. "All right," said the miner; "but bring me a plate of California raws right away, and some catchup and horse-radish and a whisky cocktail. After drinking the cocktail he put the oysters into the goblet, salted and peppered them, poured in two spoonfuls of vinegar and one of Worcestershire sauce, and added a pinch of horse-radish. On top of this he filled the goblet with catchup and stirred the mixture.[38] The restaurant-keeper looked on with interest. "What sort of a mess do you call that, pardner?" he inquired. "That?" said the miner; "oh, that's what I call an oyster cocktail; they're good. You'd better try one." Next day a sign appeared on the bar-room mirror: "Oyster Cocktail! Four Bits per Glass." And within a week every joint on the Barbary Coast was serving oyster cocktails. It was not long before the cocktails were admitted to the menu cards of the best hotels and cafés of San Francisco.

Very early in its boom days San Francisco became famous for the quality of its cuisine, and in the 1860's and 1870's it had no peer as an epicurean paradise, for high salaries had attracted many of the very best French chefs and they had a wealth of the best and rarest raw materials to work with. Game played an important part in the daily bills of fare, as it had done at earlier periods in the cities of the East and Middle West. "The hotels of the city are the equals of the very best in the Atlantic States," said Samuel Bowles; "the restaurants are the superiors. A dinner of several courses with wine is served in admirable style after the French form at the best of them for $1.50; while a meal in one of the fashionable eating houses of New York or Boston would cost four or five dollars." [39] *Leslie's Weekly* published a list of comparative prices in Boston and San Francisco restaurants in 1875, showing numerous selections from the bills of fare much cheaper in San Francisco.[40] There were many items procurable in San Francisco that one could not get for love or money in the East. One could eat at almost any price, if need be at Maloney's Franklin House, where board in the latter 1860's was four dollars a week.[41]

In the 1850's prices were higher. A restaurant called Delmonico's, as expensive, if not as consummate, as its New York namesake, was selling boiled eggs at seventy-five cents each in 1850, and dinner from one to five dollars, according to appetite, which surely was not unreasonable at a time when a quarter was the smallest coin store-keepers would accept. Elsewhere one could get a first-class *table d'hôte* dinner for two dollars and up, and steak, potatoes, and coffee for one dollar. At the first St. Francis Hotel, which Bayard Taylor called the best in San Francisco, one could get board and room for a hundred and fifty dollars a month, which was "unusually cheap." But there were restaurants even then that provided three meals a day for thirty-five dollars a week, and the City Hotel charged only twenty dollars a week for board. San Francisco was the one boom town, by all accounts, that never had to fake its bills of fare. The clipper ships rounded the Horn with plenty of cooks and cooking-apparatus as early as 1850, and they brought plenty of larder supplies, too. There was plenty of bread and cake for the honest miner, even though bags of flour were used as stepping-stones to enable him to cross the muddy streets. Perhaps the oldest surviving San Francisco bill of fare is that of a banquet at the Irving House on December 6, 1851. It lists eighty dishes. There were two choices of soup, two of fish, twelve "National Dishes" (meats), six boiled dishes (meats), four roasts, six *hors d'œuvres,* twelve entrées (meats), ten vegetables, ten game dishes, eighteen pastries and *entremets* (pies, puddings, cakes, etc.), and ten fruits and nuts as desserts.[42]

CHAPTER VIII

WATER, WATER EVERYWHERE

ACCORDING to an old proverb, all love-matches are made in heaven. There are, however, a lot of old ladies and old gentlemen who know that this statement is much too sweeping, for *their* matches were made at Newport, or Saratoga, or Cape May, or White Sulphur Springs, or at some other resort of the days when *Godey's Lady's Book* was required reading. These old ladies and gentlemen are survivors of a time when the fashionable watering-places were overrun by romantic demoiselles and amorous Lotharios, all wearing their hearts on their sleeves, and when flirtations, serious and otherwise, carried on by means of a complicated code, and gallantries of knightly urbanity, were the order of the day. A period when belles and beaux went to the beach or mountains or springs ostensibly for their health, but in reality to catch an attack of lovesickness; and then, if all went well and the wedding-bells clanged merrily, to Niagara Falls, the proverbial end of Honeymoon Trail.

Such, at any rate, is the impression one gets from the literature and journalism of the time. Love, it would seem, was all that mattered " at the springs " and down by the sad sea waves. Not pure, unadulterated love, necessarily, but often with an admixture of fortune-hunting, as is indicated by many of the love-stories with a resort as *mise en scène* and by such statements as this from a New York *Herald* editorial of 1853: "The most desperate endeavors will be made to secure the great object in the life of a belle — a rich and good-natured husband."[1] Or this, by a correspondent of the same newspaper visiting Cape May in the same year: "There are several $150,000 young ladies here, and great anxiety is evidenced for their welfare by ambitious young gallants."[2] George M. Towle, an Englishman who visited several resorts in the latter 1860's and found courtship and coquetry as prevalent here as at similar places in Europe, called the nightly balls at Saratoga "great matrimonial fairs, where the marriageable wares are shown off at their best." Ambitious mothers were present with their daughters, trying to do the best possible thing for them, Towle said, "for despite all the mother's hopes and stratagems, neither Juliana nor Lucinda has formed an engagement during the winter campaign; and the truth is they are getting on in years. Society tells her that the one way to accomplish it is to follow the fashionable stream as the gadfly dogged Io. . . . And so Newport and other American watering places have got to be — quite as much as Scarborough and Baden and Wiesbaden — marriage bourses with their speculators and victims." The fortune-hunters included not only the native swains, but also many from abroad. American resorts were frequented, as Towle said, "by the best and the lowest types of exotic Europeans. Spurious Italian counts and German music teachers with a spiritual air, if they strike the right social stratum — which they are bound to do — live in clover. For what I may call the American snobocracy — by which I mean vulgar people suddenly become rich and with it arrogant, who swarm to Newport and Saratoga and try to lord it over decent folk — the snobocracy adore nothing so much as a title, or a foreign genius, and are only too glad to shower their money on such of this sort as they find willing to receive it."[3]

The scent of orange-blossoms, which hung heavily over

fashionable resorts for fifty years, lingered on down to the gay nineties, then vanished into thin air. At least, it had ceased to be obtrusive. Goo-goo eyes became less primitive and promiscuous and the code of flirtation was forgotten. The belles had cast off that archness and air of innocence which had long been part of their stock-in-trade; the beaux were no longer punctilious and gallant in the old manner. Both had acquired a new technique, less romantic, perhaps, but more subtle and sophisticated. There was as much difference in the way of a man with a maid, and *vice versa,* as between crinolines and knee-length skirts. Dalliance had changed since the 1830's, when the beaux at White Sulphur organized the " Billing, Wooing and Cooing Society" and hung the constitution of the society—printed on pink paper—conspicuously in the ballroom of the "Old White."[4]

Saratoga and Newport in the North, Cape May and Long Branch on the New Jersey coast, and White Sulphur in the South were the great match-making and social-climbing centers of the middle decades of the nineteenth century. At those places the belles were most numerous. Throughout " the season " they were to be seen

> In clusters, in their dusters,
> Or " dressed up to the nines,"
> And sweeping all the sidewalks
> In their swelling crinolines.

White Sulphur was especially famous for its belles, for it drew its blushing beauties from the entire South, whereas in the North the beauties were scattered about at a dozen or more places. The White Sulphur Hotel, the " Old White," which was torn down in 1922, could have provided a full complement of Follies choristers in any season during its palmy days. Match-making lingered, too, at White Sulphur long after it had become archaic elsewhere. Even as late as the 1880's, according to one authority, purses were made up in little Southern towns to send likely maids and youths to the "Old White." [5]

There were, of course, other resorts in the South, but White Sulphur was the place to which the *élite* of all sections flocked; before the Civil War many Northerners went there. Its fame was not based solely on match-making. It was the center of many of the finest social, political, and historical traditions of Dixie. "Around White Sulphur Springs drifted backward and forward the fierce fortunes of the [Civil] war," says William A. MacCorkle, former governor of West Virginia, who wrote a history of the place. "It was . . . the scene of many wild' forays, fierce battles, gallant advances, sad retreats." [6] It also was there, according to MacCorkle, that the governor of North Carolina made his oft-quoted remark to the Governor of South Carolina: "It's a long time between drinks." So they went down the spiral staircase into the dark, cool bar-room of the "Old White," fragrant with the odor of mountain mint, and ordered juleps, compounded according to a time-honored formula: purest French brandy, old-fashioned cut-loaf sugar, limestone water, crushed ice, and young mint. Many other minutiæ of history are reflected in the annals of White Sulphur. As Charles Dudley Warner once said:

> The White Sulphur has been for the better part of a century, as everybody knows, the typical Southern resort, the rendezvous of all that was most characteristic in the society of the whole South, the meeting place of its politicians, the haunt of its belles, the arena of gayety, intrigue and fashion. If tradition is to be believed, here in years gone by were concocted the measures that were subsequently deployed for the government of the country at Washington, here historic matches were made, here beauty had triumphs that were the

talk of a generation, here hearts were broken at a ball and mended in Lovers' Walk, and here fortunes were nightly lost and won.

Lovers' Walk was one of a number of sylvan promenades at White Sulphur. Others were significantly labeled Courtship Maze, Lovers' Rest, and Acceptance Way to Paradise. Saratoga simply had to do something to offset all this, and so had its "Courting Yard," while the hotels installed "proposal sofas" in various sequestered nooks. Most of the leading resorts in their advertisements emphasized this important attraction. Even the press-agent of stern and rock-bound Nahant, in the heart of Puritan land, dwelt eloquently on the theme of love and Nahant's superiority as a haunt of "the fickle goddess." Said he:

> At this time [evening] the ladies and gentlemen, with their little responsibilities, generally repair to the long drawing-room. Some of the nimble fingers are always ready for the piano-forte, and some of the nimble feet are ever ready for the dance, and thus the evening's social pleasures are commenced. The young people play, dance and sing, while those who choose enjoy the familiar conversation, enlived by delicate and sparkling wit. The senior part of the company congregate in groups, while many a soft word passes between those of fewer years, and who are more sensible to the mild influences of love. There is a fashion in everything, and not less in young love than in other things. Fashion is, in some sense, the life of love. People must not be unfashionable. But we prove our position syllogistically thus: fashion is true taste, (or ought to be); true taste is lovely; whatever is lovely is the life of love; why then should not Nahant be the peculiar abode of the fickle goddess? Lovely in itself, it is, for a season, the favorite resort of young hearts, worshipping at the shrine of the blind goddess.[7]

Life was not a very gay affair at American resorts back in their earliest days. From the latter years of the eighteenth century, when resort life was just in its beginnings, on down to about 1825, mere pleasure did not count.

Health was the all-important thing, and one had to be an invalid, or pretend to be one, to qualify for a trip to the seashore or springs. After about 1825 health became more and more a secondary matter. The health pretext lived on, and is by no means non-existent today, its newest vogue being that wholesome form of sun-worship which produces a heavy coat of tan on as much of the body as the law will permit one to expose. Nowadays the quest for health and pleasure go hand in hand; back at the beginning of the nineteenth century Americans went " to the springs " solely to drink water, and they drank it in great allopathic doses, on a sort of kill-or-cure basis, like the " sad bores " whom John King found at Stafford Springs when he visited the place in 1840, after it had become old-fashioned and run down. King's "sad bores" were regular Connecticut invalids. "They drank, really without exaggeration, twenty-eight tumblers of water each day," he said.[8] They were evidently of the same type that a British visitor had found at Stafford Springs some thirty years earlier, " quaffing stupendous quantities of water " and otherwise leading a dolorous existence.

> The evenings at the Springs [he wrote] were generally spent by the young women in singing hymns, of which a favorite one was called the Garden Hymn, beginning, " The Lord is to His Garden come," &c. They sing hymns because they are more familiar with the words and tunes of these than with those of songs; and because they are accustomed to sing them in parts. A clergyman happening to come among us, prayers, hymns and chapters of the Bible were quoted before breakfast.[9]

The religious resorts, which are still fairly numerous in this country, are a heritage of those days when all American resorts — even Saratoga Springs, where the first temperance society was organized, in 1808 — were chiefly religious in tone. When the forces of the devil began to contaminate the retreats of the pious, the latter went elsewhere and established new resorts, taking care to control them so completely that they could keep satanic corruption out. Thus was invented a type of resort wholly peculiar to America, the "camp-meeting" type, combining health, pleasure, and salvation, of which Ocean Grove, New Jersey, controlled by the Methodists, is today an outstanding example. Several efforts have been made (the latest in 1827) to break down Ocean Grove's "antiquated fifty-year-old rules" by which the governing Methodist authorities keep a tight rein on all things, but these efforts have been of no avail. One of the outstanding resort hostelries of today which still maintain rigid rules is the Lake Mohonk Mountain House, in Ulster County, New York, where there are no Sunday arrivals or departures and where daily prayers are still in order. The severity of life at religious resorts has, however, relaxed considerably in recent decades.

Saratoga was perhaps the first resort to shake off the dismal air of piety and hypocrisy that enshrouded all American resorts. Probably because of the fame of its mineral springs, and its proximity to that stronghold of Beelzebub, New York, it became infested with a profane element earlier than other places, and resort proprietors soon began catering to this element. Saratoga had been a rather painfully spiritless place up to about 1820, but about that time it began to perk up and take on a mild air of liveliness. Driving in buggies and coaches, drinking water, and listening to music had been the chief worldly pastimes. Now cards, billiards, and dancing, all terrible instruments of perdition, were introduced. Compared to its later years, Saratoga was still a dull, tame place, but a guide-book of 1825 was able to assert that "the minerals of Saratoga and the healing virtues of its Springs are not the only nor the principal objects which draw to its sands the thousands who annually flock thither." [10] And a local rhymster says:

Of all the gay places the world can afford,
By gentle and simple for pastime adored,
Fine balls and fine singing, fine buildings and springs,
Fine rides and fine views, and a thousand fine things
(Not to mention the sweet situation and air),
What place with these Springs can ever compare?
First in manners, in dress, and in fashion to shine,
Saratoga, the glory must ever be thine!

Saratoga's happy-go-lucky manner made it all the more attractive, and the size of its crowds grew constantly. They were a democratic welter of visitors, the vulgar and the genteel all jumbled together. As our guide-book booster said, the crowd included "ministers of state, judges, generals, parsons, philosophers, wits, poets, players, fops, fiddlers and buffoons." They danced and flirted and gambled, and they drove madly about in showy equipages with their equally showy lady friends. By 1835 Saratoga had become an acknowledged center of gambling. Amusements of the Coney Island type were introduced at about this time, and Saratoga gave little evidence of having been the birthplace of the temperance movement.[11] John Featherstonaugh, when he opened the Covent Garden House in 1835, announced that, in addition to his regular hotel accommodations, he had a restaurant " where ladies and gentlemen will be served at all hours, with whatever they may desire." In the true flavor of announcements of those days Featherstonaugh's advertisement said:

> Attached to it [the hotel] is a fine garden laid out with great taste, and filled with a variety of trees and shrubbery, in which can be had at all times ice cream, confectionary, fruits, wines, and other refreshments of the choicest kinds.
>
> Also a great variety of amusements, such as cosmorama, solar telescope, carousal, swinging boat, billiards and bowling alleys.
>
> The garden will be illuminated every fine evening, and concerts

of music very frequently, in which boarders will have free access.

N. B. — This establishment will be found particularly eligible for single gentlemen and families with children."[12]

Saratoga's popularity at this period may be judged from an item which appeared in the Saratoga *Sentinel* of that year: "The number of strangers arrived here last week cannot have been less than 2,000; among whom were Gov. Wolfe of Pennsylvania, and several other gentlemen of distinction."[13] Even with this comparatively small number (as numbers go today) Saratoga was the greatest resort of them all, its nearest rival being Cape May. Saratoga hotel rates then, and for several seasons thereafter, were ten to twelve dollars a week, American plan, and a dollar and a half to two dollars a day, at the best hotels. Other houses charged from four to seven dollars a week, and a dollar or a dollar and a quarter a day.[14]

One of the popular amusements at Saratoga at this period was the "circular railway," which had cars "resembling the light body of a gig." Each car was provided with a seat for a lady and a gentleman, and an annalist of the day relates that "with such ease the gentleman gives power to the movement that both cars go flying round with the velocity of the wind, passing each other as feathered arrows, while a thousand fashionable promenaders, chatting and laughing, fill up the ground; the scene is truly joyous and animating." The chronicler added that " all who visit the Springs can partake of this amusement, as it is exhilarating, and a diversion in every respect unobjectionable." There was also a platform of "flying horses," thirteen bowling-alleys, plenty of billiard-tables, and much dancing. Regular assemblies and cotillion parties cost a dollar and a half to four dollars, while the "Champagne Balls" cost five dollars. The two leading hotels, Congress Hall and the United States, shared the services of a band of Negro musicians, which played alternately for tea and dinner at each hotel. Band music had been introduced as early as 1822.[15]

The promenading and driving had become a spectacular feature of Saratoga life by 1830. The promenaders were "dressed fit to kill" and the livery rigs were showy. A guidebook of 1840 states that "not less than $35,000 worth of livery property is owned for the strangers' use." Those who did not ride horseback drove in coaches, barouches, curricles, and gigs. The famous Madame Jumel was one of these. She lived extravagantly at the United States Hotel for several years, but her Paris gowns, her many jewels, and her lofty airs failed to win her admittance to the inner circle of the fashionables. She was a scandalous woman, the reputed mistress of the heartily hated Aaron Burr, and the self-righteous snobs seldom overlooked an opportunity to snub and humiliate her. They roared with laughter when Tom Camel, a Negro, garbed in a low-cut gown in imitation of Madame, and fanning himself with a huge ostrich fan, bowed and curtsied to the crowds as he was driven in a full-liveried carriage, with outriders, directly behind the carriage in which Madame drove each day to Saratoga Lake. When Madame Jumel discovered what was happening, she threatened and pleaded, but to no avail. The town louts had been engaged to teach her a lesson and so followed her until she returned to the hotel. The lesson evidently was well learned. Madame Jumel never spent another season at the Springs.[16]

Gayety increased at Saratoga from year to year, yet as late as 1843 it was not completely victorious over piety and decorum. A staff correspondent of the New York *Evening Post*, speaking of the crowded condition of the hotels in that year, said: "Union Hall, which is a sort of moral place of entertainment, where they every morning read the Bible, say prayers and drink spring water, does not look so rubicund and jolly as its more gay and dissipated neighbors." Five years later Saratoga became a racing-center. On July 4, 1848, Patten and Cole opened a racecourse, offering purses of from fifty to two hundred dollars "and other purses as liberal as the proprietors can afford." There were trotting and other track events throughout July and August, two or three days a week.[17] Racing and gambling became Saratoga's chief attractions. After the Civil War Congressman John Morrissey's elegant palace of chance, and the racecourse that the Saratoga Association opened in 1863, drew enormous crowds.[18] But the aristocracy was conspicuous by its absence. It was going elsewhere. As one observer said:

> Saratoga is a species of very Yankeefied Tunbridge Wells. Few really respectable people are to be seen about, except such as come for a day to see the place, as shoddy reigns supreme; and duels, elopements and worse things are of constant occurrence. . . . You see men here, dressed in the loudest style of Franco-Anglo-American fashion, driving four-in-hand drags filled with ladies of questionable virtue . . . and then the scenes in the gambling houses at night and the language used would require the pencil of a Hogarth and the pen of the recording angel.[19]

The racing is all that is left of Saratoga as a resort, except for those who go there to drink mineral water. August, the big Santa Claus month for the hotel-keepers in the days of Saratoga's ascendancy, has for many years been the only big money month for them. Throughout the rest of the year Saratoga is a rather dead place. It still has its long elm- and pine-shaded roads, shadier than ever; its gingerbread hotels, with their high and wide verandas; and its quaint mid-Victorian cottages; but the rich parvenus and the fast crowd, "capable of every prodigality and immorality," shun it like poison.

WATER, WATER EVERYWHERE

Although Saratoga's variety and abandon and cosmopolitanism were never equaled elsewhere, other resorts did not let Saratoga have a monopoly of high life, nor were they slow to follow in her evil footsteps. All the other resorts of general popularity quickly began to imitate Saratoga's unholy enterprise, even Nahant, which as early as 1830 had a billiard hall ("Greek temple style"), bowling-alleys, and dancing. The gayety at Cape May in the days before the Civil War, when Cape May was in a class by itself as a seashore resort, was the nearest approach to that of Saratoga. After the war Cape May did not keep pace with Saratoga in this respect. Each resort — they were close rivals — had its gambling, its fast driving, and other concomitants of high life, its catch-penny amusements *à la* Coney, its enormous piazza'd and balconied hotels, its celebrated visitors, and its belles and beaux. And each quivered and shook under the sound and fury of blaring brass bands. Three or four noted military bands played at Saratoga. A newspaper correspondent at Cape May in 1851 said: "Every hotel has a band, each conducted by a famous leader. There is a torrent of music." The Annapolis Naval Academy band was for many years one of the big attractions at Cape May. Military bands continued to be a premier attraction at resorts down to the end of the century and later. Many of the present generation remember when Paine's fireworks and the bands conducted by Pat Gilmore and John Philip Sousa drew vast throngs to Manhattan and Brighton Beaches.[20]

The beaches had their special advantages over Saratoga and other inland resorts. They afforded a better escape from city heat, and the pleasure of a dip in the ocean was an irresistible lure to many. The bathing-suits, even though they were not so scant as those of today, gave the belles and beaux a chance to display their sex appeal to good advantage. There was also a special form of beach merriment of carnival-like spirit that enlivened the daytime hours.

The frolicsome nature of the bathing parties is indicated by the historian of Cape May, who relates a story of how the flappers of long ago cut off locks of Henry Clay's hair. Clay, then at the height of his fame, was a guest of Richard Smith Ludlam, Mine Host of the old Mansion House, for several weeks in 1847. He liked to go in bathing and " went into the water as often as twice a day. The ladies would

BATHING SCENE — *From Leslie's Weekly. Aug. 1, 1857*

catch him and with a pair of scissors, carried for just that purpose, clip locks from his head to remember him by," says the writer. "When he returned to Washington his hair was very short indeed."[21] A correspondent of the New York *Herald* who visited the cape in 1853 gives us further insight into the playful liveliness of the beach parties:

> I tried to nap this morning about 11 o'clock, soon after my arrival, but my heavy eyelids were scarcely closed before I was startled with the merry shouts of a hundred voices, and looking out of my window, I was still more startled by the scene before me. I do not believe that Franconi's Hippodrome ever presents a gayer, more grotesque and animated scene than I witnessed. Hundreds of bathers,

clad in garments of every shape and color — green, blue, orange, red and white — were gayly disporting before me, and within a few yards of my window. The blooming girl, the matronized yet blushing maiden, the dignified mamma, all were playing, dancing, romping and shouting together, as if they were all of one age and were all alive with one feeling. I noticed several ladies of admirable shapes, " whose forms Praxiteles might worship," most engagingly and fittingly clad, slowly promenading on the beach before they " tempted the briny wave." Oh! ye happy waves, what a blissful destiny is yours, when you can enclasp and kiss such lovely forms. The most conspicuous gent was a noble darky, who sported any quantity of red cloth and gilt lace. He had in charge several lovely girls, " white as pearls," whom he bathed and ducked with a gallantry and grace which would have honored a Broadway exquisite.[22]

Beach revelry of similar nature prevailed at other shore resorts. A historian of Newport mentions that the " gayly appareled beaux and belles vied in fantastic tricks, making the air ring with their careless laughter."

But the music of their merry voices [he adds] and the roaring of the surf are occasionally made to play the second part to the screams of some timid girl, who would fain buffet with the waves, did her courage admit. She is vanquished at the outset and with the first wave that caresses her tiny feet vanishes forever her small stock of courage; while her companions fearlessly ride the billows' crest; now floating lightly on the ocean's heaving bosom; now diving beneath the surface, in search of old Neptune's sparkling treasures.[23]

Newport was second only to Cape May and Long Branch as a beach resort of general popularity in the middle decades of the nineteenth century. It began to win favor in the latter 1830's when two little hotels, the Bellevue and Whitfield's (later called the Touro House), sufficed for strangers. Newport's most famous hotel, the Ocean House, which George William Curtis called " a huge, yellow pagoda factory," opened in 1845, after which, as Curtis said, " a floodtide of fashion rose along Narragansett Bay." [24] Soon thereafter the Aquidneck House was built, and in the city of Newport — which then and until 1900 was one of Rhode Island's capitals — the Perry House and the United States Hotel kept open all year. Newport was quite different then from what it has been for the past thirty years or more, during which time it has had no summer hotel, but is controlled exclusively by wealthy owners of its shore line, whose cottages now monopolize the scene. The character of Newport in its rowdy days is rather harshly painted by a correspondent who, in 1853, lamented that fast driving was more in favor than loving looks.

> The destiny of this place [he said] may now be considered fixed. From a casual watering place, the resort of the invalid and the student, it has become the haunt of the vicious, the frivolous and debauched. Fashion, handmaid of vice, has set her seal upon the escutcheon of this town.[25]

But Newport outlived all this. Gradually the undesirables began to go elsewhere, leaving the historic island (ideal for exclusiveness) to high society, who finally came into full possession of it. Even before the summer hotels disappeared, Newport had taken on its present tone. The *Hotel Mail* of 1879 called it the Scarborough of America, noted the absence of "mushroom aristocracy," and said that in refinement and elegance it was "without a rival and an equal." [26]

Nahant was the only other resort along the New England coast that attained national prominence in the first half of the nineteenth century. Nahant got its first summer family in 1787 and its first small hotel in 1805, but did not become widely popular until about fifteen years later.[27] Nahant's fame was completely faded from memory, for it ha'd begun to sink into oblivion before the Civil War, despite the fact that it had a battalion of New England literati as its voluntary press agents, including Mrs. Sigourney, one of America's first poetesses, who ballyhoo'd it in prose and verse.[28] "The great hotel for the entertainment of visitants," she wrote, " is near the southeast point of the promontory. It was built in 1820 of the native stone by which it is surrounded, and contains a sufficient number of apartments for a multitude of guests. From the double piazza that engirdles it, is a succession of grand and extensive prospects, and a bracing ocean atmosphere. When long rains prevail, the mist enwraps it in a curtain, like a great ship in the midst of the sea."[29]

Some of Nahant's voluntary press agents were men after Barnum's own heart. Indeed, the great Phineas T. may very well have learned from them his first lesson in the technique of stimulating public interest, for they invented the first great publicity hoax of the century. This was the fearful Nahant sea-serpent, which created a sensation throughout the country and got Nahant a voluminous amount of space in the press of the day. Like Barnum's mermaid, it was good for several seasons, and it proved just as conclusively that the public likes to be humbugged. The advent of this imaginary monster produced " an intense, a fearful excitement among all classes in Boston," according to James Lloyd Homer, one of Nahant's historians, himself a Bostonian.[30] " Salem witchcraft was no touch to it in one respect. It caused every old lady in Boston to shake in her shoes." Homer added that many Bostonians expected the serpent would leave its native element and wreak devastation ashore.

The sea-serpent story first appeared in the *Columbian Centinel,* of Boston. It was written by Marshall Prince, who, we learn, " was near-sighted and at times somewhat passionate and enthusiastic — just the man to see a sea-serpent." Homer says that Prince " made many remarkable discoveries with the naked eye, but when he brought his telescope to bear on it, ye gods, what discoveries he made." The Boston *Gazette,* the *Palladium,* and other newspapers fell for the bait and began to be filled with sea-serpent affidavits from fishermen and the crews of Eastern coasters. These affidavits, Homer assures us, " would fill a volume of 500 octavo pages." Several expeditions to capture the monster were fitted out, at Boston, Salem, Marblehead, Gloucester, and other places, and the prices of whaleboats and harpoons "fluctuated like railway and other fancy stocks." But the crowning evidence of the success of the hoax was when a large shed was built near Faneuil Hall " for the reception of his majesty and the public." A Captain Rich, who was more gifted than the Father of his Country in some respects, reported he had harpooned the serpent, the harpoon sinking into the flesh two feet. Still the serpent got away, as so many other big fish have done. When newspapers elsewhere suggested, rather frankly, that the sea-serpent story was a myth, the *Centinel* editor hotly resented the imputations of these scoffers. But in time even Bostonians began to doubt the existence of the serpent, and eventually the story lost its potency as a publicity aid. A creature that was defined in at least one dictionary as "an enormous marine animal of serpent-like form, seen and described by credulous sailors, imaginative landsmen and common liars," could hardly be expected to survive forever, even in the minds of the old ladies of Boston.[31]

Just which place is entitled to the distinction of having been America's first resort is a matter of doubt. Several resorts still going strong, several others now abandoned, existed in later colonial years. Stafford Springs, Connecticut, probably dates further back than any other. Pilgrim colonists learned of it from the Indians. The Yellow Springs in Buck County, Pennsylvania, and the Bath Springs at Bristol, Pennsylvania, were both discovered in 1722.[32] Down in

Virginia the Cavaliers began going to Sweet Springs about 1750; and Hot Springs, Virginia, is said to have had accommodations for visitors as early as 1766. Invalids made their way to White Sulphur Springs at about the same time. The chalybeate spring at the summit of Schooley's Mountain, near Hackettstown, New Jersey, attracted New Yorkers a hundred and fifty years ago, and so did the near-by Orange springs. In Maine the Poland springs were visited by ailing Yankees long before the old Mansion House was built in 1794. Lebanon Springs in Columbia County, New York, had the original Columbia Hall as early as 1792 and was frequented long before that year. Saratoga's springs were discovered in 1767, but it was not until about thirty years later that a log tavern was built for visitors. A letter written in 1791 mentions three log houses at Saratoga, all so full of visitors that the writer had difficulty in finding accommodations. The same was true of Ballston Spa, near by.[33] It was at about this time that Benjamin Douglas, father of Stephen A. Douglas, built a log tavern there.

These were but a few of the mineral springs that bubbled forth for the benefit of the ailing. There were numerous others. Every state had several. Wherever there was a spring in an accessible location, there a resort was bound to be started, if the owner had any enterprise and if the analysis of the water showed it to contain magnesia, iodine, or other beneficial ingredients. It was seemingly not difficult to get a favorable analysis and the endorsement of physicians. Resorts vied with one another in extolling the qualities of their water. There seemed to be hardly any disease that spring water would not cure, and the ailing public was willing to believe any exaggerated claims. Boosters for the seashore resorts sometimes tried to undermine this faith in spring water. " Faith in the healing virtues of the various mineral springs is ludicrous," said a champion of the seashore. " A man, within the writer's immediate observation, attended daily the high spring at Ballston to immerse in its waters his forefinger, which had been rendered permanently stiff, apparently by a local injury. This was an affection of long standing, but was seriously believed to be within the limits of the curative effects of the spring." This, in 1821, was from the pen of a devotee of Nahant. " It is hardly to be expected, nor is it desirable," he added, somewhat sadly, "that Nahant should suddenly acquire the reputation that the various mineral springs of the country enjoy." [34]

Seashore-hotel men who tried to put in a stock of barreled water from Saratoga's most famous spring, the Congress, met with rebuff from " Dr." John Clarke, the owner, who in 1819 had introduced the first soda fountain in New York City. " Dr." Clarke refused to ship Congress water to rival places. The seaside, he said, with his tongue in his cheek, had its own attractions and he would be a fool to give its hotels an opportunity to advertise that they had " Congress Water on Draught." [35] Long Branch countered by having her own home-brewed Saratoga water, by the simple process of christening a couple of springs in the locality the " Saratoga Springs." These springs had been discovered by a Philadelphia physician in 1828, subsequently had become lost, were rediscovered a few years later, and were promptly analyzed. The analysis was, of course, highly favorable, and physicians wrote long and impressive endorsements. Newport also had its own springs, highly beneficial, and Cape May, unable to get Congress water, laid in an assorted stock from other highly recommended places. Why go to Saratoga when one could have all its advantages plus the seashore at one and the same time? In reply Saratoga cried: " Beware of musketoes and ague. Don't go where you'll get malaria and chills and fever." There was a merry warfare of this sort between resorts for many years, and especially during the quarter-century following the Civil War, when a large number of new resorts sprang up. It was toward the end of this period that Atlantic City began to attain prominence and was accused by rivals of using undue medical influence.[36]

Atlantic City had been one of America's minor resorts — very minor — for many years, unable, up to about 1880, to make much of a dent in Cape May's great popularity. Cape May was perhaps the oldest seashore resort in the country, and for fifty years was second only to Saratoga in the number and prominence of its visitors and the number, size, and pretension of its hotels. Before the Revolution sailing-ships occasionally took groups of Philadelphians to the cape, while others went by stage or drove down in their dearborns along the interminable sandy road from Camden. Farmers accommodated the visitors at first, and finally one or two small inns were built. In 1801 Postmaster Ellis Hughes of Cape Island built Atlantic Hall, a barnlike place said to have been composed of one large room, which was partitioned off with sheets into two rooms at night, the men sleeping on one side, and the women on the other. Mine Host Hughes advertised in the Philadelphia *Daily Aurora* of June 30, 1801:

> The public are respectfully informed that the subscriber has prepared himself for entertaining company who use sea bathing, and he is accommodated with extensive house room, with fish, oysters, crabs and good liquors. Care will be taken of gentlemen's horses. The situation is beautiful, just at the confluence of the Delaware Bay with the Ocean, in sight of the Light House, and affords a view of the shipping which enters and leaves the Delaware. Carriages may be driven along the margin of the ocean for miles, and the wheels will scarcely make an impression on the sand; the slope of the shore is so regular that persons may wade a great distance. It is the most delightful spot the citizens can retire to in the hot season.

Cape May's popularity grew rapidly after the War of 1812. Her first spacious hotel, Congress Hall, was built by

Thomas H. Hughes in 1816. It was a one-story frame building, with lots of gingerbread and yellow paint, but no lath and plaster. It boasted a frontage of three hundred feet, and wings two hundred feet long. It burned down two years later and was rebuilt. A number of smaller hotels were built in succeeding years, and in 1832 Smith Ludlam built the Mansion House, of only one story, but covering four acres.[37] In the same year Israel Leaming built the Ocean House, also quite sizable. They were the first with lath and plaster and with accomodations of a better sort. By this time Cape May had become a country-wide rage, and in 1840 four more large hostelries were opened, including the New Atlantic, the Center and the Delaware houses, and the Washington Hotel. The Columbia Hotel was added to the list in 1846, and in 1850 two more large houses were erected, the National and the White Hall.[38]

Then, in 1853, the Mount Vernon Hotel, greatest of all Cape May's caravansaries, was opened. It was one of the outstanding hostels of the days before the Civil War that helped to spread the fame of "America's marvelous hotel system" over the entire world. And it is the least remembered today, for it had but a brief existence. On the night of September 5, 1856, it burned down and Philip Cain, three members of his family, and the housekeeper lost their lives.[39] Only the front section, four stories high and three hundred feet long, and one wing, three stories high and five hundred feet long, had been completed. A second wing of similar size was to have been added the following season. The completed part had 482 rooms, capable of accommodating 2,100 guests, and was the world's largest hotel at that time.[40] A writer in *Chambers' Journal* of 1854 said of it: "It is a hotel so stupendous that an Englishman has some difficulty in believing that such a structure *can* be a hotel. It exceeds in size anything we can even dream of as a hotel in England." It was all the more unbelievable, he added, because Cape May is not a city, nor the suburb of a city, but "just a quiet watering place."[41]

The Mount Vernon was, if the writer in *Chambers' Journal* can be trusted, the first hotel that had a bath with every room. "Among the luxuries of the place is that every bedroom has a bath attached, with hot and cold water always laid on," he wrote. The hotel also had a sumptuous bridal chamber; and its dining-hall, 425 feet long and 60 wide, took first rank in size. Three thousand diners could be seated in it. The Mount Vernon's architecture was an imitation of the new front of Buckingham Palace, towers and all, but unlike Buckingham Palace it had balconies and a piazza the entire length of the front and side.

The Mount Vernon never was rebuilt. Congress Hall, with its "grand arched dining hall," two hundred feet long and forty-five wide, became the leading hotel and remained so until the Pennsylvania Railroad built the Stockton House, with four hundred rooms, in 1868.[42] Other important hotels at that time were the United States, National Atlantic Hall, the Ocean House, the West End, the Sea Breeze House, and Columbia Hall. These survived until the fire of November 9, 1878, which swept away forty acres of buildings. The Stockton alone escaped the flames. It still stands, and so does the fourth Congress Hall, a low, rambling red-brick structure, opened in 1879.

Cape May remains "just a quiet watering place," with many memories of the days of its greatness. And no resort has more radiant memories. Without a railroad until 1863, nearly thirty years after Saratoga had two railroads, it still drew crowds as great as those of Saratoga, and they were crowds of a more dignified and distinguished character. Its gayness never descended to notorious profligacy. It was chosen more often than any other place as a "summer White House." President Franklin Pierce spent the last summer of his term, 1856, there, and James Buchanan, his successor, spent the summer of 1859 at Congress Hall. Grant lived there during the summers of 1874 and 1875, and all the members of his Cabinet were with him, attending weekly cabinet meetings in the parlors of Congress Hall. President Benjamin Harrison occupied the " Presidents' Cottage " at Cape May Point each summer of his term (1889–93) and made Congress Hall his executive office. Other Presidents — among them John Tyler and Chester Arthur — were at least occasional visitors during their terms. Garfield and others were among the crowds before they were elected.

Cape May's palmy days corresponded in time with those of Saratoga, though Saratoga's race-track continued to bring followers of the turf after its other attractions had faded away. The two rival resorts had risen at about the same time. Saratoga's first hotel of any size was a three-story house for seventy guests, built in 1801 by Gideon Putnam, who cut the pine lumber for it on his farm. He called it Union Hall. It was the forerunner of the present Grand Union. Within the next few years other unpretentious hotels were built. The original Congress Hall was erected in 1811, and the first United States in 1823. A guide-book of 1830 listed these three and the Pavilion Hotel as Saratoga's best.[43] Congress Hall, the largest, could accommodate " nearly 200 visitants." [44] These were enlarged after the railroads came, in 1833 and 1835, and other long, low wooden hotels, bristling with cupolas, balconies, cornices, and other early Victorian baroque, were erected. Fire swept them away, one by one, Washington Hall being the last to go. Taller, larger, more ornate hotels took their place, the old Clarendon, built just before the Civil War, being the finest of this group. The third stage in hotel construction at Saratoga came after the Civil War, when several grand brick edifices of large capacity were built. The new Congress Hall, costing seven hundred thousand dollars, was the first, and the next was the Grand Union, which, with a later enlargement, cost nearly two million dollars. It had a dining-room 306 feet long and 70 wide and could serve twelve hundred guests at a sitting. The dinner menus included more than fifty dishes. The third was the present United States Hotel. The original United States burned down on June 18, 1865, and its successor was opened on June 20, 1875, under the management

UNITED STATES HOTEL, Long Branch, N. J.

of Congressman James M. Marvin. It had 768 single rooms and 65 parlor-and-bedroom suites and was the world's largest.[45]

Long Branch, New Jersey, was Saratoga's chief rival as a racing-center in the 1870's and 1880's, but, generally speaking, Long Branch never was so prominent a resort as Saratoga and Cape May, nor did its career cover so long a period. True, its first boarding-house was established in 1788, by Allison Perot of Philadelphia, but in 1820 Ocean Avenue was still a narrow wagon-track with only six buildings on it, including the Conover House, kept by Cornelius Lane, and Aunt Peggy Wardwell's boarding-house. Philadelphians were the sole clientele, and Long Branch was a saintly place, with blue laws. In 1828 Obadiah Sayrs built the Sayrs House, with sixty rooms, and in 1832 the Widow Ferguson opened the Lawn House. Many cottages were being built. Long Branch equaled Newport in fine summer homes. About this time New Yorkers began going by boat to Red Bank, and thence by stage to the Branch. A writer of 1834 mentions the good beds, fine dinners, and choice wines.[46] What had

SURF BATHERS, at Long Branch, 1870

been a sedate watering-place, with grace at each meal, hymn-singing in the evening, and prayer-meetings, began to take on a frivolous tone in the 1830's. Card-playing, billiards, bowling, dancing, and fast driving on the beach were introduced. One suspects it was the passion for fast driving that made Long Branch a Mecca of the worldly crowd. The smooth hard beaches were tempting places for this sport. Hardly anywhere else, except on city streets, could it be indulged in.

Long Branch remained, however, rather primitive and unexciting until about 1850. Just before the Civil War it began to attain some prominence. The first pretentious hotel was the Mansion House, opened July 1, 1846.⁴⁷ The National Hotel opened about four years later, the United States in 1852, and the Metropolitan in 1854. Another hotel of this period was the Howland House, an enlargement of the Sayrs House, which Henry Howland, the man whose enterprise brought Long Branch to the front, had bought in 1843. The last of Long Branch's pre-war hotels, Congress Hall, was built in 1859. After the war Long Branch came into its own. The Stetson House ⁴⁸ was opened in 1862

VISITORS GOING TO LONG BRANCH

and the Continental in 1866, and about 1870 the Monmouth Park racecourse began drawing greater crowds. The New Jersey Central Railroad made the resort more accessible to " the panting thousands of the great metropolis " when it opened a short route from New York on June 15, 1874. It afforded, as a resort directory of 1875 said, " a cheap and easy release from the narrow streets of the city, and equally narrow pursuits of gain, to the soul-saving worship of the great and good God through the never-quiet, never-ceasing roar of the mighty ocean." ⁴⁹

But Long Branch's high tide of prosperity did not last long. Within a few more years it had begun to go to seed, and its big crowds deserted it. One reason was that the conscience-stricken residents began to invoke the old blue laws, once more making the place strait-laced. Another reason was the rise of the east end of Coney Island. It had taken Coney Island a long time to attain high rank. Commodore Vanderbilt — the old Commodore — had tried, with little success, to popularize Coney in the early 1840's, when he built

ARRIVAL OF TRAIN, at Long Branch, 1873

a fine hotel there called the Oceanic and installed Charles M. Rogers as proprietor. Rogers had formerly managed the pretentious Stanwix Hall at Albany. He advertised that Coney had " the best bathing beach in the world " and ran stages every hour from the Brooklyn end of the ferry. When the Oceanic burned down, in 1851, the Commodore built another, but when it, too, fell a victim to flames, in 1855, it was not rebuilt. Down at the west end of the island, where the Oceanic stood, a lot of cheap boarding-houses and small hotels sprang up. They were filled with New

York's roughest and toughest element, who had taken Coney over for themselves. Soon after the Civil War this crowd grew rapidly, the Iron Steamboat Company having established a line to the beach. Ramshackle bed-houses, cheap restaurants, shooting-galleries, and beer gardens were built,

THREE-CARD MONTE PLAYERS, at Coney Island, 1867

and three-card monte swindlers planted their tables along the beach. Freedom reigned supreme and Coney got a very unsavory reputation.

Meanwhile the eastern end of the long beach remained barren and neglected, except for a small family hotel, where Austin Corbin, banker, in 1874 engaged rooms for his wife and little daughter, who was ill. Corbin wanted them to be near the city, so that he could visit them each day. His visits resulted in the formation of a company to build a magnificent resort hotel, the Manhattan Beach, which opened in 1877 under the management of Colonel Sam Keefer. It became fashionable immediately and was enlarged in 1878 and again in 1879. The Oriental Hotel, with even more grandeur, also was built, opening in 1880, and a third large hotel, the Brighton Beach, opened in 1878, with James H. Breslin, of the old Gilsey House, as proprietor. The rival hotels spent

MANHATTAN BEACH HOTEL, Coney Island, 1879

money lavishly to draw the crowds. It was at this time that Coney began to take on its present character. The first Paine's fireworks, set pieces showing "The Last Days of Pompeii," were displayed in 1883, and in later years the displays included "The Battle of Gettysburg," "The Burning of Rome," and other subjects. Set pieces became a standard feature at resorts and for fairs and special celebrations. Patrick S. Gilmore and his band, with Levy, the cornet soloist, played at Manhattan Beach from the beginning, and John Philip Sousa with his United States Marine Band was an attraction a few years later. It was there that *El Capitan* and several other famous Sousa marches were first played.⁵⁰ Early in the 1880's the attractions included a ballet of thirty-five dancers, seventy soldiers impersonating the Roman Guard, and a male chorus. There were daily balloon ascensions and occasionally a prize-fight. Coney had become nationally famous within three or four years after the opening of the Manhattan Beach Hotel, and no trip to New

ORIENTAL HOTEL, Coney Island, 1879

York was complete without a visit to Coney. Aristocrats and the common herd all went to the island. As a Coney poet sang:

> " For snobs ascend to feelings democratic,
> When they *descend* to Brighton's sports aquatic."

The *Hotel Mail* records that on one Sunday of July 1878 the crowd numbered more than sixty thousand. The disreputable west end of the beach drew up to the east end, but high wire fences kept them out of the private grounds where the big attractions were offered. It cost a nickel to get through the gates. Some of the riff-raff preferred to spend their nickels for schooners of beer. Competition in the form of fat ladies, tattooed ladies, two-headed boys, Ferris wheels, roller coasters, and what not quickly lined Surf Avenue, and hot-dog stands were everywhere. Coney's aristocratic hotels soon turned into white elephants. By 1895 Coney was about through as a rendezvous of the classes, but was just getting its stride as a playground of the masses.

The success of the Coney experiment encouraged a company known as the Rockaway Park Association to spend $1,250,000 on a huge hotel at Rockaway Beach. The hotel was never opened, except in August 1881. As it was nearing completion, the company got into financial difficulties, and the hotel remained vacant for several years. Finally it was torn down. The metropolitan summer crowds have since overflowed the Rockaway coast. Rockaway has, in fact, been a resort since 1802, when Jeremiah Vanderbilt kept a hotel there, and in 1833 a company consisting of Governor John A. King, Mayor Philip Hone, and others built the Marine Pavilion Hotel, where wealthy New York families spent the summer until it burned down in 1864.[51]

At about the time Coney Island rose in popular favor, Atlantic City, destined to be the country's greatest watering-place, was just beginning to supersede Cape May, Long Branch, and other seaside towns. Until after 1880 Atlantic City was distinctly second-rate, but after 1880 it came to the front rapidly, until it finally became, as the official sloganeers would have it, " America's Playground, the Mecca of Millions." With its eight-mile boardwalk, its fifteen-million-dollar — more or less — Convention Hall, and its formidable array of hotels of all degrees of magnificence, it is now a convention and recreation center which annually attracts upward of twelve million carefree Americans of every degree of social and financial standing. On a warm midsummer day it is not unusual to see more than half a million people on its beach and boardwalk. " To watch that crowd on parade is to gain a new conception of the leisure, the wealth and the craze for diversion which characterize Twentieth Century America," as one observer has said.[52] The visitors support a permanent population of about seventy thousand, for the hotels, boarding-houses, bath-houses, restaurants, gift and novelty shops — indeed, the whole business fabric of the city — are dependent on the visitors. It is estimated that the average visitor spends ten dollars a day; thus on a banner day the total may run to somewhere near five million dollars. This includes what the visitors spend on all sorts of catchpenny "rackets." A legion of skin-game barkers and pitch men rake in dimes and quarters and dollars by the bushel.

Atlantic City's memories all date from 1900 onward. When Cape May, Saratoga, and other places were at the height of their popularity, Atlantic City was merely a succession of barren sand-heaps and salt swamps. Dr. Jonathan R. Pitney of Philadelphia visited the place in 1845 and decided it could be transformed into "a second Cape May." He convinced other Philadelphians of this, and they organized a company that built a railroad from the Quaker City and bought two hundred acres of Atlantic City land at seventeen dollars an acre. The railroad, the Camden and Atlantic, opened on July 1, 1854, on which date the first train rolled in, with six hundred passengers.[53] Meanwhile a hotel run by Thomas H. Bedloe had been completed. Its first historian described Atlantic City in 1868 as "a fashionable watering place where all may go, and where even the student and the clerk, rejoicing in the leisure of summer holidays, delight to kill the heavily hanging time, as they bask in the sunbeams of the school girls' eyes." It had by this time quite a number of private villas, "carriages at city rates, a thriving railroad and its by no means insignificant commerce." Its all-year population was five hundred, and its summer population several thousand. Its principal hotels were the United States (the largest), the Surf House, the Mansion House, and Congress Hall. Others of lesser importance included the Neptune House, the Alhambra, the Seaside House, the Kentucky House, the Clarendon, the Ashland House, Bedloe's, Glenn's Inlet House, the Chester County House, Light House Cottage, and a number of boarding-houses.

Philadelphians generally remained loyal to Cape May, but as that resort declined in the 1890's, Atlantic City began to grow with renewed vigor. It had always had strong medical and railroad backing and had been for years emphasizing its value as an all-year place of rest and recuperation. In 1902 fire wiped out many of its antiquated hotels, and new ones of modern fireproof type, the best-constructed resort hotels in the country at the time, were erected. Perhaps the first of these was the Marlborough-Blenheim, followed by the Traymore and others. They attracted people of wealth, and Atlantic City's future was assured.

Thanks to the robust condition of their pocketbooks, Americans have always been able to go to resorts in greater numbers than the people of any other country. Economic conditions produced a greater crop of spenders here than elsewhere, and the resorts benefited accordingly. Of course, throughout the nineteenth century there was no such universality of touring and tripping and vacationing as there is today. Nothing better illustrates the far-reaching social changes than the enormous growth of the vacation habit. Vacations and tours were chiefly the prerogative of the well-to-do up to about fifty years ago. The week-end for the multitude was unheard of and Westinghouse's Saturday half-holiday for his workmen was as startling in 1880 as Ford's five-day week was in recent years. "In little more than a generation the vacation has become universal," said an editorial writer in the New York *World* some two or three years ago. "The mechanic — the carpenter or plumber, with his Ford — claims it with the white-collar worker; it is not a privilege, but a right. Few changes have done more to give our civilization a humane and liberal air."

Cheapness of transportation, by steamer and railroad, stimulated the business of resorts. The railroad quickly adopted the steamship lines' excursion-ticket idea and made it possible for greater numbers to go on short trips. By 1850 the vacation resorts were frequented by no inconsiderable portion of the population, and the summer flitting, with trunks of increasing number and size, had become a feature of travel. Excursions gave the great multitude an opportunity to go forth and see some of the great, wide, wonderful world. Packed into day-coaches like sardines, or on steamers far beyond rightful capacity, passengers could ride hundreds of miles for a dollar or two, spend a few hours, or a day or two, in some distant city, or at Saratoga, Newport, Cape May, or Long Branch, and go back home with something to talk about for months to come. With the increase of prosperity and railroad mileage after the Civil War, there came a great growth in the number of resorts and the size of the crowds. " Each year adds to the popularity of summer travel," said a resort directory of 1875. " The vacation fever returns annually with ' the season,' and custom demands that every well-to-do family prepare for it. No class of society is exempt. The mechanic and merchant, the banker and clerk, the student and professional man, are alike affected by its seductive influences, and, in the pleasure it brings, seek that respite from the cares of life which exhausted nature requires."

Another aspect of travel for pleasure in recent years is the great growth of touring by motor. It not only has increased the number of people visiting resorts, but has made the vacation business profitable to thousands of cities and towns that are selling their scenery and historic interest to the nomadic public. Time was when the only sightseeing trips Americans ever made were those to Niagara and Trenton

Falls, near Utica, New York, the Catskills, and the White Mountains of New Hampshire. A hundred years and more ago Niagara, especially, was visited by a great many people who wanted to see the sight. Enough were going there in 1820 to support the Eagle Tavern, built in that year. Later the Cataract House was opened, and in the 1850's the International Hotel was one of America's truly fine hotels. Trenton Falls had a hotel for many years, and the Catskills and White Mountains both were visited by sightseers at about the beginning of the nineteenth century. Abel Crawford, "Patriarch of the Mountains," and his brawny sons built the Notch House in 1803; and in the Catskills the Mountain House, with its long, Corinthian colonnade, perched at the edge of a precipice, was built about 1820. Harriet Martineau, rhapsodizing over the scene, said: "I was more moved by what I saw from the Mountain House than by Niagara itself."

It is impossible to say, with any degree of accuracy, just how extensive the summer and winter resort business has grown to be, but it is a business of mighty volume. Records kept by the *Hotel Management* magazine show that there are about twenty-five hundred summer hotels throughout the country and about six hundred winter hotels. This, of course, does not begin to tell the story, for it includes only those hotels that keep open only during certain seasons. But in addition to these seasonal hotels there are the all-year hotels that exist on a combination of commercial and vacation business, and there are the multitude of summer boarding-houses, cottages, and shacks.

Whereas the resorts of the days before the Civil War were all east of the Alleghenies, except a very few (such as the Harrodsburg Hotel which Dr. Christopher Columbus Graham founded at Harrodsburg, Kentucky, the "Saratoga of the West," in 1820), now they are scattered everywhere throughout the country. Every state has them by the dozens.

WATER, WATER EVERYWHERE

Early in the 1850's resorts began to be established along the shores of the Great Lakes, at Mackinac, Put-in Bay, Cedar Point, and elsewhere, and medicinal springs were soon discovered in distant localities. There were amusement resort centers within easy reach of Chicago, Cleveland, Cincinnati, and all the larger cities for the spendthrift crowds. The two great winter resort centers, Florida and California, both began to attract tourists (other than mere sightseers) in the 1870's. Lake Tahoe was perhaps California's first resort center. About 1880 Coronado Beach began to be popular. A large hotel, comparable with the hotels of the best Eastern resort centers, was built there in the early 1880's. St. Augustine was Florida's farthest south in the 1870's, and Jacksonville was the chief center for visitors who wanted to fish, drive, and escape the rigors of the Northern winter. Trains from the St. Johns River to St. Augustine used to stop to let passengers pick flowers. Miami, Palm Beach, St. Petersburg, Sarasota, and other places were non-existent. At about this time the Virginia coast resorts, such as Old Point Comfort, sprang up.

    The amusements at resorts have undergone considerable change. The belles and beaux have become modernized. Tennis and golf have replaced croquet, and whatever driving is done nowadays is of an entirely different sort from that of 1830. The newest thing is archery golf, played with bows and arrows, instead of with mashies and niblicks. It will probably never replace the old Scotch game. Golf, almost unknown in this country thirty or forty years ago, is now played on some four thousand courses, most of which are connected with country clubs, which are themselves a comparatively new feature of the American scene. There are also many courses connected with swagger hotels. Golf has given some of the old-time resorts a new lease of life, as, for example, White Sulphur. The game will probably be even more enduring than was the old Treadmill.

CHAPTER IX

LAVENDER AND OLD LACE

ONLY a few of the old-time hotels are holding out against the encroachments of time and the onslaughts of competition. All over the country there has been a particularly heavy death-rate among them since the World War. During the past ten years thousands of fine new hotels have been built, in every city, big and little, from Maine to California, and as a result the older houses have been thrown into the discard. Those that have survived and maintained their first-class prestige have generally been remodeled and modernized, but no doubt the weeding-out process will go on as it has done for the past fifty years.

If mere grandeur had been the only factor in hotel-keeping progress, doubtless many of the old-timers would still be in the running. They became antiquated for various reasons, but chiefly it was progress in mechanization that spelled their doom. The old-time inns of England lasted for hundreds of years. Some of those built during the Middle Ages are still doing business. The modern hotel in America has been a highly perishable product, generally with a life-span of less than half a century. The two great early exemplars of hotel grandeur — the Tremont and the Astor houses — managed to keep going somewhat longer than that length of time, because each was closed twice for general overhauling to bring them up to date in mechanical comforts. The grandest of all the old nineteenth-century hotels, the old St. Nicholas in New York, lasted, as was said before, little more than thirty years, closing in 1884.

The changing character of locations — also a result of mechanization — has brought many old hotels to a quick end, especially in New York City. For example, the Knickerbocker Hotel at Broadway and Forty-second Street, where Maxfield Parrish's *Old King Cole* smiled down on a distinguished bar-room, lived as a hotel only from 1906 to 1920, and then became an office building. The Manhattan Hotel at Madison Avenue and Forty-second Street, reputed birthplace of the Manhattan cocktail, became an office building in 1921, at the age of twenty-five, and that stronghold of smug aristocracy the Holland House, one of the noblest of Fifth Avenue's caravansaries, became an office building in January 1920, in its twenty-eighth year.

Some sections of Broadway between Times Square and the Battery are littered with old half-forgotten hotels now given over to the needle trades. One of them, the choice old Prescott House, at Broadway and Spring Street, has hummed with the whirr of sewing-machines for many years. It was built by Captain De Grott, owner of Hudson River steamers, who named it after William H. Prescott, the historian, and opened it with a dinner to the press on July 28, 1853. Reporters said that its glories were " beyond description." It had the distinction of being the first building in America with mosaic tile floors of the type used today. Before that time the marble floors had all been of the tessellated checkerboard variety — alternate large squares of black and white. The entire main floor of the Prescott was done in small tiles of all colors formed into fanciful designs — stars, octagons, swans, peacocks, roses, and various other flora and fauna. Captain De Groot was proud, also, of the fact that, although his hotel had only two hundred rooms, it had "more than twelve miles of water and gas pipe and more than 250 servants." Undoubtedly it was quite a sumptuous hotel. It survived as a hotel until about 1890, but in its latter years was known as the Hotel Diez.[1]

Another famous old hotel, the St. Denis, on Broadway just below Union Square, held out until 1917. It opened in 1852 under the management of Denis Julien, who, in naming it, was able to do honor to himself, the patron saint of Paris, and a palatial trans-Atlantic liner that had just gone into commission. Long ago the Southern belles and gay blades of old Dixie vanished from the grilled balconies of another old down-town New York hotel that still stands — the Planters at Greenwich and Albany streets, where the first Cotton Exchange in America was established. The building, erected in 1823, was put to other uses soon after the Civil War.

Gone, too, is the riotous old Gilsey House, on Broadway just below Greeley Square, for forty years one of New York's most popular houses of call. It has been a busy hive of industry since 1911, and, so far as its exterior goes, is as jaunty as ever. It opened on April 15, 1871, and the merrymakers had such a high old time at the opening reception and dinner that it had to be closed the next day for general repairs and cleaning. Colonel " Jim " (James H.) Breslin was Mine Host of the Gilsey House up to its closing day. It shared honors with the old Fifth Avenue Hotel, from 1884 onward, in being headquarters for Republican politicians.

In other sections of New York there are several survivors of the days before the Civil War, perhaps the most famous of them being the old Occidental Hotel at the Bowery and Broome Street, which was built about 1840 by Governor Yates and is still owned by his descendants. It is still running and is now known as the Commercial. The old Occidental was as elegant as any of them in its day. Its marble floors, its gorgeous bar-room, with the poker room opening off; its pretentious dining-room, its luxurious bedrooms, and its perfection of appointments in all particulars made it a

BANQUET SCENE, in the 1850's. *Dramatic Fund Dinner at the old Metropolitan Hotel, New York*

favorite rendezvous of actors, business men, politicians, Bowery boys, and sports of high degree, including the aristocracy of the gambling fraternity. It was thronged with them day and night, and the game in the poker room was almost continuous. Not so very far from the Occidental stands the old Hotel Everett, on Park Row, the first hotel to have electric lights. It is now called Morrison's Hotel. Samuel H. Crook opened it in 1862 and it was known as Crook's Hotel until 1881, when Everett became proprietor.[2] Near by, on the same street, Sweeny's Hotel still does business under the name of Hall's Hotel. Daniel Sweeny, who built it in 1858, was one of New York's pioneer restaurateurs. Few traces of the olden elegance of these three old hotels remain. They have long been lodging-houses for the floating laborers of down-town New York.

Practically all of New York's great hotels of pre-Civil War days have, however, completely disappeared. The old New York Hotel, rival of the Planters for the Southern trade, closed in 1893, and the Metropolitan, built around Niblo's Garden, where *The Black Crook* first scandalized America, went out of existence in 1895. The old Fifth Avenue, where America's first elevator was installed, passed away in 1908, and with it went the "Amen Corner," where Tom C. Platt, Republican boss, and his fellow politicians held their powwows. Throughout its career it was a nerve-center of political history. Abraham Lincoln went from it to Cooper Union to deliver the speech that started him on the road to the Presidency. Grant's candidacy was discussed at a dinner there in 1867; and later on, Grant and his Cabinet held an official session in the hotel. Roscoe Conkling, Platt's team-mate, and bitter foe of James G. Blaine, lived at the Fifth Avenue for many years, and Presidents Garfield and Cleveland held their first receptions in it. It was also the stopping-place of Blaine whenever he visited New York, and the scene of the "Rum, Romanism, and Rebellion" incident of 1884 which cost him the Presidency. The post-election fight that won the Presidency for Rutherford B. Hayes and spelled defeat for Samuel J. Tilden had its inception at the Fifth Avenue. Zachariah Chandler, Republican national chairman, was asleep in the hotel when John C. Reid, editor

BALL SCENE, at Metropolitan Hotel, New York City. *Ladies' Dressing Room*

of the New York *Times,* routed him out of bed early in the morning of November 8, 1876 and laid before him the plan to submit double sets of electoral votes from Louisiana, Florida, and South Carolina. Tilden had carried all of those states, but the commission created to decide the contest ruled in favor of Hayes two days before the inaugural.

What the Fifth Avenue Hotel was to the Republicans, the old Hoffman House was to the Democrats. Just when the Hoffman House was completed, in the fall of 1864, Generals Benjamin F. Butler and Winfield Scott came to New York with troops to suppress the draft riots. They made the hotel, then a house of two hundred and twelve rooms, their headquarters and with their staffs occupied it for several months, at the end of which time the proprietors, Reid, Wall and Company, had to renew some of the carpets and furniture and give the house a general overhauling. Daniel D. Howard was the principal proprietor, but was succeeded by Cassius H. Reid a few years later. When Edward S. Stokes, backed by his friend, John W. Mackay, became proprietor, after President Cleveland had pardoned him and he had been released from Sing Sing prison, he bought one of the finest collections of bar-room art for the Hoffman House that had ever been gathered together. It included several paintings of billowy-bodied nudes, such as Correggio's *Narcissus* and Bouguereau's *The Bathers* and *Nymphs and Satyr*. The statuary included two life-size Nubian slaves, male and female, supporting baskets of fruit on their heads. These figures were of wood and were said to have been carved two thousand years ago.[3] The *Nymphs and Satyr* became known from one end of the country to the other, for nearly every cigar case displayed it, on boxes of Hoffman House perfectos, ten cents straight. There was a comic lithograph, which had a wide distribution, picturing a ragged hobo standing at the bar and gazing at the nymphs. Underneath was the legend: " I've been looking all over the world for that creek, but darned if I can find it." The nymphs and the Hoffman House both disappeared in March 1915. A few weeks later the near-by Albemarle closed.

 The old Morton House, long a favorite of stage stars when Union Square was the Rialto of New York, was closed in the fall of 1921. It had stood at the southeast corner of

Broadway and Fourteenth Street since 1848, when it opened under the management of Congressman John Wheeler.[4] Union Square was then a fashionable residence center. Sheridan Shook, its owner, enlarged and remodeled it in 1868 and leased it to James Morton and his brother, and it was from then on that it became a favorite theatrical center. The addition to it included the Union Square Theater, one of New York's most celebrated playhouses, which opened on September 11, 1871, under the management of A. M. Palmer. During the Morton régime, which lasted about twenty years, the Morton House set what many considered the best table in New York, and its patrons included many nationally known politicians, as well as celebrities of the theater.

Two notable old hotels of the Madison Square district passed away so long ago that few remember them today. The Gramercy Hotel was farthest north when it was opened, at Broadway and Twentieth Street on June 5, 1852, under the management of Donadi and Andem. Donadi had previously been proprietor of the old Powelton House at Newburgh, New York. The Gramercy was perhaps the first hotel to give its guests a choice of either the American or the European plan. The other was the St. Germain, opened February 8, 1856, at Broadway, Fifth Avenue, and Twenty-second Street. Its first manager was Francis Rider, who had for many years been running the old Heath House at Schooley's Mountain. The St. Germain was a handsome building of French architecture, faced with Caen stone.

One of the first hotels on Broadway north of Madison Square was the original St. James, at Broadway and Twenty-sixth Street, which opened in 1863 under the management of F. T. Wells and Company. It kept going until 1896, at which time its obituaries credited it with being the birthplace of the gin rickey, named after Colonel Joseph K. Rickey of Calloway County, Missouri, where he owned a large stock-farm and had other business interests. Back in the 1870's and later Colonel Rickey used to spend a couple of months each year in Washington and New York. He spent most of the time in New York and always registered at the St. James. The barroom was his favorite part of the hotel, and there he met a Philadelphia newspaperman who produced some limes and asked the bar-tender to mix two drinks according to a certain receipt. Rickey liked the drink so well that he began ordering it steadily and bar-tenders began calling it a " Rickey." Customers began to say: " Let me try one of those things," and, having tried one, became addicts. Thus was another favorite prescription added to the pages of the *Bartenders' Guide*.[5]

" Plunger " (Francis Theodore) Walton, one of those characters whose follies endear them to the public, was proprietor of the St. James from 1877 to 1883. " The Plunger " played the races and did other spectacular things. "His ups and downs are prodigious," said one chronicler of the times, " but he accepts the blessings or floggings of fate with placidity and one cannot help admiring him. Every move he makes is a veritable plunge, involving all his fortune and everything he can beg or borrow. One of these days he will hit it again and will ride once more on the topmost wave of success." This was written after he had filed a petition in bankruptcy, in 1899. But his luck had deserted him. He died poor a few years later. " The Plunger " made his first big killing when he went to England in the 1870's and backed Foxhall and Parole for all he was worth. He came back with five hundred thousand dollars. A few years later he again went to England to back his favorite horses, but lost his shirt. He began his career in Philadelphia, where he was city recorder and proprietor of the old Globe Hotel before coming to New York. When he gave up the St. James, he returned to Philadelphia for a time and was a street-cleaning contractor. Subsequently he re-entered the hotel business and at various times was proprietor of the Stockton Hotel in Cape May, the Grand

Hotel in New York, and the Brighton Beach Hotel at Coney Island.

The first decade of the twentieth century saw the closing of five famous old-timers in New York. The first to go was the old five-story Coleman House, with its long mansard roof, which stood at Broadway and Twenty-seventh Street. It was opened in 1868 by Captain Robert W. Coleman and survived until 1902. Four years later the Sinclair House, at Broadway and Eighth Street, stepped out of the picture. It was long kept by A. L. Ashman. Artemus Ward lived in it when he came to New York in the 1860's to edit the first *Vanity Fair*. The Everett House, named in honor of Edward Everett, closed in 1908. It stood at 41 East Seventeenth Street, just off Union Square, and was fairly venerable, having opened in 1854. The Clarendon, at Fourth Avenue and Eighteenth Street, disappeared in 1910. It had been running since 1851, when it was opened by O. C. Putnam. Though small, the Clarendon was one of the hoity-toitiest hotels New York ever had. In 1860 it shared honors with the old Fifth Avenue Hotel in entertaining the Prince of Wales. It was at that period the favorite of distinguished English visitors. Its chief rival for this class of business was the Westminster Hotel, at Irving Place and Sixteenth Street, whose landlord, Charles B. Ferrin, proudly displayed in frames the letters that Dickens wrote praising the hotel when he stopped there in 1868, and that Wilkie Collins wrote in 1874. The Westminster dated from 1867 and was closed in 1910, shortly after the closing of the Clarendon.

Gone, too, are nearly all those fine old New York hotels that rose magnificently during the Gilded Age. The sedate old Park Avenue, built by A. T. Stewart, the merchant prince, as a *de luxe* home for salesladies (who refused to live in it because there were too many rules and regulations), closed in 1925. It was the pride of Murray Hill when Stewart built it in the 1870's, and it was not exactly an eyesore when it closed, in 1925. Stewart spent some three million dollars on it, inside and out. Its eight stories were of thirty-inch masonry encased in a cast-iron shell. Impressive iron staircases, wrought in Italy, guaranteed safety from flames. In its corridors hung pictures from the Stewart galleries, and its furniture was the best and sturdiest obtainable. Stewart, already seventy-four when he began to build it, was not present at the gala opening in 1877 (he had died in 1876), but New York society was on hand in full force. Nor, of course, did Stewart live to see how ungrateful working girls could be. There were hints, however, that the heirs of Stewart were not as philanthropically minded as he and that this had something to do with the fact that the building became a hotel, opening on April 2, 1878.

The lordly Buckingham, immortalized in Edith Wharton's *Age of Innocence,* closed on June 1, 1922, at the age of forty-six. It stood at Fifth Avenue and Fiftieth Street and was opened in January 1876 under the management of Fuller and Gage. George Kemp built it and made it such a substantial and luxurious place that it was touted as a marvel in the pages of the *Atlantic Monthly*. It was a hotel of heavy feudal splendor, the keynote struck in the lobby by its gilt statue of the Duke of Buckingham, waving his plumed hat under the Buckingham coat of arms, and by the high-studded rooms, the heavy, tasseled draperies, and the massive mahogany woodwork — the likeliest of all places as a haven for old Dom Pedro, last emperor of Brazil when he came to New York in 1879. It was this hotel, too, that a fugitive president of Guatemala chose as his abode when he arrived in New York with a trunk full of gold. But chiefly it was the home of the old aristocracy of the days of bustles and wasp waists and rustling silk ruffles.

Almost as grand in its earlier days was the Victoria, which Paran Stevens built as one of New York's first and finest " French flats " in 1872. It was uncompleted when

Stevens died and was transformed into a hotel within a few years, surviving until February 26, 1914.

Near the Victoria stood the Hotel Brunswick, at 225 Fifth Avenue, by all accounts the tiptop hotel of them all. It was opened in 1871 by James Mitchell and Francis Kinzler of the Hoffman House and quickly won the hearts and patronage of what Ward McAllister used to call " the *crème de la crème.*" It was built, decorated, and equipped to compete with Delmonico's for the social patronage of the elect, and it did so successfully until Billy McGlory, keeper of the notorious Armory Hall, at 158 Hester Street, put it on the bum. In a day when vile resorts abounded on the Bowery and adjacent streets, McGlory's was reputed to be the vilest of the vile.

Some time in the latter part of 1882 a man of aristocratic appearance and manner called at the Brunswick and introduced himself as Mr. Thompson. He desired to arrange for a midnight banquet and ball, for a party of several hundred persons. He wanted the best of everything, paid a substantial deposit, selected an expensive menu, and went away. The management outdid itself in preparation for the affair. It was, so they thought, to be something just as high-toned as the annual Bachelor Balls, which they had won away from Delmonico's, or the ball that Sir Henry Meysey-Thompson gave, which was a sensation akin to that created in later years by the Bradley Martin ball. The newspapers were notified and the fateful night arrived. It was in Christmas week of 1882. At midnight the management was thrown into consternation when McGlory and his wretched followers, garbed in fancy costumes, drove up to the door of the hotel in stages and hacks, " with demonstrations of lawlessness that terrorized the neighborhood for blocks around." Into the proud fastness of ultra-gentility poured the scum of the Five Points, most of them already half-seas-over. They swarmed all over the magnificent hotel and drank and danced and feasted in the glorious blue and gold ballroom, which was said to be the decorator Edward Ficken's masterpiece. The overflow poured into the equally beautiful café and bar, and groups of the *haute monde* fled out of the hotel in horror — never to return. A wave of disastrous publicity engulfed the establishment, and there was an immediate and permanent falling-off of its business. Dinner and ball reservations were canceled and the elegant apartments vacated. It was impossible to live down the disgrace of having made such a grievous error, and so, in February 1885, the management filed a voluntary petition in bankruptcy, listing liabilities of $250,000. The hotel was closed on July 1, 1885, the expensive antiques and other equipment were sold, and the building was converted to business uses.

The old Marlborough Hotel, at Broadway and Thirty-sixth Street, was one of the hotels built during the Gilded Age, but it was more of a roughneck place, remembered chiefly for the fact that it was there that Anna Held took her famous milk bath, before disappointed reporters, who couldn't see through milk. It closed on November 1, 1923, to make way for a skyscraper. It was built in 1888 by Louis M. Todd, who also built the old Vendome Hotel at Broadway and Forty-first Street, which met a similar fate in February 1930. The Marlborough, once owned by Richard Croker, was a great hang-out for theatrical stars back in the gay nineties and later. The old Navarre Hotel, built about 1890, was torn down two years ago, and the Normandie, dating from October 30, 1884, was closed in December 1927. It was built by General Ferdinand P. Earl, friend of David Bennett Hill, governor and senator, who lived in the Normandie many years and appointed Earl a general on the governor's staff. The Normandie was Samuel Gompers's favorite stopping-place for many years whenever he came to New York, and many important labor conferences were held in the parlors. In 1910 Mrs. Oliver H. P. Belmont made it the headquarters for the woman's suffrage movement, and the turmoil of that movement revolved around the hotel. But the Broadway crowd remembers it chiefly because Kid McCoy's celebrated Rathskeller was in the basement.

General Earl was also the first proprietor of the old Netherland Hotel on Fifth Avenue at the foot of Central Park. It was closed on May 9, 1925, and a week or so later its old neighbor, the Savoy, was closed. The two houses abounded in elegance, but were contrasts in style. The Savoy was a cream-colored stone building with light-brown marble interior; the Netherland was a seventeen-story brownstone structure, its interior rich in carved and paneled mahogany and walnut, and dark marble, bronze, and onyx. Boss Tweed bought the Savoy site back in 1876 and planned to build a fine hotel on it. But his downfall came just when the basement excavation was finished, and the hole stood empty until 1890, when Justice Dugro bought the property and built the Savoy, which was opened four years later. The Netherland was a little older. Across on the other side of the park stood the Majestic, at Seventy-second Street, which, from the time of its opening, in October 1894, until its closing, on October 1, 1929, was the abode of several famous authors and artists.

Greatest of all the hotels to close in recent years was the late lamented Waldorf-Astoria, with its famed Peacock Alley and its memories of presidents and princes and the Bradley Martin ball. It closed in May 1929 with a great outburst of ballyhoo that brought the auction sale of its contents up to about $350,000. Like its great predecessor the St. Nicholas, the Waldorf-Astoria closed before it had become too much run down at the heel. Part of it was only thirty-two years old. It has the distinction of being the first thousand-room house and the first hotel of modern steel and concrete construction to come down. An aura of rich anecdotage surrounds the memory of this famous old hotel.

In its early days — indeed, throughout its existence — it was filled with new-rich millionaires and limelight characters of all sorts. One of its first permanent guests was "Betcha-a-Million" (John W.) Gates, who paid the then stupendous sum of twenty thousand dollars a year for his apartment. He was the leader of what came to be known as the "Waldorf crowd" of Wall Street plungers. James R. Keene, the noted speculator and horseman and his associates were Waldorf habitués, and for several years the house swarmed with Pittsburgh steel millionaires — Charles M. Schwab and the rest of Carnegie's thirty "boys" who rolled in riches overnight when the gigantic United States Steel Corporation was organized. It is said that the steel trust grew out of a suggestion first made at a table in the men's café at which Gates and several of his associates were seated. The idea was received with enthusiasm and was followed up by several conferences in Gates's apartment and various parlors of the hotel, at which definite decision was taken to go ahead with the plans.

In other American cities old hotels, their showiness tarnished by from thirty to fifty years of usage, have been dying off with a rapidity equal to that of the old New York hotels. A few here and there hang on a little while longer. The Continental in Philadelphia, finest in the Quaker City when it opened, on February 16, 1860, disappeared in 1923 to make way for the Benjamin Franklin, Philadelphia's present largest. The Continental was the scene of Coal Oil Johnny's pranks and, of course, was distinguished for various other reasons. It outlived by several years the old Girard House, which Colonel George Presbury and John H. Billings, first proprietor of the New York Hotel, opened on January 26, 1852. A year after the Girard was opened, another fine hotel, the La Pierre, known after 1876 as the Lafayette, threw open its doors. It passed out some twenty years ago. Daniel Gale, late of the Buckingham in New York, became its proprietor in 1882, when it was enlarged and improved. Further back in the history of Philadelphia there was the old United States Hotel, which was opened in 1828, and the American Hotel, on Chestnut Street opposite Independence Square, which boasted of " over one hundred rooms" when John J. Ridgway opened it, on March 1, 1844. Another old Philadelphia hotel that cut quite a swath in its day was the five-story Marshall House on Walnut Street near Fourth, opened in 1835.

Most of Washington's old-timers have gone, the latest, early in 1930, being the National, erected in 1827 by the Calvert family. Practically all of the original building had disappeared, however, many years ago. Up to 1844 it was run by John Gadsby, an Englishman who had been running a tavern at Alexandria, Virginia, and it was called Gadsby's Hotel up to that time. Captain Robert Coleman of the Astor House changed its name and enlarged and improved it when he took charge in that year, and it was not until then that the National took on a first-class tone. During its first half-century, and even later, Washington was worse off for good hotel accommodations than any other city. It was primarily a city of boarding-houses and in its general aspects was, as Beveridge has said, " an ill-contrived, ill-arranged, rambling, scrambling village," its houses far apart, with privies, pigsties, cow-sheds and geese-pens in the back-yards, the alleys littered with rubbish and hogs nosing and wallowing in mud and garbage on the streets. Its hotels were condemned by practically all travelers who have left records of their visits to the capital. For a decade or two the National was the best, and its guest list included a great many distinguished personages. One of its permanent guests was Thaddeus Stevens, the abolitionist, and Henry Clay lived in it for years and died there. John Wilkes Booth lived at the National prior to the assassination of Lincoln, and it is believed the plot to murder the President was hatched in his room at the hotel. When Buchanan came to Washington to be inaugurated, he occupied the President's Suite and fell a victim of " National Hotel disease." This mysterious malady had resulted in a number of deaths, and it is said that only prompt attention on the part of the medical officer of the Navy saved Buchanan's life, the day before the inaugural ceremony. What caused the illness of guests was a puzzle for several weeks, but it was finally found that it was due to escaping sewer-gas.

Washington's first really great hotel was the Arlington, which stood at Vermont Avenue and Lafayette Square, opposite the White House. It opened in 1868 under the management of Theophilus Roessle, who ran it for more than thirty years. From the time of its opening until its closing, nearly twenty years ago, it was a great gathering-place of all the greatest makers of American history. In its latter days one of its most prominent permanent guests was Senator Mark Hanna, who lived at the Arlington throughout the period when he played such a great role in American politics. During the McKinley and Roosevelt administrations, up to the time of Hanna's death, in the hotel, in February 1904, the Arlington was looked upon as a sort of secondary White House. The average person remembers the old Arlington for its superb meals and accommodations in general, and few will recall it with other than pleasant memories. It had, however, at one time an embittered guest in the person of Elliott F. Shepard, then owner of the New York *Mail and Express*. The exact nature of Shepard's grievance agains the hotel is not known, but following a visit there he wrote an impassioned editorial demanding that the name of the hotel be changed. It was, he said, " a sacrilege to have a hotel, a mere inn, using the same name as Arlington Cemetery, where the heroic dead are buried." This was followed by other editorials, and for many months every dispatch, long or short, from the newspaper's Washington bureau, began and ended with the slogan: "Change the name of the Arlington Hotel." But the name was retained until the historic old hostelry was torn down to make way for a government building.

One block west of the Arlington stood the Shoreham, closed in 1928, almost exactly forty years after its opening. It was built by Levi P. Morton, of New York, vice-president during the Harrison administration, and was named after the Vermont village in which Morton was born. It maintained its prestige to the end. During the World War almost all the men prominent in the Wilson administration, except the President himself, gathered every day for luncheon in the Shoreham's H Street restaurant. Among them might be seen McAdoo, Tumulty, Hoover, Bernard M. Baruch, E. N. Hurley of the Shipping Board, and a dozen others. Back in the Shoreham's early days the Wormley Hotel stood opposite it. Charles Sumner lived there during his long term in the Senate. A year after the Shoreham closed, the Congress Hall, half a block south of the capitol, was dismantled, and some eighty senators and representatives had to move out. It had been in existence but twenty-two years. Senator Champ Clark of Missouri lived in it from the time of its opening and died in it. Among other senators who lived in it were Senators Ralston, Willis, Joseph Robinson, and Tom Heflin, who used to keep the guests in a roar of laughter whenever he told his inimitable Southern stories.

The Ebbitt House, at Fourteenth and F streets, passed out in 1925. It was built shortly before the Civil War by Caleb C. Willard, youngest of the four Willard brothers who had been bar-tenders on Hudson River steamers back in the 1850's and earlier. Joseph D. Willard was the last survivor of the four, and when he died, on January 17, 1897 — leaving an estate of about three million dollars — old Washingtonians recalled many stories of his eccentricity.

Back in the 1870's he owned a piece of property at Fourteenth and F streets which had on it a lot of old rubbish and billboards. When other property owners complained that it was an eyesore, and officials made Willard remove the billboards and rubbish, he rented the lots to a tombstone-maker, who set up sample monuments all over the property. About the time Caleb built the Ebbitt, he and Joseph had a falling out and thereafter communicated with each other solely by letter and through the newspapers. They never spoke as they passed each other on the street. Joseph predicted the Ebbitt would fail, but it was a big success, and Caleb planned to enlarge it. He bought some near-by property, but between this and the hotel there was a small vacant plot that Joseph owned and that he refused to sell when he was offered thirty thousand dollars for it by real-estate agents representing Caleb. Asked what he would take for it, he replied: " Nothing less than a million dollars." And so the parcel remained vacant and the Ebbitt was not enlarged.

Sentiment toward the old man changed in his latter years when an incident revealed that he was not so hardhearted as he had appeared to be. Joseph G. Cooke, lessee of Willard's Hotel, died a few months before the expiration date of his lease. Hotel men in various parts of the country expected that the eccentric old man would not renew the lease and that the widow would have to sell the furniture for a song. Instead, Willard gave her a long-term renewal so that she might get a proper price for the equipment, valued at seventy thousand dollars. She finally got sixty thousand.

Henry A. and Edwin D. Willard were the first of the brothers to become hotel-keepers in Washington, in 1847, when they became joint proprietors of what was originally the old Mansion House, a row of three-story residences built about 1818 by Colonel John Taylor on Pennsylvania Avenue. John Strothers connected these houses in 1820 and opened them as a hotel under the name of Mansion House.

There were various other proprietors and names during the next twenty-seven years. The Willards renamed the hotel and in 1853 remodeled it and built a large addition. Edwin D. subsequently withdrew from the firm, and Joseph became a partner. During Civil War days Willard's Hotel was the favorite headquarters of Union officers and of all the various notables and nobodies who flocked to Washington on matters in connection with the war. Nathaniel Hawthorne, who made a tour of the Virginia battlefields and military camps in 1862, wrote a colorful description of life in the old Willard at that period, a description which, very likely, would have fitted many another hotel of the time. From his tour of the battlefields Hawthorne " gained a pretty lively idea of what was going on," but, he said:

> After all, if compelled to pass a rainy day in the hall and parlors of Willard's Hotel, it proved about as profitably spent as if we had floundered through miles of Virginia mud, in quest of interesting matter. This hotel, in fact, may be much more justly called the center of Washington and the Union than either the Capitol, the White House or the State Department. It is the meeting place of the true representatives of the country — not such as are chosen blindly and amiss by the electors . . . but men who gravitate or are attracted hither by real business, or a native impulse to breathe the intensest atmosphere of the nation's life, or a genuine anxiety to see how this life and death struggle is going to deal with us.
>
> . . . Never, in any other place, was there such a miscellany of people. You exchange nods with governors of sovereign States; you elbow illustrious men, and tread on the toes of generals; you hear statesmen and orators speaking in their familiar tones. You are mixed up with the office-seekers, wire-pullers, inventors, artists, poets, prosers (including editors, army correspondents, *attachés* of foreign journals, and long-winded talkers), clerks, diplomatists, mail contractors, railway directors, until your own identity is lost among them — occasionally you talk with a man whom you have never before heard of, and are struck by the brightness of a thought, and fancy that there is more wisdom hidden among the obscure than is anywhere revealed among

the famous. You adopt the universal habit of the place, and call for a mint-julep, a whiskey-skin, a gin-cocktail, a brandy smash or a glass of pure Old Rye, for the conviviality of Washington sets in at an early hour and, so far as I had the opportunity to observing, never terminates at any hour, and all these drinks are continually in request by almost all these people. . . .

It is curious to observe what antique figures and costumes sometimes make their appearance at Willard's. You meet elderly men with frilled shirt fronts, for example, the fashion of which adornment passed away from among the people of this world half a century ago. It is as if one of Stuart's portraits were walking abroad. I see no way of accounting for this, except that the trouble of the times, the impiety of traitors, and peril of our sacred Union and Constitution have disturbed, in their honored graves, some of the venerable fathers of the country and summoned them forth to protest against the meditated and half-accomplished sacrilege. If it be so, their wonted fires are not altogether extinguished in their ashes — in their throats, I might rather say — for I behold one of these excellent old men quaffing such a horn of Bourbon whiskey as a toper of the present century would loath to venture upon. But, really, one would be glad to know where these strange figures come from. It shows, at any rate, how many remote, decaying villages and country-neighborhoods of the North, and forest-nooks of the West, and old mansion-houses in the cities, are shaken by the tremor of our native soil, so that men long hidden in retirement put on the garments of their youth and hurry out to inquire what is the matter.[6]

This old Willard's Hotel, remodeled and enlarged two or three times during its half-century, survived until 1889, when the New Willard's Hotel was built, and this in turn was succeeded by the new Willard Hotel, the last section of which was completed a few years ago. Vice-president Thomas R. Marshall lived at the Willard during the Wilson administrations, and Calvin Coolidge also lived there during his entire term as vice-president. During the first three weeks of his succession to the Presidency he remained at the hotel, and the entire White House office staff was quartered there also. The hotel became, for the time being, the temporary White House.

Among other notable Washington hotels of the nineteenth century there was the Riggs House, built by George W. Riggs and opened in May 1876 by Plummer and Spofford. Welker's Hotel was built a few years earlier. It was the favorite of President Grant and his friend Sam Ward, the famous lobbyist and gourmet, who married a member of the Astor family. The Raleigh Hotel, opened on January 1, 1895, was formerly known as the Kirkwood, rebuilt and enlarged. Andrew Johnson lived in it when he was vice-president, and was asleep in his room when friends came to tell him that Lincoln had been shot. When Lincoln died, Johnson was sworn in as President at the Kirkwood.

Most of the state capitals have had hotels of great historic interest. Just two years ago " Garry " (Garrett J.) Benson's hotel at Albany, popularly known as " the Tub," was closed and remodeled into an office building. It was for many years a popular rendezvous of members of the legislature and lobbyists. Governor Alfred E. Smith was one of its regular patrons back in the days when he was cutting his eye-teeth in state politics. Congress Hall, Stanwix Hall, and the Delaven House were the three greatest favorites from about 1830 to 1860. Crosby's Hotel, at South Pearl and Beaver streets, was of much earlier date. When it burned down, the Clinton Hotel was built on the site. Crosby's is remembered chiefly for the romance of its pretty chambermaid Amanda West, and Don Lorenzo de Zavala, governor of the city of Mexico. In 1820, or thereabouts, Don Lorenzo left Mexico in haste (for state reasons) and spent the next two or three years touring the United States. He fell in love with Amanda at first sight and wooed and won her. Historians of Albany say she was " a beautiful and intelligent girl who liked to read romances and had a presentiment that she would become a great lady." Her dreams came true, for Zavala afterwards became Mexican minister to France and she accompanied him to Paris as his wife. There, according to the annals of Albany, " she was tutored, learned French and acquired much polish." Four children were born to the union and were brought up on a large ranch in Texas, where Zavala died. A river in that state bears his name.[7]

Congress Hall, opened in 1814, was for many years said to be " the greatest focus of political life in America," outside of Washington. In it foreign visitors observed with interest the methods of lobbyists and legislators playing the political game and working out their various legislative plans. It was also the headquarters of the old judiciary, which was swept away by the " Jacobin hurricane " of 1821–2, and of " that glorious galaxy of talent, genius and learning " which adorned the bar of New York in that day. It was popularly known as " the House of Lords," and Leverett Cruttenden, a Connecticut Yankee who ran it during its first sixteen years, was known far and wide as a wit of the first water. His brilliance, it was said, matched that of any of the brilliant company that sat at his bountiful table. Congress Hall lasted until about 1860. Its most notable banquet was that at which Lafayette was guest of honor on July 1, 1824. This was perhaps the most notable of all the banquets given in honor of Lafayette during his triumphal tour of the country, for it celebrated his return to the place where he had made his military headquarters during the Revolution, in the tavern which then stood on the site of Congress Hall.

Stanwix Hall, with its five high stories and its gilded dome, was the most pretentious of Albany's old hotels. It was built by the heirs of General Gansevoort, who distinguished himself at Fort Stanwix during the Revolution, and was opened in 1833. The dome, however, did not appear until 1844, when the hotel was rebuilt and enlarged, reopening on June 10 of that year under the management of Wheeler and Bromley. On the night of December 28, 1841, a great banquet was held in the first Stanwix Hall. It celebrated the completion of Albany's first railroad. The last spike had been driven during the day into the line built by the Western Railroad Company, making it possible to travel by rail all the way from Albany to Boston. The line also provided a winter rail route to New York, by way of Hartford and New Haven. One could make the journey in thirty-two hours, without night travel.[8]

Although Richmond, Virginia, had few pretentious hotels during most of the nineteenth century, those it did have were historic. The old Ballard House and the Exchange Hotel, standing side by side, were for many years rivals in popular favor. J. P. Ballard opened the Ballard House on October 30, 1855, and one of its first guests was ex-president John Tyler, who continued to live in it until his death there, on January 18, 1862. Richmond society entertained the Prince of Wales (King Edward VII) at a grand banquet in the Ballard House on October 6, 1860, and in 1869 when the Virginia State House collapsed, the legislature held its sessions in the hotel.[9] The Exchange Hotel was much older. It opened on July 1, 1841, under the management of Frederick Boyden of Boston. It was in the Exchange Hotel that Poe lectured to a crowd of spellbound Richmond people on " The Poetic Principle " and recited *The Raven*. Richmond folks recalled Poe's younger days and his heavy drinking at the old Swan Tavern in that city. During Civil War days the Exchange and the Ballard were centers of excitement similar to that at the Willard in Washington. From their roofs great crowds watched the Union and Confederate forces fight the battle of Chickahominy and other events of the war. Many years after the war the two hotels were merged into one, and together they survived until March 16, 1896.[10]

THE AMERICAN HOTEL

Richmond's finest hotel in the old days was the Spotswood, opened in 1860. It was to this hotel that prominent Virginians escorted Colonel Robert E. Lee when he came to Richmond to take a commission in the Confederate Army, after having resigned his commission in the U. S. Army. A great crowd gathered in the streets and kept up a continuous cheering and demand for a speech, until Lee finally came out on the balcony and spoke briefly. Jefferson Davis and Mrs. Davis made the Spotswood their home when they came up from Montgomery in 1861. After the capture of Richmond by Grant's forces Union generals made it their headquarters; and when Davis was captured, he was taken to the hotel and installed as a prisoner in the same rooms he had occupied as President of the Confederacy. The Spotswood burned down on Christmas Eve of 1870 with a loss of eight lives.

The old Monongahela House on the levee at Pittsburgh, one of the numerous cradles of the Republican party, is still running, but one never hears of it nowadays. It was built in 1841 and was reputed to be the first modern hotel west of the Alleghenies. Pittsburgh then was booming at a great rate and had a population of about thirty-seven thousand. Travel was pouring westward through the city, and the need for a hotel of Astor House rank was felt. The Monongahela, "large and imposing," had two hundred and ten rooms and no less than twenty-six public rooms. James Crossan, who had been running the Exchange Hotel, a smaller, less pretentious house, was the Monongahela's first proprietor; when he died, in 1847, he was succeeded by his son, J. McDonald Crossan. The original hotel was one of the eleven hundred buildings that burned down on April 10, 1845. It was rebuilt and reopened the following year, as was also the Exchange, in larger, more ornate form. The Monongahela was the headquarters of the first Republican national convention in February 1857 and previously had

GENERAL McGOWAN ADDRESSING ABBEVILLE VOLUNTEERS IN FRONT OF CHARLESTON HOTEL, Charleston, S. C. in 1861 — *From Leslie's Weekly Illustrated Newspaper* — *Feb. 23, 1861*

been the scene of several conferences at which plans for forming the party were made.[11]

Land-hungry emigrants went down the Monongahela River to the Ohio and presently came to Cincinnati, where the old Pearl Street House and the Henrie House were the finest. Peter Gibson opened the original Gibson House on February 15, 1849; and the famous old Burnet House, in "Italian bracketed" style, was opened in 1850. The Burnet

OLD PLANKINGTON HOTEL, Milwaukee — *From an old engraving.* (1890)

passed out in 1926, but its chief rival in the old days, the Spencer House, opened in December 1853, still runs on the levee as a cheap lodging-house. Farther down the Ohio, at Louisville, the Galt House, rife with memories of old Blue Grass days, still stands, but not as a hotel. It was converted into a warehouse in 1919. The original Galt House was opened about 1838, but burned down on January 11, 1865, with a loss of six lives. The present building was erected a year or two later.

The old Kirby House in Milwaukee was dismantled in the spring of 1928 after a record of sixty-three years. It stood on the site of another Kirby House, which dated from 1844. Both were built by Mayor Abner Kirby. Another famous old Milwaukee hotel, the Plankinton, with mansard roof and towers, was pulled down in 1918. It was built fifty-one years earlier by John Plankinton, pioneer meat-packer. President Cleveland and his bride, Frances Folsom, spent a day of their honeymoon there, on October 6, 1887. In Cleveland's home town, Buffalo, the Genesee Hotel went out of existence in 1922. When it was opened, in 1882, Cleveland, then mayor of the city, led the grand march at the opening ball. The hotel was on the site of the Genesee House, built about 1850.

One of the most widely known hotels, the Neil House in Columbus, Ohio, closed in 1922, and another hotel of the same name took its place. There have been three Neil Houses. The first was built in 1839 by William Neil. It burned down on the day Lincoln was elected, November 6, 1860. Another hotbed of Ohio politics, the Boody House in Toledo, was closed in 1928. Azariah Boody built it in 1872. Toledo had another famous old house, the Oliver, a sumptuous four-story red-brick structure, opened in 1859. It ran for about forty years and then, being distant from the downtown section, became a warehouse. It was named after Major William Oliver, one of the founders of Toledo.[12]

The Ranier Grand of Seattle, which buzzed with excitement during the feverish days of the Klondike gold-rush, received its death-sentence in 1929 and was removed to make way for a federal building. It was built in 1889. The Paxton of Omaha, opened in 1882, closed in the spring of 1928 to make way for a new namesake. It was built on the site of the old Grand Central Hotel, which burned down on September 4, 1878. The Planters in St. Louis, third of its name, which had been running since September 16, 1894, closed thirty years later, and its old-time rival, the Southern, closed in 1913.

New hotels in Boston have routed out several old-timers. The United States Hotel, dating from July 13, 1840, when it was opened by R. N. Holman and Albert Clark, closed in 1929, and on September 15 of that year the Quincy House also closed. This was the second Quincy House, built in 1885. Its predecessor, opened in 1819, is said to have been the first hotel to serve free lunch. The elderly Adams House, John L. Sullivan's favorite home-town hostelry, gave up the ghost in November of 1927. The thrifty Mr. Coolidge lived there for several years in a dollar-a-day room, but, on the advice of friends, changed to a two-dollar room when he was elected governor. William Taylor Adams, whose pen name was Oliver Optic, built the first Adams House in 1846, on the site of the old Lamb Tavern. This hotel was succeeded in 1883 by the house that was Coolidge's Boston home. The old Parker House, incubator of the Parker House roll, closed five years ago, and a new Parker House arose on the site. Young's Hotel, for years the Delmonico's of Boston, closed at about the same time, and the Boston Tavern, built early in the nineteenth century, closed in April 1928. Boston still has one of its old hotels, the American House, opened in 1835. Lewis Rice ran it for forty years and was succeeded by Colonel George Keeler. Two other Boston hotels, of much later date, the Brunswick, opened in 1874, and the Vendome, opened by Charles M. Whitney in 1880, are still going as strong as ever.

Other New England cities have recently lost some of their famous old hotels. The Cooley Hotel at Springfield, dating from 1849, when Justin M. Cooley opened its original forty rooms, closed two years ago. From time to time it was enlarged. When Henry E. Marsh, nephew of Cooley, took charge, in 1866, he installed a huge goldfish fountain, imported from Italy, in the lobby. It remained until the house closed, in 1928. The Massasoit House at Springfield (its Massasoit waffles were famous all over the country at one time), was a training-school for many noted hotel men. Horace Mann, philanthropist and educator, was the first to sign its register, in July 1843. It was Springfield's first "railroad house" and was run by Marvin Chapin and E. S. Chapin. It was in Springfield that Tilly Haynes, a clothing-dealer, later widely known as Mine Host of hotels in Boston and New York, got his start as a Boniface, running the Haynes Hotel, which he built in 1864.

Major Joseph Stebbins was one of Springfield's innkeepers in its village days. The major kept the Stebbins Tavern during the latter years of the eighteenth century and early years of the nineteenth. Captain Joseph Carew ran a tannery opposite the tavern. The two made a deal whereby each profited. When customers came from a distance to buy leather, Carew told them he had none ready, but would have some the following morning. The customers stopped overnight at the tavern and meanwhile Carew soaked his leather in the brook that ran at the rear of the tavern, and sold it by the pound next day.[13]

Iowa's most historic old hotel, the Kirkwood House at Des Moines, went up in smoke on April 6, 1929. It was opened in 1862 by George W. Savery and was known as the Savery House for ten years. In 1872 it was renamed in honor of Iowa's Civil War governor. Fire, incidentally, has wiped out many old-time hotels, though it has practically no chance in the newer houses. The worst hotel fire on record was that of the Newhall House in Milwaukee, on January 9, 1883, when seventy-five persons lost their lives. New York's worst hotel fire was that of the Windsor Hotel, at Fifth Avenue and Forty-sixth Street, early in the afternoon of March 17, 1899. The St. Patrick's Day parade was coming up the avenue, and the hotel's windows were filled with guests eager to see the marchers. More than thirty-five of them lost their lives. Among those who escaped were the family of Abner McKinley, brother of President McKinley, and the President's sister, Miss Helen McKinley.

The fires that devastated Chicago in 1871, Baltimore in 1904, and San Francisco in 1906 wiped out most of the old hotels in those cities. The "Big Four" built after the Chicago fire — the Grand Pacific Hotel, the Tremont, the

OLD NEWHALL HOUSE, Milwaukee, Wis.

Palmer House, and the Sherman House — are all gone. The Tremont, first to go, has been used as a part of Northwestern University since 1902. The Grand Pacific, where Mine Host John B. Drake served Lucullan game dinners to his friends each year, closed in 1919; the Palmer House was torn down about eight years ago to make way for a larger namesake; and the present Sherman House is a few years older than the new Palmer. Several other historic Chicago hotels have disappeared recently, including the old Briggs House, demolished in 1927. The first Briggs House, erected in 1851 by William Briggs and wiped out by the fire twenty years later, was Abraham Lincoln's favorite. The old Bismarck Hotel, where for nearly fifty years the Eitel brothers served the finest German cooking in America, was supplanted by a new Bismarck about six years ago; and the Lakota, Chicago Beach, and Stratford Hotels are among the other Chicago hotels closed within the last four or five years.

The San Francisco fire laid low the original Palace Hotel, the Grand, the Occidental, the Lick House, the Cosmopolitan, and several others built when San Francisco was young and sinful. The famous old What Cheer House closed just before the fire and "Lucky" Baldwin's Hotel, rival of the Palace, stole a march on the rest by being burned out on November 24, 1898. With it went the historic Baldwin Theater, where many great stage stars rose to fame. The Baltimore fire finished the Carrolton, the Howard (since risen again), and the Maltby, opened by L. U. Maltby shortly before the outbreak of the Civil War. It was to Baltimore what Willard's was to Washington in those stirring days. The old Eutaw House, which William Hussey opened in 1835, escaped the fire and continued in operation until 1913, while the old Barnum Hotel, remembered now only by Oldest Inhabitants, checked its last guest out on April 4, 1889.

The National in Washington, the American in Boston, and the Eastern in New York are examples of hotels that live long beyond their allotted span. The National rounded out a full century, and a year or two over, and thus holds the longevity record. The American House, with its record of ninety-five years, is the oldest existing hotel in the country. The Eastern managed to keep going ninety-eight years, but prohibition sealed its doom in 1920. During its latter years it was not, of course, the classy hotel it had been when Jenny Lind was its guest and when Daniel

Webster took unto himself a second wife in its parlor. It was built by Captain Coles, who called it the Eagle Hotel when he opened it, on May 9, 1822. When the first Atlantic cable was laid, the hotel was renamed the Great Eastern, and this was subsequently shortened to Eastern. When Captain Coles doubled it in height by adding two more stories to it, some time after 1830, he used solid mahogany for floor beams and other woodwork. The mahogany had been brought back from South America as ballast in his ships and was a drug on the market.

New York's oldest survivor is the Cosmopolitan Hotel, known as the Gerard House during its first nineteen years, was opened in 1850 under the management of J. M. Davis and Brother. The Huggins brothers (N. and S. J.) gave it its present name when they took charge, in 1869. When it was opened, it was directly opposite the first Grand Central Terminal, west of City Hall Square. Legend has it that this was the hotel Coal Oil Johnny bought for a day, to fire a supercilious clerk — though Johnny in his autobiography denied he ever did any such thing.

Next in antiquity in New York is the Brevoort, kept by Mine Host Raymond Orteig, whose twenty-five-thousand-dollar prize sent Lindbergh winging across the Atlantic. It was Fifth Avenue's first hotel and recently passed its seventy-fifth birthday, having been opened on September 7, 1854. When it closes — if ever — it will leave behind more traces than most hotels do, for there was a period in the 1870's and 1880's when pretty nearly every other novel had something in it about the Brevoort. It is still, for that matter, finding its way between the covers of many books. It is particularly well described in F. Marion Crawford's *Dr. Claudius*. Ever since its opening the Brevoort has been a favorite haunt of writers. One of the first literary celebrities who lived there was Edward Z. C. Judson, the Ned Buntline of dime-novel fame, who made Buffalo Bill famous. He was a cousin of Curtis Judson, the Brevoort's first landlord.

The Grand, the Broadway Central, the Grenoble, and the Murray Hill are four other venerable New York hostelries dating from the Gilded Age. The Grenoble, bowed by the weight of fifty-four years, is soon to come down. Its chief claim to fame is that it was there that Rudyard Kipling weathered a siege of pneumonia in 1899. The Murray Hill, opened in 1884 by D. R. Hammond and Nathaniel Hunting, was for many years a political center. John W. Davis was the latest presidential candidate to make his headquarters there. "A visit to this hotel always puts me back in the antimacassar age," wrote Harry Hansen. "The gilded suns on the grill-work, seemingly a replica of the heads of Louis XIV on the doors at Versailles, stir my antiquarian interest. Stephen Graham was the latest literary light to stay there that I knew. The great staircases, the high ceilings, the marble floors, always fed his sense of grandeur."

Henry Milford Smith opened the Grand in September 1869. H. L. Powers was Mine Host at the Broadway Central (then called the Grand Central) when it opened, in 1870. For many years the Grand was a rendezvous of army officers. Its old registers bear the signatures of practically all the generals who won their spurs in the Civil and Spanish wars and in the Indian campaigns. Young Jack Pershing used to check in often in his West Point days, and later. The Broadway Central has been the scene of several noteworthy episodes. It was there that the National Baseball League was organized in 1876 and there also that Edward S. Stokes, in 1872, murdered Jim Fisk, president of the Erie Railroad, in a quarrel over the affections of the fair but frail Josie Mansfield. After nearly sixty years this celebrated homicide has fixed itself in the folklore of the country, and the ballad about it is still being sung, while other hotel tragedies, famous in their day, are forgotten. There was the slaying of Colonel Loring in the old St. Nicholas Hotel by Dr. R. M. Graham, in 1854; the murder of General Nelson by General Jefferson Columbus Davis (both federal officers) in the rotunda of the old Galt House in Louisville during Civil War days; and the Stiles murder case at the Palmer House in Chicago.

Despite the heavy death-rate of old hotels, however, new hotels have gone up faster than the old ones have come down. Especially in the past ten years there has been an enormous volume of new hotel construction. Scattered about the country there are dozens of superdreadnought hotels of from a thousand to three thousand rooms, and a host of others with five hundred rooms or more. The American Hotel Association, Mine Host's national organization, will tell you proudly that the hotel industry ranks ninth among America's major industries, and will quote figures to prove it. Big and little, good, bad, and indifferent, there are 25,950 hotels in the country, with a total of more than 1,525,000 rooms. They have a valuation of $5,100,000,000, do an annual business of $1,350,000,000, and carry 580,000 employees on their pay-rolls. These are official figures quoted in the association's official *Red Book* of 1928. An up-to-date survey of the industry would necessitate sharp revision upward, for hundreds of new hotels have been built within the past three years, and hundreds of others are being built.

The two greatest hotels yet to be built are in process of construction in New York and they will influence most of the hotel-building to be done during the next quarter-century in America. One of these hotels is the new Waldorf-Astoria, and the other is the Hotel Pierre. Each is unique in its way and each will establish precedents in construction and management that will be widely imitated.

The Waldorf-Astoria, to cost $40,000,000, will be

AN AERIAL VIEW OF PARK AVENUE — *Grand Central zone, New York, with sketch showing architects' conception of what the new Waldorf-Astoria will look like when completed in the fall of 1931*

the highest hotel ever built, rising forty-six stories above Park Avenue, where it occupies the entire block between East Forty-ninth and East Fiftieth streets, running through to Lexington Avenue. Through the center of the building on the street level will be arcaded driveways for traffic, and beneath the basement there will be switches connecting with the New York Central Railroad. These will be for the convenience of guests arriving in private cars. The hotel will contain 2,253 large guest-rooms, of which 300 will have parlors. Many of the bathrooms are "boudoir-baths," being fourteen feet wide and eighteen feet long. These will be completely equipped with dressing-rooms, having marble floors and walls. All the clothes-closets will be cedar-lined, and each room will be wired for radio and television. The tower of the building, beginning at the twentieth floor, has been designed to provide quiet, air, and sunlight and will contain five hundred *de luxe* suites. These will have eighteen-foot ceilings, open fireplaces, and drawing-rooms forty-five feet long and twenty-five feet wide. The main ballroom will be four stories in height, surrounded by three balconies. There will be three additional ballrooms, and when they are all thrown together, there will be 38,000 square feet available. The entire Park Avenue front on the eighteenth, nineteenth, and twentieth floors will be given over to the roof gardens, which will have outside terraces for dining.

The Waldorf-Astoria will constitute the final word among the hotels located in the business section, but it will be the new forty-two-story Hotel Pierre that will set the new pace for smart hotels of the residential type. This white marble edifice is located on Fifth Avenue at Sixty-first Street and overlooks the green reaches of Central Park. Being, as it is, an outgrowth of Pierre's famous restaurant on Park Avenue, this hotel will cater especially to the social side of hotel life, and fully half the guests will be permanent residents, drawn, in the main, from the ranks of New York's wealthy classes.

Hotel Pierre will be the model for the "personally conducted" sort of hostelry. It will be under the direction of Charles Pierre, the restaurateur, who was brought originally to New York from London by Louis Sherry, and he will be backed in his undertaking by several New York millionaires who want to reside in a hotel that provides every luxury and convenience available in the finest co-operative apartment. With this in view, the Hotel Pierre will specialize in large suites, so arranged that they will resemble private homes. Some of these will occupy entire floors in the tower of the building and will be the last word in convenience and elegance. Some of these suites afford private outdoor terraces, embellished with pools and growing gardens.

The most striking features superficially of the ultramodern hotel, as exemplified by the Waldorf-Astoria and the Hotel Pierre, are the new dimensions in hotel vastness that they embody. These hotels will equal, for the first time, the great business skyscrapers, rising in height to some half-hundred stories above the street level and occupying entire city blocks. They contain, not hundreds of rooms, but thousands; not one restaurant, but dozens; on the ground floor there are scores of stores of every kind, and dozens of public parlors and writing-rooms adjoin the several lobbies, which one may enter from any of a dozen doors. It is not, however, in the final analysis, the great size of these new hotels that sets them, in the main, apart from the older hotels, but their unapproached magnificence. For the Waldorf-Astoria and the Hotel Pierre will be magnificent in a way that will make many of those gorgeous hotels of the "age of innocence" merely vulgar. There will be nothing ornate about them; in fact they will rather lean toward classic severity and restraint. But only the finest materials — marble, granite, and

matched woods — will enter into their cons
furnishings will be selected for their artisti
of taste, not for their "wear and tear"
Americans for the last quarter-centu.,
ing rapidly forward in their demands for luxury, a...
constant quest for supreme elegance is now to be met by the
hotel. Most persons have hitherto felt that they were more
comfortable in their homes than in hotels; these new hotels
hope to reverse this feeling. Great suites with private terraces, sun-rooms, boudoirs, dens, two-story salons, furnished
with the spoils of European palaces, are the innovations in
these new hotels and are the real reason why they are costing
forty million dollars to build. Our national appetite for luxury will only be whetted by these two examples of what
hotels may be, and it is safe to predict that very soon Mine
Host will be planning others to equal them in magnificence.
For the history of the hotel in America is the history of progressive luxury, and it is not to be assumed that its end has
been reached.

NOTES

THE INN CROSSES THE RUBICON

1. The world's largest hotel, the Hotel Stevens, Chicago, opened in May 1927, has three thousand guest-rooms.

2. Berkeley's *History of Virginia,* quoted in Dunbar's *History of Travel in America,* Volume I, relates that in the Old Dominion innkeepers were forbidden by law to charge travelers any stated amount for board and lodging. They had to take whatever the wayfarer volunteered to give them.

3. Historians generally agree that the first inns where board and lodging might be had for payment of regular fees were established in Lydia, recognized birthplace of money.

4. In England an inn provided lodging and board, while taverns provided only food and drink — chiefly the latter. The English common law makes a marked difference between the inn, the tavern, and the hotel. In America the terms " inn " and " tavern " were synonymous. In fact, most of the inns were known as taverns, which the English considered an amusing misuse of the mother tongue.

5. See *The English Inn, Past and Present,* by Richardson and Eberlein; *London Inns and Taverns,* by Leopold Wagner; and the writings of such observers of English social life as Thomas De Quincey (" Life and Manners ").

6. De Quincey.

7. " Hotel " was a highfalutin French word that had recently been adopted. Perhaps the first tavern to use the

word was Corre's Hotel, opened in 1790 at 24 Broadway, New York, by Joseph Corre, who had previously been in charge, for a short time, of the old Cape's Tavern, or City Tavern. Corre was a pastry-cook and gave lessons to servants of families. For many years he kept various ice-cream and tea gardens in New York.

8. *Old Boston Town Early in This Century,* by 1801er (New York, 1880).

9. *History of Philadelphia,* by J. Thomas Scharf and Thompson Westcott (Philadelphia, 1884).

10. The *National Intelligencer,* Washington, D. C., June 18, 1827. Editorializing on hotels at the time of the opening of the old National in Washington, the *Intelligencer* said that hotels had become " the palaces of the people."

CHAPTER I

1. *Hotel Mail,* February 2, 1895, and other publications of approximate date.

2. *A New England Boyhood,* by Edward Everett Hale.

3. *The Witchery of Sleep,* by Edward Moyer (New York, 1903).

4. The scheme had its disadvantages. Sterne in his *Sentimental Journey* relates with gusto the tale of how he had to share his room with a lady who was a total stranger to him. They drew up a special treaty, which both promised to observe, but which each accused the other of breaking.

5. *The Journal of Madam Sarah Knight* (Boston, 1920).

NOTES

6. *Five Years' Residence in Canada, including a Tour of America, in the year 1823,* by Edward Allen Talbot, Esq. (London, 1824); Volume II, Letter xxxvi.

7. *Diary in America,* by Frederick Marryat (Second series, London, 1839).

8. *History of the People of the United States,* by J. B. McMaster, Volume I.

9. *Letters on the Eastern States,* by William Tudor (Boston, 1821).

10. *The Journal of a Residence in America,* by Frances Anne Kemble (Brussels, 1835).

11. *The Family Magazine,* 1843.

12. *Life and Letters of Charles Dickens,* by John Forster (London, 1874).

13. *A Description of the Tremont House* (Boston, 1830). See also *Boston and the Parker House,* by James W. Spring (Boston, 1927).

14. *A Few Remarks,* by Simeon Ford (New York, 1903).

15. *Reminiscences of Boston,* by Nathaniel Dearborn (Boston, 1851).

16. See *The Descendants of Thomas Boyden,* by Wallace C. Merrill and Amos Boyden (privately printed, Boston).

17. Europeans clung for many years to the theory that one must wait for travel to make the hotel. They believed, as Macaulay believed when he lamented the decline of the English inns, that "the quicker the rate of traveling, the less important it is that there should be numerous agreeable resting places for the traveler" — a theory which still seems to prevail throughout most of the Old World.

18. *Sunday Morning News* (New York), issue of September 13, 1835, and approximate dates. The rapid growth of travel a few years later, when the railroad era got well under way, is indicated by *Putnam's Monthly* for April

THE AMERICAN HOTEL

1853, which estimated the hotel population of New York at that time as "not much short of ten thousand."

19. *Journal of Commerce* (New York), issue of January 4, 1833.

20. Within little more than two years after its opening Holt was forced into bankruptcy, and on October 1, 1835 the master in chancery sold the building and contents at public auction to Levi Disbrow for $175,000. Penniless in his old age, Holt turned again to the restaurant business to try to retrieve his fortune. He died on September 5, 1852, at the age of seventy-one. Holt's Hotel became the United States Hotel a few years after the auction, when another hotel of that name went out of existence. It continued under this name, with many changes of proprietorship, until the 1880's, when the building was converted to other uses.

21. The American Hotel burned down on June 16, 1853, but at the time it was about to be closed to make way for a mercantile building. A delegation of Baltimore firemen, here to attend a tournament, were its guests at the time of the fire.

22. It still appears in historical fiction, perhaps its latest appearance in a novel having been in 1928, in *Parish's Fancy*, by Walter Guest Kellogg.

23. Boyden's lease was obtained at a compromise figure of $17,000 a year. Astor had wanted $20,000. Thus the rental was on a basis of a trifle more than $55 a year for each guest-room, an absurdly low figure as hotel rentals go today, whether in Squeedunk or New York. According to the New York *Tribune*, March 30, 1848, in an article on the death and estate of Astor, it was stated that Astor was then receiving $30,000 a year rental from the Astor House and $15,000 a year income from the City Hotel, which he had owned since about 1830.

24. At the time of the dedication of the cornerstone

NOTES

Astor intended to call his hotel the Park Hotel, but changed his mind a year or so later.

25. Issue of June 4, 1836.

26. *The Journal of a Voyage across the Atlantic in 1844,* by George Moore, Esq. (London, 1845).

27. *Letters from America,* by John Robert Godby (London, 1844), Volume II, Chapter xvi.

28. Jonathan Slick, Esq., was a comic character, the creation of the popular novelist Ann Sophia Winterbotham Stephens.

29. *Diary of Philip Hone,* edited by Allan Nevins (New York, 1928).

CHAPTER II

1. *Hotel Mail,* November 17, 1877.

2. The New England House survived until April 22, 1922. Others survived until comparatively recent dates.

3. 1839 is the generally accepted date of the opening of the Howard, but Henry Collins Brown in *The Book of Old New York* (New York, 1913) gives 1840 as the date. If so, it was very early in that year.

4. This work of art, if that is what it was, has disappeared and little is known of it beyond casual mention of it in the newspapers of the time.

5. *High Life in New York,* by Jonathan Slick, Esq. (Ann Sophia Winterbotham Stephens) (New York, 1843).

6. The *Nation,* September 11, 1884.

7. *Skyscrapers and the Men who Built Them,* by Colonel W. A. Starrett (New York, 1928).

8. *Temple Bar Magazine,* Volume II, 1861.

9. New York *Tribune,* September 19, 1848, and other New York newspapers of that period.

10. Descriptions of the St. Nicholas appeared in the New York *Evening Post,* January 5, 1853; New York *Tribune,* December 3, 1852; New York *Times,* January 7, 1853; and other contemporary newspapers.

Descriptions of the Metropolitan in the *Evening Post,* August 21, 1852; *Tribune,* August 26, 1852; etc.

Descriptions of the New York Hotel in the *Weekly Mirror,* November 30, 1844; etc.

Descriptions of the Prescott House in the *New York Herald,* July 21, 1853; etc.

Also data from the *Hotel Gazette, Hotel Mail,* etc.

11. "New York Daguerreotyped," in *Putnam's Magazine,* April 1853.

12. Quoted by George Augustus Sala, *Belgravia Magazine,* March 1873.

13. Issue of December 3, 1852.

14. The three-thousand-room Hotel Stevens, Chicago, said to be the most expensive commercial building in the world, represents an assessed value of thirty million dollars. (See New York newspapers, November 17, 1928. Newer buildings may have changed its rank.) The new hotel that is to carry on the name of the Waldorf-Astoria will, it is announced, cost more than forty million dollars.

15. New York *Tribune,* August 26, 1852 (Metropolitan data); *Tribune,* August 29, 1854 (Brevoort data), and *Gems of the Hoffman House Collection,* by F. G. De Fountain (New York, 1885) (Hoffman House data).

16. The St. Nicholas stood at Broadway and Spring Street. It was built by D. Henry Haight, and its first lessees were Treadwell, Acker and Company. When it closed, in 1884, a hotel farther north on Broadway immediately adopted its name. There was also a St. Nicholas Hotel in

NOTES

the 1840's, at 28 Cortlandt Street, operated by Wemmell and Dumphrey.

17. New York *Daily Advertiser,* June 17, 1794, and other dates.

18. *The Narrative of a Journey from Quebec to Niagara, through the States of New York, New England, etc.,* by Lieutenant R. D. White (written, 1839; published, Exeter, 1896).

19. This journal, published by Campbell and Whitmarsh at 65 Barclay Street, New York, made its first appearance in November 1844. It continued in publication nearly sixty years and finally was merged with another publication.

20. *Fresh Leaves from the Diary of a Broadway Dandy* (New York, 1852).

21. U. S. Patent Office Reports, 1790 to 1873.

22. New York *Tribune,* July 4, 1844. The Fountain Baths were at 7 Chatham Street (Park Row), within a few steps of a number of hotels.

23. *Travels in Some Parts of North America, in 1804, 1805 and 1806* (Chapter ii), by Robert Sutcliff (Philadelphia, 1812).

24. "New York Daguerreotyped," *Putnam's Magazine,* April 1853.

25. In recent years the Coolidge House has continued to exist under other names. As the Majestic Hotel it closed about a year ago.

26. *Hotel Gazette,* April 6, 1889.

27. Advertisement in New York *Daily Advertiser,* May 17, 1794, and other dates.

28. *Romantic Days in Old Boston,* by Mary Caroline Crawford (Boston, 1910).

29. Joseph Pickering and other visitors from overseas complained about this matter, a hundred years ago, as have other visitors in more recent times. Said Pickering: "Here

I will say a word or two on the excessive fondness of Americans for stoves; each church and meeting house has two to four in each; hardly a poor family in Baltimore but has one or more, at which the cooking is all done in winter, which makes their rooms like ovens, and many people look as if half stewed " (*Inquiries of an Immigrant,* Chapter ii. London, 1832).

30. The *Family Magazine,* 1843.

31. Article on plumbing and chronology of American commerce and industry, in *One Hundred Years of American Commerce,* edited by Chauncey M. Depew (New York, 1895).

32. U. S. Patent Office Reports, 1790 to 1873.

33. Standing advertisement in the *Hotel Mail* of that year.

34. *Travels in America,* Chapter vii, by George Fibbleton, Esq., Ex-Barber to His Majesty, the King of Great Britain (Asa Green) (New York, 1833). This hoist was mentioned in the New York *Journal of Commerce,* January 3, 1833, simply as a baggage hoist.

35. Issue of August 26, 1852.

36. Issue of December 3, 1852.

37. Issue of April 21, 1860.

38. *Edison's Bulletin,* March 17, 1882, published by the Edison Electric Light Company.

39. *Edison's Bulletin,* August 1882. This was not, of course, a sign with letters traced out in electric bulbs. The first sign of this type — the first real electric sign — was designed and built by W. J. Hammer for the Crystal Palace Electrical Exposition in London in 1882. Mr. Hammer was one of Edison's earliest and most capable associates.

40. *Hotel Mail,* July 4, 1891.

41. Theaters lagged behind hotels in adopting electricity. The Bijou Theater, Boston, was the first to use electric footlights, for a performance of *Iolanthe,* on the

NOTES

night of December 12, 1882. Electricity was an expensive readjustment, and incandescent lights had not yet proved themselves, at least not to everybody's satisfaction. The Murray Hill Hotel, New York, which was opened in 1884, had electric lights only in its public rooms. The Normandie, opened in the same year, was without electric lights.

42. The Exchange Coffee House in Boston and Barnum's Hotel in Baltimore had crude annunciators connecting only the bar-room with the dining-room and one or two other public rooms.

43. *Hotel Mail,* December 8, 1877.

44. *Hotel Gazette,* February 10, 1894. The Netherland had opened a few years earlier under the management of General Ferdinand P. Earle, who had long been in the hotel business in New York. It reopened under the management of Stafford and Whittaker, of the Hotel Imperial.

45. *The Story of the Waldorf-Astoria,* by Edward Hungerford (New York, 1926).

46. Issue of December 3, 1852.

47. The first patentee of a bedspring machine was A. L. Bushnell of Poughkeepsie, New York, whose patent is dated August 8, 1871. A few weeks later another patent was issued to M. Ver Pleck, of Albany, New York.

48. *Leslie's Weekly,* May 27, 1871, and the Boston *Globe,* quoted in the *Hotel Gazette,* June 27, 1908.

CHAPTER III

1. *Early Chicago Reminiscences,* by Charles Cleaver (Chicago, 1892).
2. Article on the progress of the city, in San Francisco *City Directory* for 1876.
3. *History of Chicago,* by A. T. Andreas (Chicago, 1886).
4. *The Eastern and Western States of America,* by J. S. Buckingham, Esq. (London, 1842), Volume III, Chapter xiv.
5. *Appleton's Railroad and Steamboat Guide,* issue of 1848.
6. *History of Chicago,* by Andreas.
7. New York *Tribune,* May 31, 1852.
8. United States census, 1860.
9. *Chicago Hand Book for Strangers and Tourists,* published (1869) by Halpin, Hayes and McClure.
10. *Strangers' Guide to Chicago,* by J. B. Bradford (Chicago, 1872).
11. The very first Palmer House appears to have been a three-story armory-like structure in existence in the later 1860's. A picture of it is reproduced in *Chicago and Its Makers,* by Paul Gilbert and Charles Lee Bryson (Chicago, 1929). The picture is a reproduction of the title-page of a piece of sheet music called *The Palmer House Gavotte,* published in 1868. The other Palmer House, destroyed by the fire, was on the west side of State Street, at the corner of Quincy Street. Just before the fire Palmer had begun construction of a much larger and finer Palmer House at Monroe and State streets. Completed about eighteen months after the fire, it stood until about five years ago, when it was torn down to make way for its present successor.

NOTES

12. *Appleton's Handy-Book of American Travel* (the Western Tour), 1873.
13. *History of San Francisco,* by John S. Hittell.
14. *Eldorado, or Adventures in the Path of Empire,* by Bayard Taylor (New York, 1850).
15. *The Argonauts of '49,* by Octavius Thorndike Howe.
16. *Harper's Weekly,* July 11, 1857.
17. *The Forty-Niners,* by Stewart Edward White.
18. *The Argonauts of '49,* by Octavius T. Howe.
19. *History of the San Francisco Bay Region,* by Bailey Millard.
20. *Eldorado, or Adventures in the Path of Empire,* by Bayard Taylor.
21. *Reminiscences of a Ranger,* by Major Bell (reprint, San Francisco, 1927).
22. Taylor's *Eldorado.*
23. *California Life Illustrated,* by Rev. William Taylor (New York, 1882).
24. *The Forty-Niners,* by Stewart Edward White.
25. Hittell's *History of San Francisco.*
26. Chronology of the past year, San Francisco *City Directory,* 1858.
27. Anonymous article, *Overland Monthly,* 1870.
28. *Ibid.*
29. Review of the year's progress, San Francisco *City Directory,* 1875.
30. *Our New West,* by Samuel Bowles (New York, 1869).
31. Anonymous article, *Overland Monthly,* 1870.
32. *Leslie's Illustrated Newspaper,* July 31, 1875.
33. *Hotel Gazette,* 1889.
34. *Historical Souvenir of San Francisco* (San Francisco, 1886).
35. *As I Remember Them,* by C. C. Goodwin.

36. Review of the past year, San Francisco *City Directory*, 1876.

37. New York *Sun*, March 14, 1909. Also other newspaper articles published shortly after Baldwin's death.

38. " The Story of the Destruction and Rebuilding of San Francisco," in the *Western Hotel Reporter*, April 28, 1928.

39. *History of New Orleans*, by John S. Kendall (New Orleans, 1922).

40. *The Inn of Tranquillity*, by John Galsworthy.

41. U. S. census for 1840 and 1850.

42. *Greater Cincinnati and Its People*, by Lewis A. Leonard (New York, 1927).

43. *The Eastern and Western States of America*, by J. S. Buckingham, Esq., Volume III, Chapter vii (London, 1842).

44. *Encyclopedia of the History of St. Louis* (St. Louis, 1899).

45. *America Revisited*, by George Augustus Sala (New York, 1879), Volume II, Chapter xii.

46. " Tulsa, a City of Real Charm," in *Tavern Talk* (Kansas City), November 29, 1929.

CHAPTER IV

1. *General History of Connecticut*, by the Rev. Samuel Peters.

2. Carl Russell Fish, in *The Rise of the Common Man* (New York, 1928), says: " Americans of the Thirties and Forties were laughed at by foreigners, and still are by their descendants, for their frequent assertion that every American was a king in his own country. Few remember today,

NOTES

what every schoolboy knew, that this was not a figure of speech, but a specific provision of the national and every State constitution."

3. *History of Coshocton, Ohio*, by N. N. Hill, Jr. (1881).

4. *Perley Poore's Reminiscences*, by Benjamin Perley Poore.

5. *Domestic Manners of the Americans*, by Frances M. Trollope (London, 1832), Chapter iv.

6. *Old Boston Taverns*, by Samuel Adams Drake (Boston, 1917).

7. *Travels in America in 1849 and 1850*, by Lady Emmeline Stuart Wortley (New York, 1851). In Chapter viii the writer mentions that the law against smoking on the streets was still being enforced.

8. The Marlboro was closed about 1870 and was torn down in 1879.

9. *Hotel Mail*, May 17, 1879.

10. *The Stranger in America*, by Charles William Janson (London, 1807). Janson is one of those who mention that hotel maids demanded the liberty to bundle.

11. *A Second Visit to the United States*, by Sir Charles Lyall (London, 1849).

12. *Belgravia Magazine*, March 1873.

13. The *New Yorker*, February 27, 1836.

14. Issue of March 7, 1857.

15. *Diary in America*, by Frederick Marryat (London, 1839).

16. Anthony Trollope, Colonel A. M. Maxwell (*A Run through the United States in 1840*), C. D. Arfwedson (*The United States and Canada in 1832*), J. S. Buckingham (*The Eastern and Western States of America*), John Robert Godby (*Letters from America*), H. Reid (*Sketches in North America*), and several others speak of the great volume of travel in America.

17. *Letters from America,* by John R. Godby (London, 1844), Volume I, Letter iii.

18. *America: A Four Years' Residence in the United States and Canada,* by William Brown (Leeds, 1849), Chapter iii.

19. *History of the People of the United States,* by J. B. McMaster, Volume VII.

20. Francis Power Cobbe, in the *Forum,* April 1890.

21. *Hints on Commercial Traveling,* by a Veteran Highwayman (Glasgow, 1837).

22. A similar estimate was made by Charles S. Plummer in *Leaves from a Drummer's Diary* (New York, 1889).

23. Linus P. Brockett's *Commercial Travelers' Guidebook* (New York, 1871).

24. A. M. Palmer in an article on the theater in *One Hundred Years of American Commerce,* edited by Chauncey M. Depew (New York, 1895).

25. *Notes on the United States of America,* by George Combe (Edinburgh, 1841).

26. New York *Tribune,* quoted in the *Hotel Gazette,* June 27, 1885.

27. Rand, McNally and Company's *Guide to New York City,* 1898 edition.

28. Cincinnati *Enquirer,* quoted in *Hotel Gazette,* May 17, 1884.

29. *The Great Metropolis; a Mirror of New York,* by Junius Henry Browne (Hartford, 1869).

30. Anonymous article, *Chambers' Journal* (1854).

31. *James Fenimore Cooper,* by Thomas R. Lounsbury (Boston, 1882).

32. *Life of Thurlow Weed,* by Thurlow Weed Barnes (Boston, 1884), Volume II, Chapter xxvii.

33. *Hotel Mail,* 1877.

34. Jay G. Hilliard, in the *Western Hotel Reporter,* January 12, 1929.

NOTES

CHAPTER V

1. New York *Times*, 1891; and the Onderdonck Scrapbook, 1863–4, New York Public Library. The story of David Reynolds also is related by Lydia Maria (Francis) Child, in *Letters from New York* (Boston, 1843). According to her version of it, Reynolds was a New Englander, sold flowers under the tree when he was a boy, and later built the hotel. Reynolds did not, however, build the hotel.

2. *American Society,* by George M. Towle (London, 1870), Volume I, Chapter xx.

3. The *American Almanac,* 1831 (Boston), page 304.

4. *A Subaltern's Furlough: Descriptive of Scenes in Various Parts of the United States during the Summer and Autumn of 1832,* by E. T. Coke (New York, 1833).

5. New York *Tribune,* April 19, 1847.

6. Chapter xi.

7. See *The Americans, in the Moral, Social and Political Relations,* by Francis J. Grund (Boston, 1837), Volume II, Chapter x. Old files of the hotel press mention Mine Host's railroad activities.

8. "Early Taverns of New Brunswick," by William H. Benedict, in *Proceedings of the New Jersey Historical Society,* Volume III, No. iii, New Series, 1918; *Hotel Gazette,* October 20, 1883, and other dates.

9. *Scribner's Monthly,* December 1878. The life of Drew is related in *The Book of Daniel Drew,* by Bouck White (New York, 1910).

10. *Buffalo Historical Society Publications,* Volume XVI.

11. *America: A Four Years' Residence in the United States and Canada,* by William Brown (Leeds, 1849), Chapter iii.

12. *The History of Claremont, N. H.,* by O. F. R. Waite (1895).

13. *Boston and the Parker House,* by James W. Spring (Boston, 1927). Also *Hotel Gazette* obituary, 1884.

14. *Leslie's Weekly,* February 18, 1860.

15. *Appleton's Railroad and Steamboat Companion,* by W. Williams (1848 edition).

16. Biographical sketches of John B. Drake appear in *Chicago, Its History and Its Builders,* by J. S. Currey (Chicago, 1912); *Chicago and Its Makers,* by P. T. Gilbert (Chicago, 1929).

17. The story of Drake's purchase of the Michigan Avenue Hotel is related briefly in *Chicago and Its Makers* and *Chicago, Its History and Its Builders,* and in the *American Magazine,* March 1922.

18. *The National Cyclopædia of American Biography* (New York, 1904), Volume XII. Biographical sketches of Palmer also appear in *Chicago and Its Makers; Chicago, Its History and Its Builders; Hotel Gazette,* August 15, 1885; *Leslie's Illustrated Newspaper,* March 19, 1887; etc.

19. "A Bell-Boy's Rise," New York *Times,* June 4, 1922 (and various other newspapers, magazines, etc.).

20. Mr. Statler died on April 16, 1928.

21. See "The Amiable Innkeeper," by William Weimar, in the *New Yorker,* November 12, 1927.

22. New York *World,* August 6, 1898. See also "Hobson — the Portrait of a Zealot," by M. R. Werner, in *Liberty,* February 15, 1930.

23. *The Story of the Waldorf-Astoria,* by Edward Hungerford (New York, 1925); *Hotel Review,* March 4, 1922; the *New Yorker,* September 24, 1927; etc.

24. *The Story of the Waldorf-Astoria,* by Hungerford.

NOTES

CHAPTER VI

1. *Harper's Weekly,* April 18, 1857.
2. " The Indestructible Value," by Dr. George Frederick Kunz, in the *Saturday Evening Post,* May 5, 1928.
3. Article on " New York Fashions in Jewelry," quoted from the Charleston *Mercury,* in the New York *Tribune,* September 9, 1859.
4. Dr. George Frederick Kunz, in the *Saturday Evening Post,* May 5, 1928.
5. *Hotel Mail,* October 13, 1877.
6. This was printed in a new weekly journal that attacked hotels persistently for a year or two, but changed its tone completely when hotel advertising began to appear in its pages.
7. *What I Know about Commercial Traveling,* by A. Emerson Belcher (Toronto, 1883).
8. *Hotel Gazette,* June 27, 1885.
9. " Advice to Beginners in the Hotel Business," in *A Few Remarks,* by Simeon Ford (New York, 1903).
10. *Reminiscences of a Hotel Man,* by Henry S. Mower (New York, 1912).
11. *The Western World, or Travels through the United States in 1846 and 1847,* by Alexander Mackay, Esq. (London, 1849).
12. " A Tintype of the Flash Age," by Alexander Gardiner, in the *Saturday Evening Post,* November 23, 1928. See also *Dictionary of American Biography* (New York, 1929), Volume III.
13. Report of Frank A. K. Boland, counsel, at the annual convention of the American Hotel Association, 1928.
14. *The Inns of the Middle Ages,* by W. C. Firebaugh (Chicago, 1924), page 125.

15. *Memorable Days in America,* by William Faux (London, 1823).
16. *American Towns and People,* by Harrison Rhodes (New York, 1920).
17. *The Eastern and Western States of America,* by J. S. Buckingham, Esq. (London, 1842), Volume II, Chapter vii.
18. *Hotel Gazette,* August 13, 1898.
19. *Hotel Gazette,* September 22, 1888.
20. *The Eastern and Western States of America,* by J. S. Buckingham (London, 1842).

CHAPTER VII

1. Samuel Adams Drake relates, in *Old Boston Taverns,* that in 1800 five shillings a day was the usual charge in Boston, and a pint of Madeira was served to each guest at dinner.
2. "Yankee Notions," by "Q. Q.," in the *New Monthly Magazine* (London, 1834), states that "American public dinners outdo England in numbers and lavishness." John Lambert, in *Travels through Canada and the United States in 1806, 1807 and 1808* (London, 1814), and other travelers speak of the number of dinners and the toasts.
3. Even at home the American habit of bolting food was criticized, as in the *National Intelligencer,* of Washington, issue of November 20, 1836. But several English travelers of that period and earlier praise the meals and the deportment of diners, as did Charles Augustus Murray, in *Travels in North America in 1834, 1835 and 1836* (Volume

NOTES

1). Murray said he saw no bolting of food and heard no loud talk.

4. *Impressions of America and American Churches,* by the Rev. George Lewis (Edinburgh, 1845).

5. Quoted in the *Hotel Gazette* of July 4, 1885.

6. *An Excursion to the United States of North America in the Summer of 1794,* by Henry Wansay (London).

7. *Men and Manners in America,* by Captain Thomas Hamilton (Edinburgh, 1833).

8. "New York—Its Hotels, Waterworks, and Things in General," by J. W. Hengiston, Esq., in the *New Monthly Magazine* (London, 1853).

9. *A Run through the United States in 1840,* by Lieutenant-Colonel A. M. Maxwell (London, 1841), Volume II, Chapter xxxiv.

10. *British American Guide Book,* by H. Bailliere (New York, 1859), Section 4.

11. *Travels through the Northern Part of the United States,* by Edward A. Kendall (New York, 1809).

12. *Three Years in North America,* by James Stuart (London, 1833).

13. *The Western World,* by Alexander Mackay, Esq. (London, 1849).

14. Boston Correspondent, *Hotel Mail,* February 2, 1895.

15. *Hotel Gazette,* January 9, 1886.

16. *The Virginian,* by Owen Wister.

17. *Perley Poore's Reminiscences,* by Benjamin Perley Poore.

18. *Incidents of Western Travel,* by Bishop George F. Pierce, D. D. (Nashville, 1859).

19. *Old Boston Taverns,* by Samuel Adams Drake (Boston, 1917).

20. *From Pillar to Post,* by John Kendrick Bangs.

21. Big breakfasts were by no means peculiar to

America. English annals and literature are full of them, and the same may be said of France. The usual breakfast of Louis XIV was four cutlets or a fat chicken, six eggs, two slices of ham, and a quart and a half of champagne. His dinner consisted of eight plates of meat, six of poultry, and four of fish, with soup and pastry.

22. The *Temple Bar*, 1861.
23. Quoted in the *Hotel Gazette*, July 4, 1885.
24. *Impressions of America, during the Years 1833, 1834 and 1835*, by Tyrone Power (London, 1836), Volume I.
25. *Three Years in North America*, by James Stuart (London, 1833).
26. *Men and Manners in America*, by Thomas Hamilton (Edinburgh, 1833).
27. Various advertisements in the *Sunday Morning News*, New York, 1835. The first of these advertisements was that of the United States Hotel, at 178 Pearl Street, operated by Raymond and Groot. This was not the more famous United States Hotel, which was first known as Holt's Hotel.
28. New York *Evening Post*, March 9, 1840.
29. London *Illustrated News*, August 10, 1844.
30. New York *Weekly Mirror*, December 7, 1844.
31. New York *Tribune*, November 27, 1864.
32. New York *Herald*, March 26, 1865.
33. *Hotel Gazette*.
34. *Old Boston Taverns*, by Samuel Adams Drake (Boston, 1917).
35. *Hotel Gazette*, August 22, 1885. (Antiquarians of more recent date say the incident occurred at Moon's Lake House, on Saratoga Lake.)
36. Mrs. C. B. King of Philadelphia, in an address on October 2, 1928, at the convention of the National Restaurant Association, Atlantic City.

NOTES

37. *Hotel Gazette,* May 6, 1899.
38. *Hotel Gazette,* June 22, 1889.
39. *Our New West,* by Samuel Bowles (New York, 1869).
40. *Leslie's Illustrated Newspaper,* January 2, 1875.
41. San Francisco *City Directory,* 1867.
42. New York *Herald,* December 6, 1851.

CHAPTER VIII

1. Issue of August 23, 1853.
2. Issue of August 13, 1853.
3. *American Society,* by George M. Towle (London, 1870), Volume II, Chapter v.
4. *In Vacation America,* by Harrison Rhodes (New York, 1915), Chapter iii.
5. *Ibid.*
6. *The White Sulphur Springs,* by William Alexander MacCorkle (New York, 1915).
7. *Letters from Nahant,* by W. W. Wheildon (Lynn, 1842).
8. *Life and Letters of Edward Everett Hale,* by Edward Everett Hale, Jr. (Boston, 1917).
9. *Travel through the Northern Parts of the United States,* by Edward A. Kendall (New York, 1809).
10. *A Northern Tour,* by Henry Dilworth Gilpin (Philadelphia, 1825), page 66.
11. S. De Veaux naïvely exonerates resident Saratogans from guilt in the sinful amusements that went on around them. In *The Travelers' Own Book to Saratoga, Niagara Falls and Canada* (Buffalo, 1841) he writes: " The

citizens of Saratoga are a steady, quiet people, and in no way inclined to participate in the follies and dissipation which is annually poured in upon them."
    12. Advertisement in the New York *Evening Post,* various issues, June 1835.
    13. Saratoga *Sentinel,* July 21, 1835.
    14. *The Travelers' Own Book to Saratoga, Niagara Falls and Canada,* by S. De Veaux (Buffalo, 1841).
    15. *Reminiscences of Saratoga,* by William L. Stone (New York, 1875), Chapter xxviii.
    16. *Ibid.,* Chapter xxi.
    17. Advertisement in the New York *Herald,* June 27, 1848.
    18. Morrissey, "Old Smoke" of the prize-ring, was not the first to have a gambling-casino at Saratoga, but his establishment was the maximum of elegance. This luxurious place came eventually into the hands of Richard Canfield, America's most celebrated gambler. Morrissey was still proprietor of it when he was elected to Congress from a Tammany-controlled district.
    19. "Summer Life in the States," by John C. Hutcheson, in *Belgravia Magazine,* Volume XV (1871).
    20. Amusement parks at Coney Island and elsewhere still have military bands, but in this age, when the air is literally cluttered with jazz, military bands are merely a sort of necessary evil.
    21. *History of Cape May County,* by Lewis Townsend Stevens (Cape May, 1897).
    22. New York *Herald,* July 19, 1853.
    23. *Newport, the City by the Sea,* by James W. Bowditch (Providence, 1882).
    24. *Lotus Eating,* by George William Curtis (New York, 1852).
    25. New York *Herald,* August 23, 1853.
    26. *Hotel Mail,* May 3, 1879.

NOTES

27. *Boston Monthly Magazine,* June 1825.
28. Mrs. Sigourney's poem on Nahant begins:
    Rude, rock-bound coast, where erst the Indian roamed,
    The iron shoulders of thy furrowed cliffs
    Made black with smiting, still in stubborn force,
    Resist the scourging wave.
29. *Scenes from my Native Land,* by Lydia H. Sigourney (Boston, 1845). The hotel, greatly enlarged about 1850, was destroyed by fire on September 12, 1864, and was never rebuilt.
30. *Nahant and Other Places on the North Shore,* by James Lloyd Homer (Boston, 1848). Homer declares he participated in the perpetration of this hoax.
31. The sea-serpent also is described by W. W. Wheildon in *Letters from Nahant* and by Alonzo Lewis in *A Picture of Nahant* (Boston, 1848). The serpent was reported to be fifty to seventy feet long, and as large around as a barrel, and carried its head six to eight feet above water.
32. A pamphlet entitled *Experiments and Observations on the Mineral Waters of Philadelphia, Abington and Bristol,* by Dr. Benjamin Rush (Philadelphia, 1773), was perhaps the first of a great mass of resort literature, medical and otherwise.
33. *Things as They Are, or Notes of a Traveler* (New York, 1834), Chapter xiii; or *Three Years in North America,* by James Stuart (London, 1833).
34. *A Topographical Sketch of Nahant,* by Walter Channing, M.D. (Boston, 1821), believed to have been a pamphlet reprint from the Boston *Weekly Messenger*). Dr. Channing's claims for Nahant were almost as impressive, however, as those made for the springs. He declared Nahant was good for three classes of ailments — "in weaning children suffering from the diseases of dentition"; for dyspepsia (already a popular disease in America); and for

321

THE AMERICAN HOTEL

debility and emaciations, "with which some organic affections are attended."

35. *Reminiscences of Saratoga,* by William L. Stone (New York, 1875), Chapter xxviii. Clarke had gone to Saratoga in 1826, and his enterprise did perhaps more than that of any other individual to popularize Saratoga.

36. One of Atlantic City's booklets in the 1880's listed the testimony of 312 physicians, and several letters by prominent men. Other resorts had spread a report that Atlantic City's beach was infested by malarial mosquitoes.

37. The Mansion House burned down in 1856 and the American House, with 125 rooms, was built on the site.

38. *History of Cape May County,* by Lewis Townsend Stevens (Cape May, 1897).

39. Cain and Colonel Frank T. Foster were the proprietors.

40. Philadelphia *Bulletin,* September 6, 1856.

41. *Chamber's Journal,* 1854, Volume VI, page 190, and Volume VIII, page 153.

42. The Keystone Hotel Company, a subsidiary of the Pennsylvania Railroad Company, sold its hotel holdings, at Cape May, Bryn Mawr, and Cresson Springs, Pennsylvania, in 1887, and the railroad went out of the hotel business.

43. *The Fashionable Tour, a Guide to Travelers Visiting the Middle and Northern States* (Saratoga, 1830).

44. A British visitor at Saratoga at this period noted that " the bar-keepers at these hotels are seemingly as respectable as anyone else." He said they played checkers with the guests " and seemed to feel at ease in doing so." Backgammon, then popular in England, was almost unknown at Saratoga, and cards were seldom seen. Invalids drove about a great deal in carriages and drank lots of water. But " there were no showy equipages." Pedestrians were looked upon with surprise and were invited to get in and ride. Doors

NOTES

were left unlocked at night, shutters left open, and clothes left overnight to bleach on the unfenced greens.

45. *Leslie's Illustrated Newspaper,* July 31, 1875, page 371.

Marvin was born at Ballston on February 27, 1809 and was connected with the old States from the time it opened in 1824. He served in Congress from 1862 to 1868.

46. *Things as They Are, or Notes of a Traveler* (New York, 1834).

47. *The Album of Long Branch,* by J. H. Schenck (New York, 1868).

48. This was kept by C. A. Stetson, Jr., son of General Charles Stetson, of the Astor House, New York. After the war it was enlarged. Under the name of West End Hotel it survived until about three years ago, when it was destroyed by fire.

49. *Popular Resorts and How to Reach Them,* by John B. Bachelder (Boston, 1875), third edition, page 231.

50. *The Story of Manhattan Beach* (New York, 1879).

51. *History of the Rockaways,* by Alfred H. Bellot (New York, 1918).

52. "The Big Parade on Atlantic City's Boardwalk," by Robert L. Duffus, in New York *Times Magazine,* August 12, 1928.

53. *Atlantic City, Its Early and Modern History,* by Carnesworthe (Philadelphia, 1868).

CHAPTER IX

1. New York *Herald,* July 21, 1853, and other New York newspapers of approximate dates. The Prescott opened for business on August 2, 1853.
2. The name Crook's Hotel was resumed in the 1890's.
3. *Gems of the Hoffman House Collection,* by F. G. De Contain (New York, 1885).
4. The original building, however, disappeared some years later.
5. *Hotel Gazette,* September 2, 1895.
6. "Chiefly about War Matters," by Nathaniel Hawthorne, *Atlantic Monthly,* July 1862.
7. *The Annals of Albany,* by Joel Munsell (Albany, 1856), Volume VII.
8. *Ibid.,* Volume X.
9. *Richmond, Her Past and Her Present,* by William Asbury Christian (Richmond, 1912).
10. *Richmond, Its People and Its Story,* by Mary Newton Stanard (Philadelphia, 1923).
11. "Abraham Lincoln in Pittsburgh and the Birth of the Republican Party," by Charles W. Dahlinger, in the *Western Pennsylvania Historical Magazine* (October, 1920); also *The Standard History of Pittsburgh,* by Erasmus Wilson (Pittsburgh, 1898).
12. *History of the City of Toledo,* edited by Clark Waggoner (New York and Toledo, 1888).
13. *Handbook of Springfield,* edited by Moses King (Springfield, 1884); also *Springfield — History of the Town and City,* by Mason A. Green (Springfield, 1888).

INDEX

Actors and hotels, 125–6
Adams, Charles Francis, 41
Adams, William T., 139, 177, 288
Adams House (Boston), 41, 177, 288
Adams House (Chicago), 82
Adelphi Hotel (New York), 11
Agassiz, Louis, 132
Age of Innocence, The, 270
Albany, hotels in, 281–3; *and see names of hotels*
Albemarle Hotel (New York), 266
Aldrich, Thomas Bailey, 132
Alger, Horatio, Jr., 31–2, 138, 139, 159
Algonquin Hotel (New York), 131
Alhambra Hotel (Atlantic City), 256
Allen (Astor House, N. Y.), 178, 179
Alta Californian, 86
Amen Corner (Fifth Ave. Hotel), 133, 264
American Almanac, 142
American Exchange Hotel (San Francisco), 87, 89
American History, Magazine of, 195, 205
American Hotel (Buffalo), 47–8, 99, 118, 149, 150
American Hotel (New York), 11, 31, 35, 156
American Hotel (San Francisco), 88
American House (Boston), 24, 41, 64, 152, 288, 291
American House (Cleveland), 122
American House (Philadelphia), 46, 275
American Notes, 16, 110, 111
American Temperance House (Chicago), 79
Andem (Gramercy Hotel, N. Y.), 267
Annunciators in hotels, 27, 69–70
Ansonia Hotel (New York), 167
Appleton, James, 142
Aquidneck House (Newport), 238
Argonaut Hotel (San Francisco), 97
Arlington Hotel (Binghampton, N. Y.), 166, 167
Arlington Hotel (Boston), 62
Arlington Hotel (Washington), 276–7
Arnold, Miss (St. Louis), 165
Arthur, Chester, 246
Ashland House (Atlantic City), 256

i

INDEX

Ashman, A. L., 269
Astor, John Jacob, 29, 32, 141
Astor, William Waldorf, 166
Astor House (New York), 14, 23, 29, 31–7, 41, 42, 44, 47–8, 49, 56–7, 63, 73, 117, 133, 141, 144, 149, 151, 152, 156, 178, 197–8, 199, 207, 209–10, 211, 214, 260, 275
Astor House (San Francisco), 85
Atlantic City, hotels in, 243, 254–6
Atlantic Hall (Atlantic City), 243
Atlantic Monthly, 270
Auditorium Hotel (Chicago), 153

Baldwin, Elias J., 94–6
Baldwin Hotel (San Francisco), 95–6, 291
Ballard, J. P., 283
Ballard House (Richmond), 283
Ball's Hotel (Brownsville, Pa.), 183, 188
Baltimore, hotels in, 47, 291; and see names of hotels
Bangs, John Kendrick, 203
Barnum, David, 11, 47
Barnum, P. T., 139, 239
Barnum's Hotel (Baltimore), 47, 152, 291; and see City Hotel
Baruch, Bernard M., 277
Bates, Harvey, 157
Bates House (Indianapolis), 157
Bath facilities in hotels, 24, 33, 36, 55–7, 59–62
Battle House (Mobile), 14
Baumann, Gustave, 163, 164
Beaubein, Mark, 78

Bedloe, Thomas H., 255
Bedloe's Hotel (Atlantic City), 256
Beecher, Henry Ward, 67
Bellboys in hotels, 27
Bellevue Hotel (Newport), 237
Bellevue Hotel (Philadelphia), 132, 166
Bellew, Kyrle, 170
Bellona Hotel (New Brunswick, N. J.), 148
Belmont, Mrs. Oliver H. P., 272–3
Belmont Hotel (New York), 97, 211
Benjamin Franklin Hotel (Philadelphia), 47, 274
Benson, Garrett J., 281
Benson's Hotel (Albany), 281
Berry, William F., 146
Bertillon, Alphonse, 191
Beveridge, Albert J., 275
Billings, John H., 47, 153, 274
Biltmore Hotel (New York), 163–4
Bismarck Hotel (Chicago), 291
Blaine, James G., 264–5
Blatch, Harriot S., 128
Bobo, William M., 44
Boldt, George C., 132, 165–6, 180
Bonaparte, Joseph, 111
Boody, Azariah, 287
Boody House (Toledo), 287
Boomer, Lucius M., 164–5, 180
Booth, John Wilkes, 211, 275–6
Booths, the, 139
Boston, hotels in, 11, 41, 288; and see names of hotels
Boston Tavern (Boston), 288
Bouguereau, Adolphe William, 266

ii

INDEX

Bowles, Samuel, 84, 90, 222
Bowman, John McEntee, 163–164
Boyden, Dwight, 27, 32, 141, 151, 199, 206
Boyden, Frederick, 27, 32, 141, 151, 283
Boyden, Simeon, 26–7, 32, 141, 151
Boylston Hotel (Boston), 41
Brady, Diamond Jim, 170
Branch Hotel (New York), 139–140
Bread and Cheese Lunch club, 131–2
Breslin, James H., 39, 153, 252, 262
Brevoort Hotel (New York), 46, 54, 153, 292–3
Bridal chambers in hotels, 50–2
Briggs, William, 81, 290
Briggs House (Chicago), 81, 82, 290–1
Brighton Beach Hotel (Coney Island), 252, 269
Broadway Central Hotel (New York), 293
Broadway Hotel (Kansas City), 103
Broadway Hotel (New York), 118, 151
Brockway, Horace H., 153
Bromfield House (Boston), 153
Bromley (Stanwix Hall, Albany), 283
Brooklyn House (San Francisco), 89
Brown, Jesse, 201, 202
Brown, M. O., 68
Brunswick Hotel (Boston), 288
Brunswick Hotel (New York), 271

Bryant, William Cullen, 131
Buchanan, James, 245–6, 276
Buckingham, J. S., 78–9, 101, 187–8
Buckingham Hotel (New York), 270, 275
Buffalo, hotels in, 47–8, 286; *and see names of hotels*
Bulfinch, Charles, 15
Bull's Head Tavern (New York), 148
Bunker's Mansion House (New York), 11
Buntline, Ned, 292–3
Burke's Hotel (Chicago), 83
Burnet House (Cincinnati), 14, 48, 99–100, 152, 157, 286
Burr, Aaron, 233
Butler, Benjamin F., 266

Cain, Philip, 244
Caldwell, Archibald, 77
Calhoun, John C., 111
Calvert family, 275
Camel, Tom, 233
Canfield, Richard A., 178–9
Cape May, hotels at, 235, 236, 242, 243–6; *and see names of hotels*
Carew, Joseph, 289
Carlton House (New York), 36, 44, 156
Carnegie, Andrew, 274
Carrolton Hotel (Baltimore), 291
Caruso, Enrico, 135
Cary, Alice, 142
Cary, Phœbe, 142
Castle Square Hotel (Boston), 62
Cataract House (Niagara Falls), 185–7, 258

iii

INDEX

Center House (Cape May), 244
Chambers' Journal, 244-5
Chandler, Zachariah, 265
Chapin, E. S., 289
Chapin, Marvin, 289
Charleston Hotel (Charleston, S. C.), 14
Chester County House (Atlantic City), 256
Chicago, hotels in, 76-83, 290-291; *and see* names of hotels
Chicago Beach Hotel (Chicago), 291
Childs, George W., 215
Cincinnati, hotels in, 99-100, 286; *and see* names of hotels
City Hotel (Baltimore), 11, 24, 47, 56; *and see* Barnum's Hotel
City Hotel (Boston), 27
City Hotel (Chicago), 79; *and see* Sherman House
City Hotel (New York), 10, 11, 13, 31, 131-2, 156, 199, 206, 209, 213
City Hotel (San Francisco), 83, 84, 85, 223
Clarendon Hotel (Atlantic City), 256
Clarendon Hotel (New York), 44, 45, 269
Clarendon Hotel (Saratoga), 246
Clark, Albert, 41, 288
Clark, Champ, 277
Clarke, John, 242
Clay, Henry, 110, 189, 236, 275
Cleaver, Charles, 75-6
Clemens, Samuel L., *see* Twain, Mark
Clerks in hotels, 169-80
Cleveland, Frances Folsom, 287

Cleveland, Grover, 218-19, 264, 266, 287
Clifton House (Chicago), 82
Clinton, De Witt, 132, 185
Clinton Hotel (Albany), 281
Clinton Hotel (New York), 156
Clover Club, 132
Clubs and hotels, 131-2
Coal Oil Johnny, 83, 89, 274, 292
Coates, Kersey, 103
Coates House (Kansas City), 103
Coke, E. T., 143
Cole (Saratoga racecourse), 234
Coleman, Robert, 151-2, 207, 275
Coleman, Robert W., 269
Coleman House (New York), 269
Coles, Capt., 292
Collins, Wilkie, 269
Columbia Hall (Cape May), 245
Columbia Hall (Lebanon Springs, N. Y.), 184, 188, 241
Columbia Hotel (Cape May), 244
Columbian Centinel (Boston), 239, 240
Combe, George, 127
Commercial Hotel (New York), 262; *and see* Occidental Hotel
Commercial House (Chicago), 82
Commercial House (San Francisco), 89
Commercial travelers and hotels, 123-5
Commodore, Hotel (New York), 167
Condé, 213

iv

INDEX

Coney Island, hotels on, 250–4; *and see names of hotels*
Congress Hall (Albany), 281, 282
Congress Hall (Atlantic City), 255
Congress Hall (Cape May), 243, 245, 246
Congress Hall (Long Branch), 249
Congress Hall (Saratoga) 232–233, 246
Congress Hall (Washington), 277
Congress Hotel (Chicago), 158
Conkling, Alfred, 185
Conkling, Roscoe, 144, 185, 264
Connecticut, General History of, 108
Connors, Chuck, 137
Conover House (Long Branch), 247
Constellation (New York), 32–3
Continental Hotel (Long Branch), 249
Continental Hotel (Philadelphia), 47, 274
Cooke, Joseph G., 278
Cooley, Justin M., 288
Cooley Hotel (Springfield, Mass.), 288–9
Coolidge, Calvin, 280, 288
Coolidge House (Boston), 61
Cooper, James Fenimore, 131, 132
Corbin, Austin, 251–2
Corday, Charlotte, 60
Cornell, Ezra, 184
Correggio, 266
Corwin, Tom, 157
Cosmopolitan Hotel (New York), 45, 153, 292

Cosmopolitan Hotel (San Francisco), 88, 291
Cotter, John, 208
Couch, Ira, 79–80, 82
Couch, James, 79–80, 82
Cozzens, William B., 31, 102, 153
Cozzens brothers, 102
Cozzens House (Omaha), 102
Craig Hall (Atlantic City), 162
Cranston, Hiram, 152
Crawford, Abel, 258
Crawford, F. Marion, 292
Crockett, S. Frank, 153
Crockett, Selden, 153
Croker, Richard, 272
Crook, Samuel H., 264
Crook's Hotel (New York), 67, 264; *and see* Everett, Hotel
Crosby's Hotel (Albany), 281
Crossan, James, 284
Crossan, J. McDonald, 153, 284
Croton Hotel (New York), 144
Crum, George, 219
Cruttenden, Leverett, 282
Crystal Palace, New York hotels built for visitors to, 45, 61, 65
Curtis, George William, 237–8

Daily Aurora (Philadelphia), 243
Dakin (architect), 99
Dam, Andrew J., 178, 179
Darling, Alfred B., 152
Davenport, E. L., 156
Davis, J. M., 292
Davis, Jefferson, 284
Davis, Jefferson Columbus, 294
Davis, John W., 293
De Grott, Capt., 261
Delaven, Edward C., 144

v

INDEX

Delaven House (Albany), 144, 281
Delaware House (Cape May), 244
Delmonico, Charles, 218, 219
Democracy in America, 113
Dennison, William, 188
Dennison House (Cincinnati), 188–9
De Quincey, Thomas, 7
Description of the Tremont House, A, 15
Diamonds and hotel clerks, 170–3
Dickens, Charles, 16, 23, 52, 110, 111, 115, 125, 202, 269
Diez, Hotel, 262; *and see* Prescott House
Dr. Claudius, 292
Donadi (Gramercy Hotel, New York), 267
Donahoe, James A., 88
Douglas, Benjamin, 241
Douglas, Stephen A., 241
Douglas House (Omaha), 102
Dow, Neal, 142
Drake, John B., 77, 153, 157–8, 290
Drake, John B., Jr., 157
Drake, Samuel Adams, 112, 213
Drake, Tracy A., 157
Drew, Daniel, 148–9
Duffy, Tom, 160
Dugro, Justice, 273
Duncan, John M., 118
Durand, Asher Brown, 132

Eagle Hotel (New York), 292; *and see* Eastern Hotel
Eagle Tavern (Buffalo), 149
Eagle Tavern (Niagara Falls), 258

Earl, Ferdinand P., 272, 273
Eastern Exchange Hotel (Boston), 63
Eastern Hotel (New York), 291–2
Eaton, William S., 83
Ebbitt House (Washington), 277, 278
Edison, Thomas A., 66, 67, 68
Edward IV, 19
Edward VII, 269, 283
Eitel brothers, 291
Eldridge, Thomas B., 103
Eldridge House (Lawrence, Kansas), 103
Electric lighting in hotels, 66–8
Elevators in hotels, 64–6
Emerson, Ralph Waldo, 132
Enquirer (Cincinnati), 128–9
Enterprise (Virginia City, Nevada), 94
European plan in hotels, 207–9
Eutaw House (Baltimore), 47, 151, 152, 291
Evening Post (New York), 50–1, 233–4
Everett, C. E., 67
Everett, Edward, 14, 269
Everett, Hotel (Park Row, New York), 66, 67, 264, 265
Everett, Samuel H., 66, 67
Everett House (Union Square, New York), 66–7, 177, 269
Everett's Hotel (Vesey St., New York), 67–8
Examiner (San Francisco), 190–1
Exchange Coffee House (Boston), 11, 26
Exchange Coffee House (Philadelphia), 11

INDEX

Exchange Hotel (Montgomery, Ala.), 200
Exchange Hotel (New Orleans), 46
Exchange Hotel (New York), 42
Exchange Hotel (Pittsburgh), 284
Exchange Hotel (Richmond), 283

Fairmont Hotel (San Francisco), 96
Family Magazine, 23
Faux, William, 182
Fay, Patrick, 139
Featherstonaugh, John, 231-2
Ferber, Edna, 216
Ferguson, Widow, 248
Ferrin, Charles B., 269
Ficken, Edward, 272
Fifth Avenue Hotel (New York), 45, 53, 64, 65-6, 68, 116, 133-4, 152, 180, 211, 262, 265-6, 269
Firebaugh, W. C., 181, 182
Fish, Carl Russell, 54
Fisk, Jim, 148, 219, 293
Floor-clerks in hotels, 92
Floyd (St. Charles Hotel, New Orleans), 99
Food and hotels, 192-223
Ford, Henry, 256
Ford, Simeon, 25-6, 70, 174-5, 202-3
Fosbrooke, Jonas, 19
Franklin, Benjamin, 60
Franklin House (Cleveland), 122
Franklin House (New York), 156
French, J., 71

French, Richard, 152, 212
French cuisine in hotels, 213-15
French Lick Hotel (French Lick Springs), 146
French's Hotel (New York), 152, 212
Fuller (Buckingham Hotel), 270
Fuller, Leigh A., 179
Fuller, Seth, 27, 69

Gadsby, John, 275
Gadsby's Hotel (Washington), 275; *and see* National Hotel
Gage (Buckingham Hotel), 270
Gale, Daniel, 275
Gallier (architect), 99
Galsworthy, John, 99
Galt House (Louisville), 14, 48, 110, 286, 294
Gansevoort, General, 282
Garden City House (Chicago), 82
Gardner House (Chicago), 82
Garfield, James A., 246, 264
Garrison, W. D., 153
Gaslight in hotels, 24-6, 32-3
Gates, John W., 274
Gazette (Boston), 240
Gem of the Prairies, 80
Genesee Hotel (Buffalo), 287
Gerard House (New York), 292; *and see* Cosmopolitan Hotel
Gibson, Peter, 286
Gibson House (Cincinnati), 286
Gideon Society, 125
Gilmore, Patrick S., 235, 252
Gilmore House (Baltimore), 47
Gilsey House (New York), 39, 153, 252, 262
Girard House (Philadelphia), 46-7, 153, 274

vii

INDEX

Glenn's Inlet House (Atlantic City), 256
Globe Hotel (Philadelphia), 268
Godby, John Robert, 34, 120
Godey's Lady's Book, 224
Godkin, E. L., 9, 48-9, 119
Goff, Nathan, 160-1
Gold, 86
Golden West Hotel (San Francisco), 97
Gompers, Samuel, 272
Goodwin, C. C., 94
Gough, John B., 142
Gould (Shawmut House, Boston), 41
Gould, Jay, 148
Graham, R. M., 294
Graham, Stephen, 293
Graham House (San Francisco), 85
Gramercy Hotel (New York), 45, 267
Grand Central Hotel (Omaha), 103, 287
Grand Central Hotel (San Francisco), 97
Grand Hotel (Indianapolis), 145
Grand Hotel (New York), 153, 268-9, 293
Grand Hotel (San Francisco), 88, 97, 291
Grand Pacific Hotel (Chicago), 77, 82, 83, 92, 95, 153, 157, 290
Grand Union Hotel (New York), 25-6, 69-70, 118, 153, 174, 203; *and see* Robinson's Hotel
Grand Union Hotel (Saratoga), 156, 246-7
Grant, Ulysses S., 100, 123, 145, 211-12, 245, 264, 281, 284
Greaves, Joseph, 164
Greeley, Horace, 42, 50, 116, 144
Green, Asa, 64
Green, John Bowling, 146
Green Mountain Coffee House (Landsgrove, Vt.), 155
Grenoble Hotel (New York), 293
Grimsley, Thornton, 101
Grimsley, William G., 101
Guerin, Francis, 213
Gwinnet, Button, 190

Halleck, Fitz-Greene, 32, 131
Hamilton, John C., 31
Hamilton, Thomas, 15, 206
Hamlins, the, 139
Hammond, D. R., 293
Handy, Moses P., 132
Hanford Hotel (New York), 211
Hanna, Mark, 276
Hansen, Harry, 293
Harding, Warren G., 133
Harper's Weekly, 39, 116-17
Harrison, Benjamin, 145, 246, 277
Harrodsburg Hotel (Harrodsburg, Ky.), 258
Harte, Bret, 89
Hartwell, H. J., 46, 61
Hawk, Samuel, 212
Hawthorne, Nathaniel, 132, 279-80
Hayes, Rutherford B., 265
Haynes, Tilly, 153, 289
Haynes Hotel (Springfield, Mass.), 289
Heath House (Schooley's Mt.), 267

viii

INDEX

Heating systems in hotels, 62-4
Heflin, J. Thomas, 277
Held, Anna, 272
Henry, Patrick, 145
Herald (New York), 212, 224-5, 236-7
Herndon House (Omaha), 102
High Life in New York, 34-5, 42-3
Hill, David Bennett, 272
Hill, Samuel E., 125
History of Transportation, The, 147
Hitchcock, Hiram, 152
Hobson, Richmond Pearson, 165
Hoffman House (New York), 50, 54, 95, 128, 133-4, 153, 166, 215, 266, 271
Holland House (New York), 69, 163, 261
Holman, R. N., 41, 288
Holmes, George, 61
Holmes, Oliver Wendell, 132
Holt, Mary, 30
Holt, Stephen B., 29
Holt's Hotel (New York), 29-30, 64; *and see* United States Hotel
Homer, James Lloyd, 239-40
Hone, Philip, 36, 254
Hoover, Herbert, 277
Hotel Gazette, 124, 159, 174
Hotel Greeters of America, 179
Hotel Mail, 39, 70, 173, 215, 238, 253
Hotel Management, 258
Hotels: development of, from inns, 3-8, 11-12, 14, 17-18; earliest American examples of, 10-11
House rules in hotels, 113, 114

Howard, Daniel D., 42, 50, 153, 266
Howard, John P., 42
Howard Hotel (Baltimore), 291
Howard Hotel (New York), 41-4, 50, 153, 156, 211
Howland, Henry, 249
Howland House (Long Branch), 249
Huggins, N., 153, 292
Huggins, S. J., 153, 292
Hughes, Ellis, 243
Hughes, Thomas H., 244
Hunt, John E., 155
Hunting, Nathaniel, 293
Hurley, E. N., 277
Hussey, William, 47, 291
Hyde (Tontine House, New York), 195
Hyer, Tom, 139

Illustrated News (London), 100
Indian Queen Tavern (Baltimore), 11
Indian Queen Tavern (Boston), 27
Indian Queen Tavern (Washington), 201
Ingram Hotel (Chicago), 157
International Hotel (Niagara Falls), 258
International Hotel (San Francisco), 87, 89
Irving House (New York), 44, 49-51, 156, 209
Irving House (San Francisco), 85, 223
Ives, George D., 144

Jarvis, John Wesley, 132
Jefferson, Thomas, 106
Jenks, Francis H., 71-2

ix

INDEX

Johnson, Andrew, 281
Johnson, Samuel, 175
Jones, Cyrus, 200–1
Journal of Commerce (New York), 30
Judson, Curtis, 293
Judson, Edward Z. C., 292–3
Julien, Denis, 262
Julien, Jean Baptiste, 213
Jumel, Mme, 233

Keefer, Sam, 252
Keeler, George, 288
Keene, James R., 274
Kemble, Frances Anne, 22
Kemp, George, 270
Kendall, Edward A., 198
Kennedy, Robert Cobb, 212
Kent, James, 132
Kentucky House (Atlantic City), 256
Keys for guest-rooms in hotels, 22–3
King, Charles, 132
King, John, 229
King, John A., 254
Kinzie, James, 77
Kinzler, Francis, 271
Kipling, Rudyard, 293
Kirby, Abner, 51, 287
Kirby House (Milwaukee), 51, 287
Kirkwood Hotel (Washington), 281
Kirkwood House (Des Moines), 289
Knickerbocker Hotel (New York), 261
Knight, Sarah, 20
Knox, James, 56, 59
Kohler, Stanton U., 179
Kuhn's Hotel (Chicago), 83

Laclede Hotel (Chicago), 82
La Farge House (New York), 45–6, 211
Lafayette, Marquis de, 184, 282
Lafayette Hotel (Philadelphia), 47, 274–5
Lake House (Chicago), 78, 79
Lake Mohonk Mountain House, 230
Lakota Hotel (Chicago), 291
Lamb Tavern (Boston), 288
Lane, Cornelius, 247
Laperreque, Eugene, 215
La Pierre Hotel (Philadelphia), 47, 274–5
Lawn House (Long Branch), 248
Leaming, Israel, 244
Lee, Robert E., 212, 284
Leland, Aaron, 155, 156
Leland, Charles, 155, 156
Leland, Charles E., 157
Leland, Lewis, 94, 156–7
Leland, Simeon, 155
Leland, Simeon, Jr., 155, 156
Leland, Warren, 155, 156
Leland, Warren F., 157
Leland, William, 155
Leland family, 94, 152, 155
Leland's Hotel (Chicago), 157
Leslie's Weekly, 66, 222
Levy (cornetist), 252
Lewis, George, 195
Lick House (San Francisco), 88, 291
Light House Cottage (Atlantic City), 256
Lincoln, Abraham, 81, 146–7, 264, 275, 276, 281, 287, 291
Lind, Jenny, 291
Lindbergh, Charles, 292
Lindell, Peter, 101

INDEX

Lindell Hotel (Chicago), 101-2
Livery in hotels, 39-41
Long Branch, hotels at, 247-50
Longfellow, Henry Wadsworth, 132, 185, 189, 220
Loring, Col., 294
Louis XIV, 213
Louis Philippe, 109, 110
Lovejoy, Jonathan, 35, 211
Lovejoy's Hotel (New York), 35, 211
Lowell, James Russell, 132
Ludlam, Richard Smith, 236, 244
Lyall, Charles, 114

MacCorkle, William A., 227
MacGill, Caroline E., 147
Mackay, Alexander, 177
Mackay, John W., 266
Mail and Express (New York), 276-7
Majestic Hotel (New York), 273
Majestic Hotel (San Francisco), 96
Maloney's Franklin House (San Francisco), 222
Maltby, L. U., 291
Maltby Hotel (Baltimore), 291
Manhattan Beach Hotel (Coney Island), 252, 253
Manhattan Hotel (New York), 153, 261
Mann, Colonel, 139
Mann, Horace, 289
Mansfield, Josie, 293
Mansion House (Atlantic City), 255
Mansion House (Cape May), 236, 244
Mansion House (Chicago), 79
Mansion House (Long Branch), 249
Mansion House (Philadelphia), 11
Mansion House (Poland Springs), 241
Mansion House (Washington), 278-9; *and see* Willard Hotel
Manx Hotel (San Francisco), 97
Marat, Jean Paul, 60
Marine Pavilion Hotel (Rockaway), 254
Marlboro Hotel (Boston), 113, 114, 143, 177
Marlborough-Blenheim Hotel (Atlantic City), 256
Marlborough Hotel (New York), 167, 272
Marryat, Frederick, 21, 116, 118-19
Marsh, Henry E., 288
Marshall (discoverer of gold in California), 83, 84
Marshall, Thomas R., 280
Marshall House (Philadelphia), 275
Martha Washington Hotel (New York), 129
Martin, Bradley, 271, 273
Martin Chuzzlewit, 110
Martineau, Harriet, 118, 258
Martling, Abram (Brom), 31
Martling's Tavern (New York), 31
Marvin, James M., 247
Massasoit House (Chicago), 82
Massasoit House (Springfield, Mass.), 289
Matteson House (Chicago), 82
Maury, Evarist, 101
Maverick, John, 177

xi

INDEX

Maverick, Samuel A., 177
Maverick House (Boston), 177
Maxwell, A. M., 197
Maynard, Lambert, 71
McAdoo, William G., 277
McAllister, Ward, 271
McAlpin Hotel (New York), 165
McCoy, Kid, 273
McCullough, John B., 156
McDonald (St. Charles Hotel, New Orleans), 99
McGlory, Billy, 271
McKinley, Abner, 290
McKinley, Helen, 290
McKinley, William, 276, 290
McKnight (Planters Hotel, St. Louis), 101
McLure House (Wheeling), 160–1, 162
McMackin, General, 201–2
McMackin Hotel (Vicksburg), 201–2
McMaster, J. B., 21
Menu cards in hotels, 198–201
Merchants' Exchange Hotel (New York), 165
Mercury (Charleston), 172
Merrifield, E. L., 153
Merry, Henry L., 165
Metropolitan Hotel (Long Branch), 249
Metropolitan Hotel (New York), 45, 54, 63, 65, 71, 152, 156, 162, 211, 264
Meysey-Thompson, Sir Henry, 271
Michigan Avenue Hotel (Chicago), 158; *and see* Tremont House
Miller, Hank, 78
Miller, Sam, 78

Mitchell, James, 271
Monnot, S. Baptiste, 209, 210
Monongahela House (Pittsburgh), 48, 153, 284–5
Montgomery Hall Hotel (Saratoga), 219
Moon, Carey E., 219
Moore, John L., 144
Morrison, Martin, 220
Morrison's Hotel (New York), 264; *and see* Everett, Hotel
Morrissey, John, 234
Morse, Samuel F. B., 132
Morton, James, 267
Morton, Levi P., 277
Morton House (New York), 266–7
Mott, J. L., 60
Mountain House (Catskills), 258
Mount Vernon Hotel (Cape May), 244–5
Mower, Henry S., 176, 177
Mudge, E. R., 99
Murat, Caroline, 111
Murray Hill Hotel (New York), 293

Nahant, hotels at, 228, 235, 238–40, 242
Nassau Hotel (Long Beach), 165
Nation (New York), 9, 48
National Atlantic Hall (Cape May), 245
National Hotel (Long Branch), 249
National Hotel (New York), 11
National Hotel (St. Louis), 100–1
National Hotel (Washington), 152, 275–6, 291

INDEX

National House (Cape May), 244
Navarre Hotel (New York), 272
Neil, William, 287
Neil House (Columbus), 287
Nelson, General, 294
Neptune House (Atlantic City), 256
Netherland, Hotel (New York), 70, 273
New Atlantic House (Cape May), 244
New England Coffee House (Boston), 27, 62, 154
New England Hotel (Philadelphia), 71
New England House (New York), 139, 211; *and see* North American Hotel
Newhall House (Milwaukee), 289
Newport, hotels at, 237–8, 242; *and see names of hotels*
New York City, hotels in, 10, 11, 29–37, 41–6, 49–57, 144, 261–74, 291–4; *and see names of hotels*
New Yorker (Greeley's), 33, 116
New York Hotel (Baltimore), 152
New York Hotel (New York), 44, 49, 56, 61, 156, 209, 210–211, 264
New York Hotel-keepers' Association, 212
New Orleans, hotels in, 46, 97–99; *and see names of hotels*
Niantic Hotel (San Francisco), 84
Niblo's Tavern (New York), 196
Normandie, Hotel (New York), 272–3

North American Hotel (New York), 137–40
Notch House (White Mountains), 258
Nye, Bill, 25

Occidental Hotel (New York), 262–4, 265
Occidental Hotel (San Francisco), 88, 157, 291
Ocean House (Cape May), 244, 245
Ocean House (Newport), 177, 237
Oceanic Hotel (Coney Island), 250
Oliver, William, 287
Oliver House (Toledo), 287
Omaha, hotels in, 102–3
Optic, Oliver, *see* Adams, William T.
Oriental Hotel (Coney Island), 164–5, 252
Oriental Hotel (San Francisco), 87
Orteig, Raymond, 292
Overland Monthly, 90

Palace Hotel (San Francisco), 76, 91–4, 95, 97, 156, 291
Palladium (Boston), 240
Palmer, A. M., 267
Palmer, Alexander Hamilton, 180
Palmer, Potter, 68, 82, 83, 136, 145, 153, 157, 158–9
Palmer House (Chicago), 68, 77, 81–2, 83, 92, 136, 153, 159, 173, 208, 290, 294
Park Avenue Hotel (New York), 269–70

xiii

INDEX

Parker, Harvey D., 41, 152, 154-5
Parker, Robert, 85
Parker House (Boston), 41, 132, 152, 155, 288
Parker House (San Francisco), 85, 86
Parkman, Francis, 132
Parmalee, Frank, 80
Parrish, Maxfield, 261
Patten (Saratoga racecourse), 234
Pavilion Hotel (Saratoga), 246
Paxton Hotel (Omaha), 103, 287
Pearl Street House (Cincinnati), 157, 286
Pedro, Dom, 270
Pelton, A. D., 63
Permanent residents in hotels, 115-19
Perot, Allison, 247
Perry House (Newport), 238
Pershing, John J., 293
Peters, Samuel, 108
Philadelphia, hotels in, 46-7, 274-5; and see names of hotels
Pickwick Papers, The, 123
Pierce, Franklin, 45, 245
Pierce, George F., 202
Pierre, Charles, 296
Pierre, Hotel (New York), 294, 295-7
Pitney, Jonathan R., 255
Plankinton, John, 287
Plankinton Hotel (Milwaukee), 287
Planters Hotel (New York), 262, 264
Planters Hotel (St. Louis), 48, 101, 287-8

Platt, Thomas C., 133, 144, 264
Plaza Hotel (New York), 165
Plumbing in hotels, 24, 33, 55, 62-4
Plummer (Riggs House, Washington), 281
Poe, Edgar Allan, 283
Politics and hotels, 132-4
Polo, Marco, 181, 182
Ponce de Leon Hotel (St. Augustine, Fla.), 68
Poore, Perley, 201
Porter (Porter House, North Cambridge), 220
Porter House (North Cambridge, Mass.), 220
Powelton House (Newburgh, N. Y.), 267
Power, Tyrone, 206
Powers, H. L., 212, 293
Powers' Hotel (New York), 212
Presbury, George E., 47, 153, 274
Prescott, William H., 45, 261
Prescott House (New York), 45, 60, 63, 261-2
Prices in hotels, 28, 86-7, 91, 120, 156, 205, 210, 222-3
Prince, Marshall, 239-40
Putnam, Gideon, 246
Putnam, Israel, 145
Putnam's Magazine, 22, 51, 61, 214

Quincy House (Boston), 288

Rabineau, Henry C., 57
Ragot, Louis, 215
Raleigh, Walter (1861-1922), 52
Raleigh Hotel (Washington), 281

INDEX

Ralston, Samuel M., 277
Ralston, William C., 91, 94, 95
Ranier Grand Hotel (Seattle), 287
Rathbun, Benjamin, 118, 149–151
Rathbun's Hotel (New York), 150–1, 156
Reading-rooms in hotels, 16–17
Red Book, American Hotel Association, 294
Reddington, Joseph, 136
Register, hotel, 180–91
Reid, Cassius H., 266
Reid, John C., 265
Renfost Hotel (Chicago), 157
Reunion Hotel, 118; and see Grand Union Hotel
Revere, Paul, 154
Revere House (Boston), 41, 152, 154, 176
Revere House (Chicago), 82
Reynolds, David, 137–9, 140
Rhodes, Harrison, 181
Rice (Shawmut House, Boston), 41
Rice, John A., 95
Rice, Lewis, 41, 152, 288
Rich, Capt., 240
Richelieu Hotel (San Francisco), 97
Richmond, hotels in, 283–4
Rickey, Joseph K., 267–8
Rider, Francis, 267
Ridgway, Charles, 50
Ridgway, John J., 275
Riggs, George W., 281
Riggs House (Washington), 281
Ritz-Carlton Hotel (New York), 126
Rivers, R. J., 98, 153
Robinson, Joseph, 277
Robinson's Hotel (New York), 117–18; and see Grand Union Hotel
Roessle, Theophilus, 144, 276
Rogers, Charles M., 250
Rogers, Isaiah, 14, 15, 32, 99
Rogers, Nathaniel, 113, 143–4
Roseberry, Lord, 217
Royal, Hotel (New Orleans), 98; and see St. Louis Hotel
Rusk, Jeremiah Lane, 145
Russ, J. C. Christian, 88
Russell, Jacob, 79
Russ House (San Francisco), 88
Rutledge, Ann, 147
Rutledge, James, 147

Safe-deposit boxes in hotels, 71–2
Sagamore Hotel (Green Island, Lake George, N. Y.), 68
St. Charles Hotel (New Orleans), 14, 46, 97, 98, 99, 153
St. Cloud Hotel (New York), 118
St. Denis Hotel (New York), 45, 262
St. Francis Hotel (San Francisco), 85, 87, 97, 136, 222
St. George Hotel (Philadelphia), 166, 215
St. Germain Hotel (New York), 267
St. James Hotel (Chicago), 82
St. James Hotel (New York), 211, 267, 268
St. Louis, hotels in, 100–2; and see names of hotels
St. Louis Hotel (New Orleans), 46, 98–9
St. Nicholas Hotel (New York), 45, 51–3, 54, 60, 63, 65, 71,

xv

INDEX

152, 162, 211, 212, 261, 273, 294
Sala, George Augustus, 49, 63, 115, 116, 130, 203–4
Saltus, Nick, 131
Sands and Nathan Circus, 139
San Francisco, hotels in, 83–97, 291; *and see names of hotels*
Saratoga Springs, hotels at, 230–5, 241, 242, 245, 246; *and see names of hotels*
Saturday Club, 132
Sauganash Tavern (Chicago), 78
Savery, George W., 289
Savery House (Des Moines), 289
Savoy Hotel (New York), 273
Sayrs, Obadiah, 248
Sayrs House (Long Branch), 248, 249
Schubert, Franz, 199
Schwab, Charles M., 274
Scott, John B., 139
Scott, Walter, 205
Scott, Winfield, 132, 266
Sea Breeze House (Cape May), 245
Seaside House (Atlantic City), 256
Sentinel (Saratoga), 232
Seward, William H., 150
Shakspere, William, 19, 131
Sharon, William, 91, 94, 95
Shawmut House (Boston), 41
Shenstone, William, 105
Shepard, Elliott F., 276
Sherman, F. C., 79
Sherman, William Tecumseh, 100, 211
Sherman House (Chicago), 77, 79, 82, 83, 290

Shew, Joel, 58
Shook, Sheridan, 267
Shoreham Hotel (Washington), 277
Sigourney, Lydia H., 239
Sinclair House (New York), 269
Sleeping-accommodations in hotels, 19–22
Smith, Alfred E., 281
Smith, Henry Milford, 153, 293
Soule, Pierre, 98
Sousa, John Philip, 164, 235, 252–3
Southern Hotel (St. Louis), 102, 288
Spencer House (Cincinnati), 48, 100, 210, 286
Spofford (Riggs House, Washington), 281
Spotswood Hotel (Richmond), 284
Spring beds in hotels, 70–1
Springfield, Mass., hotels in, 288–9
Stafford Hotel (Philadelphia), 166; *and see* St. George Hotel
Stafford Springs (Conn.), 229, 240
Stanford Hotel (San Francisco), 97
Stanwix Hall (Albany), 99, 250, 281, 282–3
Statler, Ellsworth M., 62, 153, 159–62
Statler, Hotel (Buffalo), 62, 161, 162
Stebbins, Joseph, 289
Stebbins Tavern (Springfield, Mass.), 289
Sterry, Fred, 165
Stetson, Charles A., 141, 152, 207

xvi

INDEX

Stetson House (Long Branch), 249
Stevens, Elihu, 154
Stevens, Josiah, 154
Stevens, Paran, 41, 152, 153-4, 155, 176, 270, 271
Stevens, Thaddeus, 275
Stewart, A. T., 269, 270
Stickney (Planters Hotel, St. Louis), 101
Stiles murder, 294
Stockton House (Cape May), 245, 268
Stokes, Edward S., 219, 266, 293
Stowe, Harriet Beecher, 204
Strangers' List, 29
Stratford Hotel (Chicago), 291
Strothers, John, 278
Sturtevant Hotel (New York), 156
Sullivan, John L., 288
Sullivan, Yankee, 139
Sumner, Charles, 277
Sunday Morning News (New York), 29
Surf House (Atlantic City), 255
Sutcliff, Robert, 59
Sutter, Johann, 83, 88
Swan Tavern (Richmond), 283
Sweeney, George W., 166-7
Sweeny, Daniel, 264
Sweeny's Hotel (New York), 264
Sweet, Alanson, 79

Taggart, Thomas, 145-6
Talbot, Edward Allen, 20-1
Talmage, T. De Witt, 67
Tammany Hall Hotel (New York), 11, 31, 35, 102, 153, 208, 211

Taverns, early, in the West, 74-6, 77
Taylor, Bayard, 84, 85, 87, 222
Taylor, John, 278
Taylor, William, 87
Taylor's Hotel (New York), 144
Taylor's International Hotel (New York), 45
Telephone in hotels, 27, 69, 70
Temperance and hotels, 112, 142-4
Thackeray, William Makepeace, 205
"That Old Time Place," 99
Thefts from hotels, 134-6
Throckmorton, Major, 110-11
Tierney, Edward M., 166
Tilden, Samuel J., 265
Tobacco and hotels, 112-13
Tocqueville, Alexis de, 113
Todd, Louis M., 272
Tontine House (New York), 195
Touro House (Newport), 237
Towle, George M., 141, 225
Train, George Francis, 162
Travel and the growth of hotels, 119-23
Travel in America, History of, 299
Traymore Hotel (Atlantic City), 256
Tremont House (Boston), 13-14, 15-17, 18, 22, 23, 24, 26, 27, 28, 29, 30, 31, 32, 38, 41, 56, 62, 69, 70, 73, 101, 115, 117, 141, 151, 175-6, 179, 195, 196-7, 198, 199, 206, 214, 260

INDEX

Tremont House (Chicago), 77, 79–80, 81, 82, 83, 157, 158, 290
Tremont House (Claremont, N. H.), 154
Tremont House (San Francisco), 85
Tribune (New York), 50, 53, 64–5, 66, 71, 127, 144, 207, 208
Trollope, Anthony, 111
Trollope, Frances M., 111
Tschirky, Oscar, 166
Tudor, William, 21–2
Tumulty, Joseph P., 277
Tupper, Martin, 49
Twain, Mark, 94
Tweed, William M., 140, 144, 273
Twelfth Night, 19
Tyler, John, 42, 246, 283

Uncle Tom's Cabin, 98
Union Club, 131
Union Hall (Saratoga), 233–4, 246
Union Hotel (San Francisco), 87
Union Square Hotel (New York), 178
Union Square Hotel (San Francisco), 97
United States Hotel (Atlantic City), 255
United States Hotel (Boston), 41, 177, 288
United States Hotel (Cape May), 245
United States Hotel (Long Branch), 249
United States Hotel (Newport), 238

United States Hotel (New York), 211; *and see* Holt's Hotel
United States Hotel (Philadelphia), 275
United States Hotel (Saratoga), 91, 111, 233, 246, 247

Van den Heuvel, John C., 31
Vanderbilt, Cornelius, 147–8, 250
Vanderbilt, Mrs. Cornelius, 148
Vanderbilt, Jeremiah, 254
Vanderbilt, William H., 148
Vanity Fair (ed. Artemus Ward), 269
Van Osdel, J. M., 79
Vatel, 213
Vendig, Charles, 162
Vendig Hotel (Philadelphia), 162
Vendome Hotel (Boston), 68, 288
Vendome Hotel (New York), 272
Verandah Hotel (New Orleans), 46
Verplanck, G. C., 132
Victoria, Queen, 38
Victoria Hotel (Kansas City), 61–2
Victoria Hotel (New York), 167, 270–1

Waite, Charles B., 153
Waldorf-Astoria Hotel (New York), 70, 97, 132, 164, 165, 166, 180, 273–4, 294–5, 296–7
Walker, Joshua, 36, 44
Wall, E. Berry, 170
Wallack, James W., 139
Walton, Francis Theodore, 268

xviii

INDEX

Walton House (New York), 220
Wansay, Henry, 195–6
Ward, Artemus, 269
Ward, Sam, 217, 281
Ward House (San Francisco), 87
Wardwell, Peggy, 247
Warner, Charles Dudley, 227–8
Warren, John C., 44
Washington, hotels in, 275–81; *and see names of hotels*
Washington Hall (Saratoga), 246
Washington Hall Hotel (New York), 11, 208–9
Washington Hotel (Cape May), 244
Washington House (Philadelphia), 46, 61
Water Cure Journal and Teacher of Health, 58
Watering-places, hotels at, 224–259
Watrous (St. Charles Hotel, New Orleans), 99
Weaver, Henry, 101
Webster, Daniel, 14, 220, 291–2
Weed, Thurlow, 32, 133, 214
Welch, Uriah, 152
Welker's Hotel (Washington), 281
Wells, F. T., 267
Wenberg, Ben, 217–19
Wentworth, Elijah, 77–8
West, Amanda, 281–2
West End Hotel (Cape May), 245
Western Hotel (Chicago), 79
Westinghouse, George, 256
Westminster Hotel (New York), 269

Wharton, Edith, 270
What Cheer House (San Francisco), 89–91, 104, 291
Wheeler (Stanwix Hall, Albany), 283
Wheeler, Henry, 46
Wheeler, John, 267
Whipple, Edwin P., 132
Whipple, J. Reed, 153
White, "Bishop," 177–8
White, R. D., 56
White, Stewart Edward, 86
White Hall (Cape May), 244
White Sulphur Springs Hotel (W. Va.), 189, 226, 227–8
Whitfield's Hotel (Newport), 237
Whitney, Charles M., 288
Whittier, John G., 132
Willard, Caleb C., 153, 277, 278
Willard, Edwin D., 278, 279
Willard, Henry A., 153, 278
Willard, Joseph D., 153, 277–8, 279
Willard Hotel (Washington), 153, 278, 279–80, 283, 291
Williams, Charles, 109, 110
Willis, Frank Bartlett, 277
Willis, Nat P., 209–10
Wilson, Woodrow, 277
Wilson's Exchange Hotel (San Francisco), 87; *and see* American Exchange Hotel
Windsor Hotel (New York), 289–90
Wister, Owen, 102, 200, 214
Wolcott, J. W., 68
Wolfe, Gov., 232
Women as hotel guests, 126–9
Woods, James, 97
Woodward, R. B., 89

xix

INDEX

World (New York), 133-4, 256
Wormley Hotel (Washington), 277

Yates, Gov., 262
Youle, George, 62

Young's Hotel (Boston), 155, 288

Zangwill, Israel, 208
Zavala, Don Lorenzo de, 281, 282

THE LEISURE CLASS IN AMERICA

An Arno Press Collection

Bradley, Hugh. **Such was Saratoga.** 1940

Browne, Junius Henri. **The Great Metropolis:** A Mirror of New York. 1869

Burt, Nathaniel. **The Perennial Philadelphians.** 1963

Canby, Henry Seidel. **Alma Mater:** The Gothic Age of the American College. 1936

Crockett, Albert Stevens. **Peacocks on Parade.** 1931

Croffut, W[illiam] A. **The Vanderbilts.** 1886

Crowninshield, Francis W. **Manners for the Metropolis.** 1909

de Wolfe, Elsie. **The House in Good Taste.** 1913

Ellet, E[lizabeth] F[ries Lummis]. **The Court Circles of the Republic, or The Beauties and Celebrities of the Nation.** 1869

Elliott, Maud Howe. **This Was My Newport.** 1944

Elliott, Maud Howe. **Uncle Sam Ward and His Circle.** 1938

Fairfield, Francis Gerry. **The Clubs of New York** and Croly, [Jane C.] **Sorosis.** 1873/1886. Two vols. in one

[Fawcett, Edgar]. **The Buntling Ball:** A Graeco-American Play. 1885

Fawcett, Edgar. **Social Silhouettes.** 1885

Fiske, Stephen. **Off-Hand Portraits of Prominent New Yorkers.** 1884

Foraker, Julia B. **I Would Live It Again:** Memories of a Vivid Life. 1932

Goodwin, Maud Wilder. **The Colonial Cavalier.** 1895

Hartt, Rollin Lynde. **The People at Play.** 1909

Lehr, Elizabeth Drexel. **"King Lehr" and the Gilded Age.** 1935

Lodge, Henry Cabot. **Early Memories.** 1913

[Longchamp, Ferdinand]. **Asmodeus in New-York.** 1868

McAllister, [Samuel] Ward. **Society as I Have Found It.** 1890

McLean, Evalyn, with Boyden Sparkes. **Father Struck It Rich.** 1936

[Mann, William d'Alton]. **Fads and Fancies of Representative Americans at the Beginning of the Twentieth Century.** 1905

Martin, Frederick Townsend. **The Passing of the Idle Rich.** 1911

Martin, Frederick Townsend. **Things I Remember.** 1913

Maurice, Arthur Bartlett. **Fifth Avenue.** 1918

[Mordecai, Samuel]. **Richmond in By-Gone Days.** 1856

Morris, Lloyd. **Incredible New York.** 1951

Neville, Amelia Ransome. **The Fantastic City:** Memoirs of the Social and Romantic Life of Old San Francisco. 1932

Nichols, Charles Wilbur de Lyon. **The Ultra-Fashionable Peerage of America.** 1904

Pound, Arthur. **The Golden Earth:** The Story of Manhattan's Landed Wealth. 1935

Pulitzer, Ralph. **New York Society on Parade.** 1910

Ripley, Eliza. **Social Life in Old New Orleans.** 1912

Ross, Ishbel. **Silhouette in Diamonds:** The Life of Mrs. Potter Palmer. 1960

Sherwood, M[ary] E[lizabeth W.]. **Manners and Social Usages.** 1897 **The Sporting Set.** 1975

Van Rensselaer, [May] King. **Newport: Our Social Capital.** 1905

Van Rensselaer, [May] King. **The Social Ladder.** 1924

Wharton, Edith and Ogden Codman, Jr. **The Decoration of Houses.** 1914

Williamson, Jefferson. **The American Hotel.** 1930